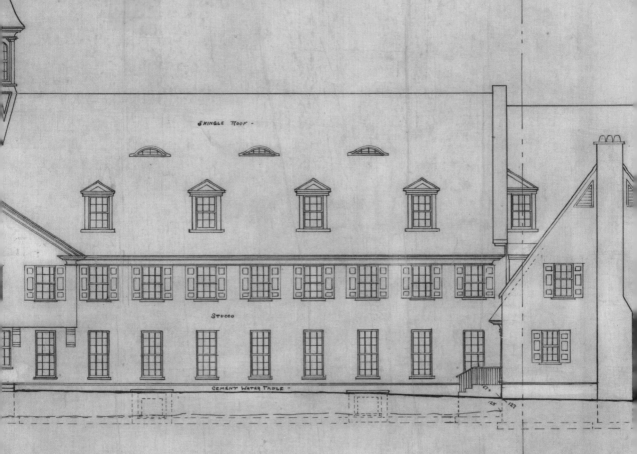

SHINGLE ROOF

STUCCO

CEMENT WATER TABLE

EVATION.

D'S SCHOOL FOR GIRLS.

CONN.

THEODATE POPE ~ARCHITECT~

FARMINGTON ~ CONN.

ADDRESS N° 25 WEST 26TH STR.

NEW YORK CITY ~

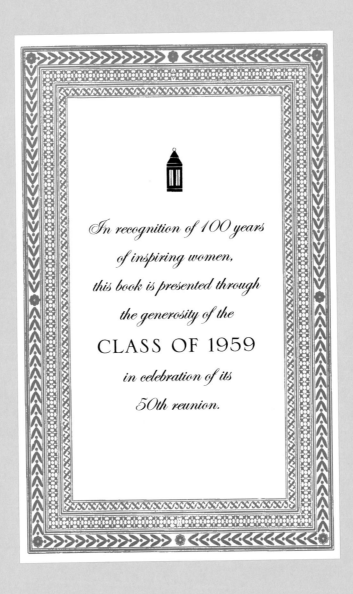

WESTOVER

Garnet Books

OTHER BOOKS BY THE AUTHOR

Portrait of an Artist: A Biography of Georgia O'Keeffe

Louise Nevelson: A Passionate Life

Without Child: Challenging the Stigma of Childlessness

Four Tenths of an Acre: Reflections on a Gardening Life

WESTOVER

Giving Girls a Place of Their Own

LAURIE LISLE

WESLEYAN UNIVERSITY PRESS ✦ MIDDLETOWN, CONNECTICUT

Published by Wesleyan University Press, Middletown, CT 06459
www.wesleyan.edu/wespress

Printed in U.S.A.   5 4 3 2 1

Library of Congress Cataloging-in-Publication Data
Lisle, Laurie.
Westover : giving girls a place of their own / by Laurie Lisle.
p.   cm.
Includes bibliographical references and index.
ISBN 978–0–8195–6886–1 (cloth : alk. paper)
1. Westover School. 2. Girls' schools—Connecticut—Middlebury—History. I. Title.
LD7251.M635L57 2008
373.18235'2097468—dc22   2008029051

Materials in the Westover archive are published with the permission
of Westover School, Middlebury, Connecticut.

Materials pertaining to Theodate Pope Riddle are published with permission
of the Archives, Hill-Stead Museum, Farmington, Connecticut.

Excerpts from a letter of John Masefield to Mary R. Hillard, dated April 28, 1917,
are quoted with the permission of The Society of Authors, London, the literary
representative of the Estate of John Masefield.

Quotations from the essay "Taking Women Students Seriously" are from
On Lies, Secrets, and Silence: Selected Prose 1966–1978 by Adrienne Rich. Copyright
© 1979 by W. W. Norton & Company, Inc. Used by permission of the author
and W. W. Norton & Company, Inc.

Every effort has been made to secure permissions from copyright
owners to publish photographs in the archive of Westover School. Sometimes
the photographer is unidentified and unknown. In other cases, neither the
photographer nor his or her estate could be located. Any copyright owners
who were not contacted by the author are invited to come forward and
be gratefully acknowledged.

Designed by Charlotte Strick

To my Westover
aunts, cousins, mother,
and sister—
once girls known as
Eleanor Cole,
Esther Merriman,
Barbara Simonds,
Lally Simonds,
Nan Morse,
Linda Simonds,
Phillis Simonds,
Abigail Congdon,
and
Adeline Gwynne—
who attended from
1909 to 1968

CONTENTS

FRONT ELEVATION
SCALE

Theodate Pope Architect
Farmington Connecticut

Westover
Miss Hillard's School for Girls
Middlebury Connecticut

PREFACE

My Westover

THIS BOOK HAD ITS BEGINNING IN THE AUTUMN OF 1971, WHEN I was working for *Newsweek* in New York. In the wake of the women's liberation movement, I was seeing everything with new eyes, and I wanted to re-evaluate my life as a girl, especially my three years at Westover. The impact of leaving home at the age of fifteen for a hermetic female community had been huge. As far as I could tell, the school had changed very little from the time my mother had attended in the late 1920s and early 1930s. I wondered why I had never heard the words "women's rights" spoken by my intelligent and independent women teachers, even by the indomitable Louise Dillingham, who had ruled the place for many years with a peculiar combination of absolute authority and enigmatic detachment. I was wondering about other matters, as well.

After graduating in 1961, my memories of my years in Middlebury, Connecticut, remained unresolved. They were as charged as if radioactive, and as ongoing as a persistent itch. I remembered my restlessness because I didn't believe I was being readied for Real Life. Although I realized I was getting an excellent education, I also wanted something else. After graduation, my adolescent ambivalence turned to antagonism, when alumnae news was more about weddings than professional work or other kinds of adventures. As boys' prep schools went coeducational, I applauded, regarding female institutions as anachronisms, something I had endured simply because I was born too soon.

Intending to write a freelance article about girls' schools from my new point of view, I wrote to Westover's acting headmaster for an interview. I was more comfortable returning as a reporter than an alumna and had skipped my tenth reunion the previous spring. When I drove up to the school's imposing façade along the side of a village green, all the nervousness and anticipation I had felt when returning from vacations came rushing back. I pushed open the heavy front door, walked in, and there was Red Hall flooded with sunlight, with the green grass and little apple trees within the Quad visible through its large windows. Standing in that familiar, feminine place, I felt enveloped by emotion. To my astonishment, I felt a sense of solace. I tried to resist this feeling because it undermined my new ideas. An enthusiastic supporter of the Equal Rights Amendment, I espoused equality and togetherness with males, and I rejected the ideas of womanly retreat and feminist separation.

Why did it feel so, well, *pleasant* to be back?

Perhaps it had to do with tricks of memory or the beauty of the place. Still, my reaction didn't make sense to me. After all, I had suffered adolescent angst while there. Maybe I was tired of gender battles in Manhattan, where my boyfriend seemed to live in the Dark Ages, and where female editorial employees of *Newsweek* had filed a complaint with the federal Equal Employment Opportunity Commission protesting the magazine's discriminatory policies against them.

In the interview, soft-spoken Joseph Molder gave me the impression that he was "more on the girls' side" than I had expected, my notes of the meeting say. My notes also reveal my point-of-view at the time: It would be a mistake for alumnae to make the school "a bulwark against change in their daughters and granddaughters, rather than a good opportunity to mold the new woman creatively." Afterward, he introduced me to a long-haired, bearded English teacher about my age, who startled me by saying he was getting girls to read women writers like Sylvia Plath. I was also surprised to see students in their own clothes, to hear about their baking cookies at the headmaster's house, and to see them riding off on bikes to volunteer jobs outside the high walls of the school. In a note to Mr. Molder after I returned to New York, I thanked him for answering my questions so "patiently and graciously" and praised his "sensitive touch" as headmaster. Then I asked him if the school was ever going to teach sex education or women's studies. (I never got an answer to that question.)

Then I got in touch with the president of the board of trustees, who politely invited me to lunch at his Wall Street club, a hushed place with red walls and large models of sailing ships. As we talked, he indicated that Westover's future was up in the air, and that it might become a school for remedial students. Noticing that I was almost the only female in the room, I asked if we were in a men's club. When he nodded yes, I felt a stab of resentment. Maybe my conflict had less to do with my dislike of the female sphere than my perception of its inferiority to the male one, where the prizes, I thought, were the ones worth winning. Since I had intended my article to be critical of girls' schools, I was confused. I had no idea how to begin it and, in fact, I never did.

Years later, after returning from my thirty-fifth Westover reunion in 1996, I read in *The New York Times* about the opening of the Young Women's Leadership School, the first public school for girls to open in the city in a century. I instantly understood what the young girls in East Harlem would get from a school of their own, and I felt happy for them. I also realized that I was glad that Westover was still a school for girls, and that it had been mine for a while. Even at the time of the interview I had noted that "I guess the place either gave me or nourished my desire to dream and grow." Entering at the end of the 1950s, I must have absorbed the message that girls like me were important because such a magnificent piece of architecture had been designed for us and dedicated to educating us. Also, I remembered being interested in the school motto, "To Think, To Do, To Be" (inscribed in Latin on our brass belt buckles and the awesome emblem over the front door). It boldly challenged the expectation for a girl's life in an era when women were only assumed to exist, instead of also thinking and doing. The words must have interested me because they assumed no inherent conflict between intellectuality and femininity: they indicated that clear thoughts and bold actions were part of a womanly life.

Soon afterward I returned to Middlebury to examine the school archive on the balcony of the former library, the airy, white clapboard colonial that had once been a church. I loved being back in the beautiful old building, and I remembered being happy reading on its sofa in the warmth of the fireplace on winter afternoons. The large portrait of founder Mary Robbins Hillard still hung there, the doe-eyed likeness that makes her look smaller and sadder than the way my mother remembered her. Maybe I would find material for the article left unwritten so long ago or for a book about girls' schools. The archive was indeed full of treasures—letters, diaries, manuscripts, photographs, memorandums, minutes of meetings, and many other materials carefully collected over the years by alumna archivist Maria Randall Allen. Eventually, when she suggested that I write a history of Westover, I realized it was what I really wanted to do—to examine the place that still evoked such strong emotion.

One day while perusing the large, gold-embossed, old leather-bound school guest book, I saw what looked like the signature of my grandfather. He and my grandmother may have visited in May of 1923, when my mother and her older sister were still in grade school. It was my grandmother who must have heard about Westover from an older cousin in Massachusetts, whose daughter, Eleanor, had entered when it first opened in 1909. I will never know how the Coles heard about Miss Hillard's new school in Connecticut, but it doesn't matter. In Eleanor's old age—eighty years after her graduation in 1912—she remembered that she had "worshipped" her headmistress and "adored" her years in Middlebury. She had not been especially studious, she said, but she had loved all the singing and the "feeling of freshness and, in a way, hope" in the "lovely little chapel," whose beloved chaplain had officiated at her wedding.

My mother was in her eighties when I began working on this book, and I enjoyed entertaining her with what I was discovering in the archive. I liked taking her to visit her sister-in-law, a member of Westover's class of 1930, and one afternoon my stories inspired the two old ladies to break into a spirited "Raise Now to Westover." After my mother's death, when I was going through her attic, I found her khaki day and white evening school uniforms, carefully tucked into a trunk along with a wedding dress. I held up the uniforms and marveled at their exquisite tailoring: all little tucks, intricate seams, deep hems, and lovely embroidery. Then, most miraculously of all, I discovered in the attic many girlish letters, written in achingly familiar handwriting, that she had mailed to her parents from Middlebury.

My mother had wanted me to go to Westover, too. In fact, she never even suggested the possibility of my going away to any other school. It was go to Westover or stay home—despite the fact that her memories were a mixture of pleasure and shame. While at boarding school, she had learned a love of reading, made good friends, and been elected head of the Over field hockey team, but she had left without a diploma. She did not attend her class's graduation or ever return for a reunion, as far as I know. Still, she felt that Westover was an experience her daughters should not miss.

During my childhood, she had often talked about a larger-than-life personage, a Miss Hillard, a kind of Protestant princess or priestess in my imagination, who could read girls' minds. Mother never spoke about her own mother with the same kind of awe. She also made affectionate references to a young headmistress, whom she called "Dilly," who sounded like the nicest person in the world. My mother often recited poems to me that she had memorized during her four years away at school, like Emily Dickinson's paean to reading, a little, rhyming poem called "A Book." She also used to recite a Biblical passage that she knew by heart, and that I would also learn at Westover—"Though I speak with the tongues of men and of angels, and have not Love, I am become as sounding brass or a tinkling cymbal," it begins. I still have my tiny blue booklet about it given to me and everyone in my class by Miss Dillingham in 1959, full of my scribbled, idealistic reflections.

On an autumn day when I was fourteen, my mother drove me to Middlebury to meet "Dilly" and see the school I had heard so much about. I remember a long talk with a formal and formidable Miss Dillingham in her dimly lit sitting room, when my mother nervously did most of the talking. At home in Providence, I had taken to bickering with her, and I didn't get along with my stern stepfather, either. "Growing up was growing out, I had nothing to lose, so I was ready to go," I had remembered a decade after graduating. When the acceptance letter arrived a few months later, I was glad to be going.

Walking through Westover's front door in September of 1958, I was a quiet girl, distressed, maybe even depressed, by feeling voiceless at home. In the presence of my volatile stepfather, it was impossible to say much of anything. Before long, after discovering the daily pile of *The New York Times* on a high-backed bench, I became electrified by news about the nascent civil rights movement. I tentatively started to talk about it, and soon I was offering my opinions in Current Events and Miss Norman's history class, on the volleyball court and everywhere else. Rooting for the Overs seemed less important than defending the pacifism of Martin Luther King. My classmates gently teased me for my passionate and probably dogmatic views, but they, as well as my teachers, put up with my argumentativeness.

My newfound voice was not just verbal, either. I began keeping a diary, writing about my thoughts as well as my emotional ups and downs. After returning from a "perfect" Christmas vacation during junior year, it suggests that I had a mid-winter meltdown. I was seventeen, in my seventh year in a girls' school (including a day school in Providence), and eager to experience life. I was also starved for *difference*, but most of my classmates were, like me, daughters of alumnae from established Protestant families. Everything suddenly seemed too female, too boring, and too tense. I telephoned my mother in tears, telling her that I wanted to go to another school senior year, definitely one with boys. She sighed and suggested that I go talk to Miss Dillingham. At the age of sixty-two—incredibly, younger than my age now—the headmistress appeared to me as a powerful but benevolent grandmother figure, not unlike my own widowed grandmother. The next day I fearlessly went to see the person we called Miss D in her sitting room. Our talk elated me, evidently because of her empathy. "It came down to the point that maybe I was ready to go on and that enough of boarding school is enough," I told my diary. "I've just outgrown this place." Wisely, she asked me to wait until after spring vacation to make a final decision, and I willingly agreed.

It wasn't long before I went to see her again, this time to ask if I could take a rare weekend pass to go to Harlem for a seminar for teenagers at a Quaker settlement house. She said she would think about it and, after undoubtedly calling my mother, gave permission. Despite being "petrified," my diary says, I was soon on a train to New York, where I was met by two boys wearing American Friends Service Committee tags and taken by subway to a narrow brownstone on East 105th Street and another kind of life.

That evening or the next, a square dance was organized for those of us from elsewhere and the Puerto Rican teenagers in the neighborhood. Smoking incessantly, the young men, who wore black felt hats pulled down over their foreheads and long hair, seemed older and more guarded than others my age. As an accordion player warmed up, a dance set was formed, and our two groups eyed each other nervously. I smiled uncertainly at the girl with jangling earrings and elaborately curled hair opposite me, and she quickly beamed back. The dancing started awkwardly—they had never square danced before—and it ended in twirling circles that made all of us dizzily collide and collapse on the floor. After a moment of silence, a titter broke out, and soon everyone was laughing together.

Back in Middlebury, I landed in the infirmary with a sore throat after four days of sleeping little and eating erratically. In the silent, snowy, wintry beauty around me, I reflected on the overcrowded tenements, overflowing garbage cans, and noisy streets of East Harlem. I had been shocked by its ugliness, but not as much as by a despairing parody of the Twenty-Third Psalm, which a young addict had slipped into my hand. "Heroin is my Shepherd: I shall always want. It maketh me to lie down in gutters," it began, and it ended: "Surely hate and evil shall follow me all the days of my life, And I will dwell in the house of misery and disgrace forever." When I recovered, returned to the dormitory, and dressed in my white eyelet evening uniform for dinner, an elderly housemother reprimanded me for wearing seamless stockings, presumably because they made me look bare-legged. After my days in Harlem, I was infuriated by her pettiness. It was 1960, however, and it did not enter my mind to rebel against the rules. My plan was to go to another school.

That year I was taking a creative writing elective. It meant so much to me that I have saved my notebook from the class, as well as the classic grammar we were given, *The Elements of Style*, by E. B. White and William Strunk, Jr. The first page of the notebook has a quotation by Joseph Conrad about the purpose of writing, undoubtedly dictated by our teacher, white-haired and soft-spoken Miss Kellogg, English department chair and Bryn Mawr alumna, whom Miss Hillard had hired in 1925. On the second page, I dutifully wrote down more time-honored rules about writing, and then, as in any working writer's notebook, I used the rest of the ruled pages for essay and story ideas as well as bits of dialogue and description. I have never forgotten the excitement of a homework assignment from that class: taking a topic from a basket in the schoolroom, and then writing about it for half an hour. I must have loved that exercise in extemporaneous writing because it was an invitation to voice.

As I wrote, the act of writing enabled me to sublimate my desires and summon the patience to postpone what I imagined was really living. A few weeks after returning from New York, but well before spring vacation, I announced to my diary, "I'm staying. What's one year out of a lifetime?" I found a roommate and applied for a summer program with the Quakers. And I wrote. The extreme contrast between Harlem and Middlebury called for comprehension, and it fueled my words. It was then when I intuited that I had the mind set of a writer, and the inclination to be more of an observer than a participant. The pleasure of expressing myself on paper was enhanced the following June, when one of my essays about Harlem was published under my byline in the school literary magazine, *The Lantern*.

Senior year was surprisingly happy. In October, I loved thinking hard in the mornings and playing tennis vigorously in the afternoons. As always, I found my classes intellectually exciting, or mentally "invigorating," as I put it in my diary, and I was doing well in all of them except for French. I also noted that "being away from the world gives you a chance to think about things." Since everyone's femaleness was taken for granted, it was downplayed, and we were free to dream outside the narrow gender expectations of the era. In November, I was thrilled when President Kennedy was elected, and I planned to join his Peace Corps. And, despite my Unitarian reservations about the Anglican liturgy, I liked what I called the "peace and beauty" of the lovely little chapel with its large arched window, especially at Christmastime, when it was full of sweet-smelling greenery. That winter I contentedly worked on a paper for Miss Dillingham's senior ethics seminar about nonviolence in the civil rights movement. When the pond froze, the ice hockey was exhilarating. In Introduction to Philosophy, Mr. Schumacher asked us to write about what we wanted in life, and, at a time when few women I knew had careers, I wrote in turquoise ink that I wanted two of them: to be a writer and a social worker. That school year had its disappointments, too. After getting permission from Miss Dillingham to drop mathematics after sophomore year, I was disappointed when I did poorly on my math SAT. She told me it didn't matter, since I was going to major in history or political science. But I was right to be worried, and I did not get into the college of my choice.

At Ohio Wesleyan, I stayed away from sororities after so many years at girls' schools. But after being mocked in a mostly male history class when speaking up, I gravitated to literature classes with more female students and became an English major. If women did not make history, I told myself, they had at least written novels for centuries. Literature was as close to a female sensibility as I could find in academia at that time before women's studies courses. After graduating, I went to work for a daily newspaper in Providence before moving to New York. It was a struggle to write on my own, until I left *Newsweek* after six years to write a book. After it was published, I moved from Manhattan, eventually settling into a small historic house (called "the Academy," since part of it had once been a schoolhouse) on a village green in northwestern Connecticut. Without really realizing it, I had found a place like Middlebury, where I developed a pattern of writing in the mornings and walking or gardening or researching or running errands in the afternoons, not unlike the rich rhythm of life I had learned so long ago at Westover.

Working in the archive on this book, I was alternately surprised, amused, saddened, and almost always interested in what I was finding. I interviewed alumnae, administrators, trustees, and teachers, including my former English teacher, Miss Newton, who amazed me by saying she not only remembered me but also recalled my total absorption and involvement in classroom discussions. This demanding teacher had wanted me to think harder in her Nineteenth Century Literature class, so I was glad to give her a copy of my first book and get a nice note from her about it. I decided that she and my other teachers had not used feminist language in the 1950s because it was risky and, besides, many of them were living the lives of liberated women anyway. Being in Middlebury and returning to my own and others' reunions, I got to know the school again. It was gratifying to see the way it had transformed itself through the decades into a place that is better than before—more informal, more open, and much more diverse—while still offering excellence in the classroom. While Miss Dillingham had endorsed a kind of tough love, I learned that Ann Pollina has brought great warmth to Westover, and it is what she calls "a place with heart." As always, students get used to expressing themselves and being smart and strong. It is without question a good place for girls.

Reading letters and diaries of other alumnae and listening to their stories, I understand that we shared much, but that we experienced it differently. Sometimes it seems as if we went to different schools. My Westover is unlike anyone else's, yet, like everyone else, I feel a sense of possessiveness about it. Inevitably, this history of our school is about what I read and remembered as well as what others revealed to me and reminded me about. And, as I learned about our school's past, I learned more about myself. At times I was sorry for that struggling teenager, but I was glad to discover in my student file that Miss Dillingham had had a better opinion of me than I had of myself. Looking back, I'm grateful that my Real Life was delayed for a few years so that I could imagine the life I really wanted to live.

L. L.
Sharon, Connecticut

ACKNOWLEDGMENTS

MANY MORE PEOPLE THAN I CAN EVER THANK PERSONALLY HAVE helped me bring this book into being. Archivist Maria Allen's assistance has been invaluable. Over the years, she has collected not only memorabilia and other materials but also many stories from alumnae, and it was wonderfully helpful when she sent out a mailing to all the alumnae from the Dillingham decades asking for more of them. She has aided me in innumerable other ways, from showing me around the archive to arranging initial meetings with her classmate, Adele Ervin, and her friend, the late John Ferguson. Adele, the school's first alumnae secretary, has enriched this history through our talks and by giving me a box of vivid and important letters. During his boyhood in Middlebury, John knew his mother's close friends—Mary Hillard, Helen LaMonte, and Lucy Pratt—so his reflections, and the letters and papers he gave me, were very revealing.

Maria did not ask me to write this book before proposing the idea to Ann Pollina, who immediately endorsed it. It has been a pleasure to get to know Ann and hear about her exciting ways of educating girls. She has enthusiastically assisted me in every way, giving steadfast support, a number of interviews, any documents I asked for, and allowing me to go where the truth has taken me. My first interview with Joseph Molder, long before I began this book, was followed by another four of them, the last at his lakefront home in Middlebury. True to character, he was always thoughtful, insightful, and honest with me about the goings-on at Westover during three decades.

I am grateful to the nearly one hundred people who have graciously shared their memories and insights with me in person, by telephone, letter, and e-mail. The oldest was Mary Willcox Wiley '18, and the youngest were girls who were not yet alumnae. Mary, who had just had her hundredth birthday when I visited, had a merry smile and an amazing memory, and when it faltered, she would say, "I can't quite get hold of that tail feather"; we had a good laugh after I mentioned uniforms, and she replied that she had never seen any "unicorns" at Westover. Since Louise Dillingham's personal papers have disappeared, I am very glad to have talked at length with her niece, Dorothy Goodwin '49. Also, my sister and her roommate in the class of 1968 explained to me why they had felt so rebellious. I had fascinating talks with Anita Packard Montgomery '47, Eunice Strong Groark '56, Betsy Shirley Michel '59, Victoria DiSesa '70, and Mary Gelezunas '84. Other contributors are too numerous to name, but I have cited them in the endnotes, and my heartfelt thanks go to every one.

I also wish to thank those who let me publish photographs and quote from letters and other writings of their relatives, especially the nephews of Mary Hillard and Helen LaMonte, William H. MacLeish and Edward S. LaMonte. During her very long life, Miss LaMonte was like a one-woman Greek chorus commenting kindly and wisely from afar about the happenings in Middlebury. My thanks go as well to David Norman, a nephew of Patience Norman, and to Mark Schumacher, the son of Joachim Schumacher. Many alumnae kindly shared their youthful writings and the written words of their mothers and fathers, including my classmates, Catherine Drew and Skipper Skelly. I am very pleased that Adrienne Rich and her publisher and John Masefield's literary executor also granted me permissions. *Mary Robbins Hillard*, a 1944 memoir published by Bishop John T. Dallas about his longtime friend, and *Westover*, Elizabeth Choate Spykman's delightful little 1959 history written for the fiftieth anniversary, were very useful. When working at the archive of Theodate Pope Riddle's Hill-Stead Museum, the staff generously gave me valuable information, such as the existence of Miss Hillard's letters to a close friend, August Jaccaci. Thanks also go to all those with offices on the ground floor of Hillard House, who, between my rushed trips up and down the stairs from archive to photocopy machine and back, answered my many questions. It was Kitty Benedict '52 who suggested that I send the manuscript to Wesleyan University Press, and Charlotte Strick '91 who designed the book.

WESTOVER

1

Mary Hillard and Her Era:
Protestant and Progressive

ON A DAY IN LATE APRIL OF 1909, A WOMAN NAMED THEODATE
Pope and a group of teachers from St. Margaret's School in the city of Waterbury,
Connecticut, excitedly got into the Pope family's chauffeured motor car, carrying a
samovar, a ham, hatboxes, and precious colored photographs. The overloaded car made
what one of the women later described as a "perilous" trip over the hilly six miles to
the village of Middlebury. The village green, shaded by elms and encircled by white
colonial homes and shops, was now bordered on one side by an enormous, pale stucco
school with a steep slate roof and a bell tower. Over the large dark green door, an
emblem on a projecting gable held three Tudor roses, a lamp of learning, and the
commanding words *"Cogitare, Agere, Esse"* (or, "To Think, To Do, To Be"). A few days
later, when a Waterbury newspaperman described the impressive neocolonial façade of
the school called Westover, he noted that it would look better with shrubbery grown
up around it.

After the teachers arrived, walked through the wide doorway, and looked around,
they started to oversee the unpacking and arranging. At the end of the day, Lucy Pratt,
Helen LaMonte and others happily settled down in a small front office and lit candles
on its mantel and a fire in its grate. They waited for the new headmistress to arrive and
"be delighted" by the sight, but when Mary Hillard finally rushed down the hall carrying her typewriter and papers, she was so busy that she didn't even notice them. Since
there was not yet any telephone or telegraph service to the village, it seemed as if they

were far out in the country. When Miss LaMonte opened her eyes on the first morning, however, she joked: "'Taint lonesome! Miss Pratt.' So we began with gaiety—and it never was lonesome," Lucy Pratt recalled forty years later.

The next day, the women continued to hurry around the huge, half empty edifice, unpacking blue Canton china for the dining room and endless boxes and crates. Theodate Pope locked the chapel door so no one would touch the drying varnish inside. "Workmen were underfoot everywhere, uncrating chapel chairs or putting turf in the Quad or carpet on Red Hall, but we somehow managed to go on in spite of all the activity," recalled Helen LaMonte. Curious visitors were constantly arriving and asking to be shown around, she remembered, and her feet ached even though someone had thought to bring foot powder for everyone's shoes.

Less than a week later, Miss Hillard and others stood inside the front door to greet the seventy or so pupils, who had formerly boarded at St. Margaret's School, arriving after spring vacation on electric trolley cars from Waterbury. The young girls excitedly explored the many rooms as their trunks and more furniture slowly arrived up the hill by horse-drawn wagons, a procession that was halted for a few days by a spring snowstorm. As the unpacking paused, Lucy Pratt took the time to write to Theodate Pope, who had left for a vacation in Cuba to rest from her exhausting preparations as the school's architect. "We have been in our beautiful home one week . . . [and we think] with love of our blessed architect . . . for every peg in every closet, every latch of every door, every screw in its place sings Theodate. My sweet bedroom almost keeps me awake with the peace of its beauty."

In the middle of May, the three apple trees inside the inner courtyard put forth arrays of pale pink blossoms as one of the loveliest springs in memory got underway. Amid the excitement there were a few emergencies. A girl suddenly needed an appendectomy, and without a motor car available to get her to a hospital, the operation was performed on ironing boards in the unfinished infirmary. Someone threw a few muslin blouses, called waists at the time, down a chute labeled "waste." Then the well water ran out. Nonetheless, Mary Hillard was elated. "We are in! It is all so beautiful and good," she wrote to a friend in late May. "It is all so good a start," she added a few weeks later. "A beautiful spirit was here, that matched our beautiful setting, and I think our life had a benediction in the sweetness and consideration that my dear girls showed through the days of adjustment, and that every helper, from the servants up, seemed full of. So that I shall always look back to those days of real stress with such deep thankfulness as being full of something living and spiritual." When the school term ended in June, the twenty seniors returned to Waterbury for a graduation ceremony with their former classmates at St. Margaret's School, mostly day students who lived in the bustling city.

✦   ✦   ✦

BY THE TIME WESTOVER OPENED, the task of educating girls already had a long and contentious history. In 1792 during the Enlightenment, eighteenth-century English feminist Mary Wollstonecraft had called for their equal education with boys. In *Thoughts on the Education of Daughters,* she urged mothers to teach their daughters so they would learn to think, and she herself started several schools for girls. Early on in New England, there had been dame schools, where young children were taught to read, write, and do arithmetic in the homes of women. After the American Revolution, it was regarded as patriotic to educate the future "mothers of the republic," those who would educate the male citizens of the young democracy. Connecticut had enlightened attitudes about educating females, and many of the best schools for girls were in the state. One was Sarah Pierce's school in Litchfield, which opened in 1790 to educate the daughters of merchants, landowners, and ministers, including educator Catharine Beecher and her sister, author Harriet Beecher Stowe. Because of the difficulty and expense of travel at the time, they were by necessity boarding schools. In the nineteenth century, a new generation of female educators urged women to take responsibility for educating members of their own sex, and one of them named Emma Willard briefly ran a female seminary in the village of Middlebury.

The school called Westover was Mary Hillard's idea long before it was anyone else's. She envisioned it as a wholesome setting for study and sports, as well as a school in which to instill in young women useful knowledge and idealistic values. It was as if she were trying to recreate the most ideal conditions of her own childhood. Born and raised in Connecticut villages like Middlebury, she knew them intimately as places where a traditional way of life went on apart from all the rapid changes going on in America. This was particularly true of Plymouth, where she lived during the impressionable ages of seven to seventeen with her family in a parsonage on a hill above the Naugatuck River valley in central Connecticut, where brass factories were attracting thousands of immigrants from southern Europe.

The Rev. Elias Brewster Hillard was the minister of the big white First Congregational Church of Plymouth. A member of the New England intelligentsia, he had acquired a fine education at Andover Academy and Yale University, where he graduated with the class of 1848. His thinking was liberal, learned, and open-minded, particularly about the education of his daughters. He was also curious, candid, excitable, and courageous; even as an old man he had "vividness and aliveness," remembered his grandson, poet Archibald MacLeish. The minister liked to tell his children stories about their ancestors, Puritans who had sailed from England in the early 1600s. There was the tale of great-grandparents captured by Indians, and one about their grandfather Moses, an enterprising ship's captain who attempted to smuggle Napoleon out of France. In his spare time Elias wrote a book about four forgotten Connecticut heroes of the American Revolution.

When the young minister was the principal of a private school in Southington, Connecticut, he met his future wife, Julia Whittlesey, a student there. The daughter of a Yale-educated judge who had moved to Cleveland, Ohio, Julia was sent back East to finish her schooling, and she received what was considered the best possible education for a female in her day. Julia was diminutive and delicate with big, bright, brown eyes and dark hair. Besides being very feminine and lovely looking, she was possessed of a "sweet selflessness" and "charm and inward grace," according to this grandson. When she became the mother of a large family, she was also firm, frugal, humorous, and extremely organized. Despite her practical nature, she also had an interest in spiritualism. The couple was well matched. "I can see Elias flying off on tangents and Julia holding onto his coat-tails," said Mary Robbins Whittlesey, Julia's older sister, for whom her daughter Mary was named.

The couple's eldest child, Martha, born in 1856, went to Vassar College, which had opened its doors when she was nine. Her college tuition was paid for by the estate of a tall, aristocratic, and emotionally disturbed aunt who lived with the Hillards, a woman who suffered from what was called "insanity of the will." After teaching mathematics at Vassar, Martha became principle of Rockford Seminary in Illinois until she married

Andrew MacLeish. A leader in progressive education, social reform, and missionary work, she helped Jane Addams establish Hull House and was president of the Chicago Women's Club, among many other activities. Frederick, born a year later, would invent typewriter parts but fail to profit from his patents. The third child, Helen, became a nurse and was a founder of a settlement house. Mary was born three years later in the summer of 1862, and the petite Emily was born four years after that. Then there was Fanny, who was mentally ill most of her life. The next child, precocious and sickly William, died at the age of twenty. Another son, Arthur, lived only a year. The youngest and ninth child was John, born when Mary was a teenager, who became almost like a son to her.

The Hillards raised their children based on the theories in Horace Bushnell's *Christian Nurture*, which was a more affectionate approach to childrearing than the strict Puritan way; years later, however, when a young man remarked to Mary that "one hardly dares to be too happy," she asked him with surprise, "have you got that in your background, too?" Martha later portrayed the Hillards as a happy, if financially strapped, family. Their religious expression was "simple, sincere, and beautiful," and the children were instilled with the highest ideals. Mary was especially idealistic and wanted to become a missionary in China. In the evenings their father would read aloud Dickens, Stowe, and other novelists, while Julia and their daughters would sit around a large table doing needlework. Elias also enjoyed taking his children picnicking and camping. When he went about his parish in a sleigh or horse and buggy, he liked to take young Mary with him; she later said that she had noticed and remembered everything, like the differences in intellect and personality among his parishioners.

At the time Mary was born, on June 14, 1862, in the Connecticut village of Kensington, her father was deeply upset by the outbreak of the Civil War the year before. Inheriting her mother's dark eyes, she would also acquire, in her eldest sister's opinion, her mother's take-charge manner, sense of spirituality, gift for organization, and strong belief in right and wrong. When she was a teenager, a classmate described her as "very tall, angular, almost ungainly . . . [but with a] directness, a dashing quickness of motion, [an] entire absence of self-consciousness and great dignity . . . Plain of face she may have been, dark olive and even sallow in coloring, but a face which lighted up radiantly and which was redeemed by the deep-set, very dark, very penetrating eyes—sympathetic

The Hillard family around 1894. From left: Emily, Martha (Ishbel MacLeish in lap), Elias Brewster Hillard, Mary, John, Helen, Archibald MacLeish, Julia Whittlesey Hillard, Frederick, and Fanny. CONNECTICUT HISTORICAL SOCIETY.

often, quizzical oftener and with a look so far away at times that she was even then thought quite mystic and unsearchable." This classmate, Martha Coffin, also went on to say that "there was infinite pathos" in Mary's eyes, orbs that "were always darkened by deep circling shadows"; some friends even "called her sad-eyed." The classmate also remembered "the fine modeling of the head, that something quite lovely about the brow and temples." Mary grew to be one of the tallest members of her family as well as the most attractive of the clan, according to a family photograph taken around 1894, when she was thirty-two. In this photograph she is the most stylishly dressed among her dark-garbed parents and siblings, wearing a handsome light-colored suit and a dark high-necked blouse. Sitting near the center of the group, she exudes such a strong force of personality that she eclipses everyone else, even her brilliant older sisters.

After attending the local schoolhouse in Plymouth, Mary followed her sister Helen to the Collegiate Institute for Young Ladies in Waterbury, a school run by the Episcopal Church and renamed St. Margaret's School for Girls when Mary was thirteen. Uncle Moses Hillard, a bachelor, helped with the tuition. When the headmaster of St. Margaret's, the Rev. Francis Thayer Russell, realized that high-spirited Mary was not settling down to study, he suggested to her parents that she might do better elsewhere. At the age of eighteen her parents enrolled her in Abbott Academy, a girl's school on a hill in Andover, Massachusetts, where she came under the influence of the elderly, authoritative headmistress, Philena McKeen, a husky-voiced woman with ringlets on both sides of her face. Mary was expected to earn her tuition, so she ran the supply shop and led a gymnastics class. She admired Miss McKeen, and a number of her later educational practices—quiet Sabbaths and simplicity of dress—became traditions at Westover. In her studies, Mary was fair in algebra and Latin but poor in French and German as well as in music and drawing. What interested her intensely were the ideas inherent in the study of history: the history of art, the history of religion, the history of linguistics, and the history of England. She also read voraciously on her own, as she would do all her life.

From an early age she was exceptional in her gift for public speaking. When asked to recite in class, she would turn recitation into something else, "a thought and question-provoking forum," in the words of Martha Coffin. A natural leader, she was regarded as the head of the school even before she was elected president of her class. She was also firm and opinionated. Girls who went to her for advice often got "a strong bracing up, a sound whacking" instead of sympathy, recalled this classmate, who noted that nothing dampened her high spirits. One of her friends summed her up as "the biggest tease, the one who always kept her things in perfect order, who always had time for any fun going on (mostly setting it going), made the best use of her time, worked the hardest, and had the best time of any girl in school."

The Rev. Hillard supposedly wanted Mary to go to college like her older sisters but, for reasons that are not entirely evident, she did not wish to go. Perhaps she realized that she was not a scholar, or her certainty and independence made college appear unnecessary. In an era when differences between academies and universities were not as distinct as they are today, she stayed at Abbott for four years, until she earned her high school diploma around the time of her twenty-second birthday. On graduation day she gave an impressive valedictory speech and then returned home to teach children in the Plymouth schoolhouse.

A year later, in 1885, Sarah Porter hired her to teach at her long-established girls' school in the village of Farmington, a few miles west of Hartford. It was to Mary Hillard's advantage that when Miss Porter hired a teacher, she was less interested in her education than in her character—"a clear and well-trained mind, quick sympathies and a pure heart" were what she wanted. Perhaps the headmistress at the age of seventy-two saw the twenty-three-year-old Mary as a younger version of herself; both were descendents of old American families and daughters of Congregationalist ministers. There were some differences, however: Sarah Porter, whose brother was the president of Yale University when she hired the young teacher, was a scholar who had studied languages and other subjects with Yale professors throughout her life. A pious woman who dressed in handsome black dresses in winter and gray ones in summer, she was also a person who valued simplicity and humility and was supposedly indifferent to the social backgrounds of her wealthy pupils, preaching that "wealth did not make worth."

Young Mary Hillard was deeply impressed by this woman, who became a mentor. She admired the way the older woman impressed old-fashioned values upon her pupils to prepare them for family life rather than for teaching, missionary, and other kinds of women's work. Yet unlike traditionalists who believed that the female body did not have enough blood to sustain both the brain and the womb, Miss Porter also rejected the idea that mental activity undermines a woman's family responsibilities, and she attempted to prepare girls for lifelong intellectual and spiritual growth. Mary Hillard later said that she was very grateful to Sarah Porter for teaching her everything she knew about successfully running a school during the six years under her wing.

Those years of her early twenties were the time when the lovely Mary Hillard would have been most likely to marry. An old friend of hers acknowledged that Mary had been in love as a young girl, and that she had struggled "to decide between love and duty." Teaching evidently tapped her idealism: the little girl who had wanted to be a missionary in China now wanted to enlighten and lead young women. If she married, she knew that she would eventually have to give up teaching; wives almost always left or lost their jobs especially after the arrival of children. At that time she expressed caution about romantic feelings. Miss Hillard has "some queer ideas, such as that a girl should never love a man before he asks her to and then she cannot be certain whether she can care for him or not but must wait to find out," confided Elizabeth Failing, a Miss Porter's pupil, to her diary. Miss Porter viewed romantic infatuation as a feeling to be directed toward the good of the family, a view the young teacher would also articulate. At the Westover graduation of 1917, she declared that marriage is not for personal happiness but a way to pass along values to the next generation.

Even at that early age, Mary Hillard had a knack for understanding girls; Elizabeth Failing also wrote in her diary that she was in awe of her teacher's insight into her at a party where Miss Hillard told fortunes and placed an apt quote about each girl at her plate. The girl also wrote about her admiration for her energetic and entertaining young teacher: Miss Hillard is, she wrote, "like a breeze [that] stirs up the air and implants a new vitality." Still, Mary Hillard came to regard herself as less gifted as a teacher in the classroom than as a leader who could inspire young women with her melodic speaking

Mary Robbins Hillard as a young woman. L. ALTMAN & CO.

voice. Miss Porter noticed her leadership qualities and soon gave the youthful teacher a small administrative role in one of the school's dormitories.

By that time Miss Porter had already chosen her successor, assistant principal Mary Dunning Dow, a former pupil and a widow who was much older than Mary. At the same time, the scholarly and elderly headmaster of St. Margaret's School in Waterbury was looking for an assistant. His wife had recently died, and one day during a visit with a parishioner he confessed his difficulty in trying to run the girls' school alone. The woman, whose daughter had roomed with Mary Hillard at St. Margaret's, mentioned the young teacher as someone with energy and ideas; one thing led to another, and Dr. Russell offered Mary Hillard—whom he had asked to leave the school some fifteen years earlier—the position of assistant principal. When she told Miss Porter about the offer, the older woman urged her to take it, telling her that she had a talent for leadership. Mary's reservations were about leaving the peaceful village of Farmington for the busy city of Waterbury. Also, she had enlarged her circle of friends in Farmington to include more sophisticated people than those in the parsonages of her youth. Miss Porter assured her that she would find similar people in Waterbury, like the fine old New England family of Edith and Frederick Kingsbury, who had two daughters her age living at home. As Mary Hillard turned twenty-nine, she decided to go.

As Miss Mary Hillard walked rapidly through the streets of Waterbury in the autumn of 1891, she carried herself with more dignity and solemnity than usual, aware that she was being observed. A tall, slender, single woman with searching eyes, she was remembered for parting her long, dark brown hair in the middle and pulling it back into a knot at the back of her head. Instead of elaborate Victorian fashions, she wore the more practical clothing of the professional women of her day. "There was an air of austerity mingled with something athletic," an observer recalled. "The shirtwaist with a collar and bow tie, the longish skirt, the absence of anything colorful, the modest hat, gloves, all bespoke restraint." She brought a pearl-handled knife to St. John's Episcopal Church in the city, where St. Margaret's trustees and most of its pupils worshipped, to cut tight corset strings of girls who fainted during services. Although young men were awed by her, she got to know several Yale graduates who worked for *The Waterbury American* as well as families who knew her father. Direct and businesslike, she gave people the impression that she knew what she wanted and had no time to waste. "There were inner fires always burning in her," observed a younger friend, the Rev. John T. Dallas, assistant pastor at St. John's, who would get to know her very well.

Her sense of urgency was undoubtedly exacerbated by the realization that St. Margaret's was in debt and in decline. She had quickly discovered problems with the school's faltering furnaces and its drafty, dilapidated Victorian wooden structure. About a year after her arrival, Dr. Russell became ill, entered a New York City hospital, and sent in his resignation. The board of trustees asked Mary to take his job. In an act of astonishing audacity by a woman barely over the age of thirty, she said no. Instead, she responded with a counteroffer in which she proposed to rent the rambling building from the trustees and run St. Margaret's as her own school. As gestures to reassure the trustees, she offered to hire Dr. Russell, who had remained in New York to teach theology, as rector and to meet with them once a year.

Mary Hillard obviously did not want to be under the thumb of older, more cautious male trustees who, she feared, might not be willing to borrow enough money to turn the school around. She felt supremely confident that any debts she took on would be eventually repaid as she increased enrollment. The trustees, including Frederick Kingsbury, must have been taken aback by the demands of the young woman, but by 1894 they agreed to them. Kingsbury, whose mother had gone to Miss Pierce's School in Litchfield, was a firm believer in women's education and most likely in women educators as well. The young headmistress was equally persuasive with Waterbury bankers. At the end of every school year, when tuition income ended and teachers had to be paid and repairs undertaken, she would take out a personal bank loan endorsed by Dr. Russell simply on the strength of a handshake.

It was during this time in the late 1890s when she began to hire the teachers a few years younger than herself who would follow her to Westover and be lifelong friends. She asked Helen Dean LaMonte, a member of the Smith College class of 1885, to teach art history and literature. Lucy Bailey Pratt, a teachers' college graduate, took charge of the kindergarten. She also hired Henriette Coffin, a young Frenchwoman, to teach the French language and literature, and Helen Andrews, an artist, to teach drawing and painting. In 1900 her younger sister, Fanny, was teaching psychology and history at the school, but she, like their oldest sister Martha, gave up teaching when she married. During the first decade of her sixteen years at St. Margaret's, Mary borrowed and

Theodate Pope (left) and Mary Hillard at Miss Porter's School, 1888.
ARCHIVES, HILL-STEAD MUSEUM, FARMINGTON, CT.

repaid huge amounts of money for repairs and, with the help of a gift in 1902, finally got the school out of the red. Meanwhile, enrollment increased so much that she had to rent a house near the school for all the new boarders.

After Mary Hillard moved to Waterbury, she kept in touch with friends she had made in Farmington. One of them was Theodate Pope, a former pupil who was an unhappy only child from a wealthy Cleveland family. She did not get along with her conventional mother, questioning her lavish spending habits. In the fall of 1886, when the girl was almost twenty, her parents sent her to Miss Porter's School instead of to Wellesley College because she was so poor in math. Theodate had been named Effie for an aunt, but the year she left home she renamed herself for a Quaker grandmother in Maine. At Miss Porter's she struggled with her studies as well as her moods and was often depressed. She was troubled by finding more inspiration in paintings, books, music, and nature than in religion. She also agonized about whether it was her duty to live at home or marry or fulfill her dream of living on a farm with children adopted from poor families.

Mary Hillard noticed Theodate's depression and asked her to sit at her table in the dining room. Only four and a half years younger than the teacher, Theo, as she came to be called, was plain, short, sturdy, and broad-shouldered with light brown hair and expressive blue eyes. Feeling empathic toward the troubled girl, perhaps because of the mental illness in members of her own family, Miss Hillard recommended to her the inspirational words of the medieval monk Thomas à Kempis. Two months later, Theo noted in her diary that "Miss Hillard said that she thought there was nothing that could not be borne in this world, although borne perhaps with a struggle, except the consciousness of sin." By spring the teacher and pupil had become close. "Miss Hillard made me promise I would come and see her when I feel blue and desperate. She is wonderfully nice to me. I have a walking day with her and I go every Sunday evening to see her."

The next school year, which would be Theo's last year of education, the teacher tutored her in math while the girl developed a schoolgirl crush on her. Miss Hillard "knows everything," Theo wrote in her diary. "She already knew something that I confessed to her today." In March Theo's parents withdrew her from school, supposedly because of illness, but the truth is that Mrs. Pope disapproved of Miss Hillard's influence over her daughter, even bluntly telling the teacher to see less of the girl. During the summer a family friend's eligible son, Harris Whittemore, proposed marriage to Theo, and the following year of 1888, the Popes departed for a year-long tour of Europe with the engaged couple. During the trip Theo confessed to her father that she didn't love Harris enough to marry him, so the engagement was broken off, and the young man returned to America.

Theodate had been making drawings of buildings since childhood. One day while the Popes were abroad, her father noticed her sketches of the farmhouse of her dreams and suggested that she study architecture. Although she now felt she had permission to lead a life different from her mother's, she was still struggling with the strictures of upper class society. After the family's return to Cleveland, Theo made her debut but soon afterward fell into such a deep depression that her parents sent her to a rest home in Philadelphia for a month. Perhaps on advice from a doctor, in May of 1890 the Popes allowed their daughter to rent a small eighteenth-century farmhouse in Farmington within walking distance of her former school. Over the next few years, rebelling against her privileged Victorian background, she restored the old farmhouse, which she named the O'Rourkery. Theo, who had become an ardent suffragette and socialist as well as a Unitarian, now wanted to become an architect. After studying privately with art and architectural historians at Princeton University, she began to design a home for her parents in Farmington with the assistance of the architectural firm of McKim, Mead and White. Finished in 1900, Hill-Stead was so impressive that writer Henry James, in his book *The American Scene*, likened it to George Washington's Mount Vernon.

After returning to Farmington, Theo was glad to renew her friendship with her former teacher. The Popes knew people who were part of the country's intellectual and establishment elite, including writers Edith Wharton and Ida Tarbell, and even President Theodore Roosevelt. Over the years Mary Hillard would meet many of them at Hill-Stead, where she often went and spent many holidays, especially Christmas. She sometimes also stayed at the Popes' suite in the Buckingham Hotel in New York City.

As Mary and Theo became more intimate, they vacationed together, going to Bermuda in spring and to rustic camps in Maine and New Hampshire in summer, often with relatives and friends, including teachers at St. Margaret's. Then in December of 1902, the headmistress of St. Margaret's announced to her students that she was "rundown" and needed a long period of rest. A few months later, the friends sailed for Europe. It was around this time that Theo began thinking about designing a school for Mary, and they toured England and France with an eye toward what they most admired in architecture. The eventual design of Westover was influenced by the colleges in England and Europe where students both studied and lived. Spending a week in the guesthouse of an English convent and girls' school, Mary was impressed by its chapel; she was also inspired by the cloister of the Salisbury Cathedral. In Paris they visited American artist Mary Cassatt, whose work the Popes collected. The friends also studied the French language along with the country's history and literature at the Convent of the Soeurs de St. Augustin in Tours.

In July of 1903, when the friends had been in Europe for six months, they heard from Alfred Pope, whom Mary now called Uncle Alfred, about new developments in the struggle for control over Miss Porter's school after the headmistress's death. Miss Porter had hoped that Mary Dow would be the new headmistress, and that Mary Hillard would be her associate and eventually succeed her, but the founder's will had been challenged. When Mary heard the news, she immediately left for America. Soon after her arrival, she met with the school's trustees and told them that she was alarmed that Miss Porter's legacy was in danger and proposed that they help Mrs. Dow and herself start a new school together. Perhaps because Miss Hillard admitted to doubts about giving up her position at St. Margaret's, or because her relationship with the older woman was strained, or because of the astonishing fact that she intended to open a school in Farmington whether the other woman went along or not, nothing ever came of her proposal.

Still, in that encounter Mary Hillard revealed how sure of herself she had become after her successful years at St. Margaret's. "I know school affairs thoroughly," she told the trustees of Miss Porter's. "It is my business. I know [the] ins and outs of school management as only one in school work can know them . . . points so essential that to ignore them means failure, while at the same time they are so obscure that only the experienced mind understands their importance . . . Moreover, the talent for success is extremely rare. I might almost say that in the last six or seven years there has not been a change of importance in any important boarding school for girls in the East without my having been asked to come in or lend a hand by advice or help find someone to run the school."

Despite her faith in herself, she was soon to be shaken to her core. Toward her younger brother John, who was born when she was fifteen, Mary had always acted like a parent, directing his education and planning his life. After graduating with high honors from Yale, he began to practice law in New Haven. In August of 1903, a few weeks after his sister returned from Europe, he contracted typhoid fever after boating on the Farmington River. He hung onto life at Hartford Hospital for a few weeks, but in late September he died at the age of twenty-six. John's death, their eldest sister Martha acknowledged, was the worst grief of Mary's life.

Like many other freethinkers at the time, Theo had become fascinated by what was called "psychical science," the investigation into the unknown and the unconscious. In an effort to ease her friend's grief, Theo suggested that they try to communicate with her brother. Harvard psychologist William James, who had started the American branch of the Society for Psychical Research in Boston, recommended that they see Beacon Hill psychic Leonora Piper. A few months after John's death, they had their first sitting to try to talk to his spirit. In the first session Mrs. Piper told Mary to tap her fingers, and then told her that her brother wanted her to remove her hat so she could hear him better. Mary became a true believer, and on John's tombstone she had the following words inscribed: "He Being dead yet speaketh." The séances continued intermittently until the end of 1907, when the plans for Mary's new school got underway, and she supposedly became more concerned about her reputation. There's another story that she stopped because she found it all "a little too exciting." It's doubtful that she abandoned her belief in the unknowable; it's more likely that she convinced some of her colleagues of it. Years later Theodate's young twin cousins spent a weekend with her and heard about inexplicable phenomena. When they returned to Westover, where they were pupils, and described this to Helen LaMonte, she did not disillusion them. Instead, Miss LaMonte pointed out that before the invention of the telephone, the idea of someone in America talking to someone in Europe would have been unbelievable, so that if one does not understand something, it does not mean that it does not exist.

After the months in Europe, it was more evident than ever that the growth of Waterbury in the 1890s had become "phenomenal," to use Mary Hillard's word, as immigrants arrived to work in factories that were polluting its air with coal smoke. The city had, in fact, more than doubled in size since she had moved there. At a time when there was no cure for tuberculosis, Waterbury and other cities were dangerously overcrowded. Teachers and parents alike had begun to believe that the countryside was a more wholesome place for schoolchildren than a city. And, as a result, Mary believed that St. Margaret's School was in peril.

Not only did Mary want to get away from the unhealthy conditions of Waterbury, she also wanted to offer girls the athletics and other advantages that were more available in the country. Most important of all, she fervently wanted to create a self-contained community devoted to teaching traditional moral values to daughters of the newly wealthy merchant class. By then in her forties, Mary Hillard was a self-possessed person with a regal bearing. Her dream was a real possibility because of her manner and persuasiveness with the St. Margaret's board of trustees as well as her friendships with the Popes and other wealthy and influential Connecticut families. At a time in America when a newly emerging crusade for rights for women was gathering force, Theo's resources and determination to build another building and Mary's success as an educator and her missionary zeal were a potent combination.

Their plan emerged for a girl's school for one hundred and forty boarders and their teachers. Mary and Theo had joined the Connecticut Society of Colonial Dames together in 1900, and the ultimate design was heavily influenced by the colonial revival style. It was not necessary to be licensed to work as an architect in Connecticut at the time, and Theo hired draftsmen and consultants as needed. On January 30, 1906, Mary proposed to the St. Margaret's board that they build a new school building outside Waterbury for the boarding pupils; they eventually agreed to the idea, even permitting her to take along the boarders and teachers who wished to go with her. Then, after someone remembered that the school charter did not allow a move out of Waterbury, the board agreed to release Mary from her contract. When she handed in her resignation exactly a year later, she was asked to withhold it until the end of the school year, and she agreed.

Mary's plan was already in place, however. In 1903 she had told the Miss Porter's trustees of her plan to form a company and issue stock in it to raise the $200,000 to $300,000 that a new school would cost, explaining that a well-managed school was "an extremely good investment." Four years later in 1907, she set up the Westover Corporation to sell three thousand shares of stock at a hundred dollars each, which would pay an annual dividend of six percent. She sold stock to everyone she knew—friends, relatives, parents of pupils—even St. Margaret's trustees. The man who immediately bought the most stock was John Howard Whittemore of Naugatuck, a man of her father's generation whom she had met

Theodate Pope around 1895.

through the Popes. After making his fortune in malleable iron castings, he had commissioned a number of McKim, Mead and White buildings in his native city. Mary knew how to appeal to Mr. Whittemore, since they were both descendants of old Connecticut families and children of Congregational ministers. She praised his philanthropy as "a true and honest source of right and high minded influence," and, after receiving a grateful letter from her in 1907, he called his help "a labor of love." After selecting the rose as the new school's flower, she sent the Whittemores roses at Christmastime; she would also ask him to light the first fire in a school fireplace. After the pupils arrived in Middlebury, Mr. Whittemore used to ask her, "Are the girls happy?" He was the first president of the Westover Corporation and then the first president of the board of trustees until his death in 1910, a year after the school opened.

It was because of the Whittemores that Mary's school was built in Middlebury, where the family had a summer home, Tranquillity Farm. Before land was bought, the Popes' chauffeur, Turner, used to drive Mary, Theo, and teachers at St. Margaret's around the countryside in the family convertible motor car, nicknamed the "Yellow Peril" for its color, looking for sites for the school. (It was the first automobile that Mary had ridden in, and at first she had been fearful of its great speed.) They had driven through Middlebury in 1906 but considered it too isolated; the village had been bypassed by industrial development because it lacked waterpower, and most of its eight hundred residents still worked the land. But after Mr. Whittemore and his influential friends pulled strings, an electric trolley line was built from Waterbury to Woodbury with a stop in Middlebury, and it was possible to transport laborers and, eventually, students to the village.

With the help of John Whittemore and his son Harris, Mary pieced together a parcel of land along the south side of the Middlebury green that soon amounted to twenty-five acres. Involved in all the legal and financial details, she was so able that one of the shareholders, banker James S. Elton, said he regretted that because she was a woman she could not be president of the Waterbury National Bank. Mary wrote Harris Whittemore that she was "on fire" about her school, and when someone declined to buy stock, she would simply ask again. In 1907 Theo's architectural plans were finished and Richard F. Jones of Hartford, a contractor who had built Hill-Stead and also worked for the Whittemores, was chosen. John Whittemore signed the construction contract in September, but before building could begin it was necessary to move the Methodist meetinghouse and its parsonage, the Middlebury general store and post office, a blacksmith shop, a clapboard farmhouse, and several towering elms. All but three apple trees

in an old orchard were cut down, and the soggy pastures of a farm were filled to become playing fields.

When word finally got out about the plans, there was an uproar. It was feared that the trustees as well as the principal were abandoning St. Margaret's. At a meeting in November, alumnae and others presented two petitions protesting the loss of the boarders to trustee Chauncey B. Brewster, the bishop of Connecticut, but by then most trustees were already backers if not stockholders of "Mary's school." Finally Miss Hillard was forced to publicly explain. In a lengthy letter to *The Waterbury Ameri-*

Westover School under construction about 1908.
WESTOVER SCHOOL ARCHIVE.

can, she complained about being misquoted and misunderstood and heatedly defended herself and her plan for a new school. She wrote that she felt "naturally" entitled to take boarders and teachers with her to Middlebury because it was she who had attracted them to St. Margaret's in the first place. She explained that prospective parents of out-of-town pupils worried about their daughters' lack of athletics and "freedom of life" in Waterbury. The handwriting on the wall became clear, she went on, when her "own old girls" began urging her to do something so that they could send "their daughters to me" to be educated. She also pointed out that without boarders at St. Margaret's, there would be more room for the Waterbury girls. Finally, she added that the pupils at the new school would continue to patronize Waterbury churches, concerts, hotels, and businesses. The storm blew over, but a newspaperman wrote sarcastically that the young ladies will go to Middlebury, "where the bloom of the cowslips is unpolluted and the rarified atmosphere untainted with the soot of industrial progress."

This ivory tower had been estimated to cost a quarter of a million dollars, but by the time it was finished it would be more than twice that amount. Although Theo designed the building without a fee, she never felt constrained by a budget. As expenses mounted, more stock was issued; then in late 1908 when a large amount of money had to be borrowed, Mary refused to agree to the loan until the stockholders had taken out an insurance policy on her life and until dividend payments had begun. (Afterward Mr. Whittemore admitted to her that he had never believed dividends would ever be earned, and he was surprised and pleased to be wrong.)

As construction got underway, the Pope's chauffeur drove Mary and Theo to Middlebury almost every day. One moonlit evening when the two women went to Middlebury to inspect the new foundation, Mary felt overwhelmed by its size—it was a hundred and twenty-five feet square—so Theo calmed her by telling her to let her "spirit" fill the space. After the walls went up, stucco was applied, made of white sea sand, goats' hair, and lime, supposedly a formula that Michelangelo had used for frescoes. They envisioned the large interior of the four-sided structure with its covered walkway as a place for walking in bad weather. "This quadrangle is filled with sunshine falling over the low roofs," Mary wrote in the first school catalog. "The spring sunshine in these sheltered conditions will bring bulbs and shrubs into early bloom." She was more than pleased. And after telling Mr. Whittemore that the building of the school was going "very well," she added: "I took advantage of the fine sleighing and a beautiful day to take the schoolgirls out to see it. They could talk of nothing else for some time they were so charmed with it all, the location, the building, the New England green and all. It had just the effect I knew it would have upon them, and they are already planning coasting and skating and all the sports. There was but one dissenting voice among them. 'But where is a corner grocery for getting olives and crackers?' said one mournful fifteen year old, little knowing that one of my joys is the absence of corner groceries and soda fountains!"

Nicknamed "the Nomadic Queen" by the Rev. John N. Lewis, Jr., of St. John's Episcopal Church in Waterbury, Mary Hillard ended up taking almost all the St. Margaret's boarders with her to the new school like a pied piper, leaving only six girls behind with the day pupils. The teachers, maid, and handyman who followed her to Middlebury were those who were devoted to her. Many times throughout her life she would say that after loyalty to "Truth, Justice, Patience, Courage" and other ideals, she believed in loyalty to people. Most of them stayed for the rest of their working lives at the school called Westover, which was given its name because it was west and over the hill from Waterbury.

2

Creating a School:
"A Real Girls' Republic"

IN THE WESTERN WORLD THERE IS AN AGE-OLD DREAM OF womanly togetherness. Alongside the history of female exclusion from male institutions, there are stories of females voluntarily withdrawing together to embrace values that are absent in society. This tradition includes Amazon myths, Christian convents, and the Beguine communities of lay women during the Middle Ages. In 1405 Christine de Pisan wrote about an imagined City of Ladies devoted to the principles of Reason, Rectitude, and Justice. In nineteenth-century America, the antislavery, temperance, and other reform crusades gave birth to a feminist movement, and its aspirations were reflected in the nation's poetry, plays, and political organizations. The early years of the twentieth century were the era of the educated "New Woman," who was agitating for the right to vote, to contraception, and other forms of equality and emancipation. When the American Charlotte Perkins Gilman published a humorous fantasy about a peaceful female civilization in her periodical *The Forerunner,* many of its characteristics were already in place at Westover. Although no one knows whether Mary Hillard read those passages—which eventually turned into the utopian novel titled *Herland*—many of her ideals were taken from its pages.

In the fictionalized country that the author called Herland, women are not isolated, uneducated, ignored, inhibited, or dominated. When three young men discover this land, its women innocently challenge their assumptions about the nature of women. Gilman pictured a community of rose stone buildings set in a great garden and encircled by carefully tended forests of trees dedicated to the free and full development of everyone. This utopia pictures chaste courtship with men without the restrictions of marriage and the pleasures of motherhood through the parthenogenic births of daughters. Education, as well as enlightenment and empowerment, was a centerpiece of this ideal community. In her novel, Mrs. Gilman, the mother of a daughter herself, described spirited and fearless girls who were also eager learners. They were instructed in morality and other matters by the kind of reasonable, gentle, serene, and wise women that Miss Hillard wanted to bring to her school. The adults of Herland, in fact, looked like contemporary American women, the author observed, but without their "strained nervous look."

In 1909, as the first full year of her school got underway, Mary Hillard herself, at the age of forty-seven, appeared dignified and self-confident. Likewise, Middlebury resembled the imagined Herland to a striking degree. The school's first catalog, no doubt written by the principal, pictured it as "an old, quiet, orderly little village lying peacefully among the hills of western Connecticut . . . set in an intimate and beautiful park-like landscape broken by frequent streams and ponds, and dotted with the buildings, pastures, and woodlands of old farms, still largely owned and worked by the descendants of the early settlers. Removed from the activities and turmoil of our modern urban life, Middlebury furnishes an ideal environment characterized by the intimacy and the decorous simplicity of New England." Originally inhabited by Algonquin Indians, the village was settled by English families in the early 1700s, and little had changed since then.

With its neocolonial façade of large shuttered windows, the school's exterior echoed the village's colonial past. Its square shape with everything—classrooms, bedrooms, offices, music practice rooms, a dining hall, schoolroom, gymnasium, library, infirmary, and chapel—under one roof was also reminiscent of the old scholarly and religious communities of Europe. Perfectly planned and proportioned as a place for girls and women, it was intended to create a sense of comfort and closeness. Certainly the sheltered cloister in the center of the school, where Mary Hillard hoped bulbs and bushes would blossom in early spring, suggested a sense of safety. One side of it called the Sally Port opened out to a view of the lovely Connecticut landscape. Many years later an architectural historian would note that the handsome and "prepossessing" quadrangle still fostered a feeling of community within.

Mary Hillard and pupils gathered in Red Hall, 1910. WESTOVER SCHOOL ARCHIVE.

In the early catalog, Miss Hillard went on to describe the inspiring aspects of the architecture. It blends "purpose with beauty, so that the sweet austerity, the charm and stately dignity of its academic and domestic atmosphere shall be an unconscious but constantly elevating influence endearing the place to all." Older girls were supposed to initiate younger ones into this state of mind. And everyone else, pupils and teachers and administrators alike, was supposed to be affected as well. Like Sarah Porter, who had encouraged friendships between students and faculty, Mary Hillard wanted to break down barriers between the generations. "From today on you will realize more and more clearly there is no difference between us," she would say to her girls. "We are all just pupils in the great school of life."

Inside the large front door, the building was oriented both inward and outward—inward toward the grassy courtyard and out toward the rolling hills. The heart of the school was Red Hall, an airy two-story assembly room with a grand staircase encircled by a balcony, named for the blood-red color of its carpeting, curtains, upholstered couches, and extravagantly fringed and tufted velvet Victorian lampshades. Others believed the soul of the school was the small Gothic Revival chapel with its carved dark walnut woodwork and graceful arched window of clear glass. As so many backers of the school were Episcopalians on the board of St. Margaret's School, the prayer books and hymnals were of that denomination, and the chapel was named after the same saint. It would be open to girls and speakers of all Christian faiths, so it was decided that the chapel would be dedicated instead of consecrated during a ceremony on a late October afternoon in 1909.

Expressing the understatement of the Arts and Crafts aesthetic of the time as well as the values of her childhood in a Protestant parsonage, Mary Hillard also explained in the catalog that "luxury" had been banished from the school for the "straightforward, perfect simplicity" of New England village life. For years afterward, she liked to tell the story about a girl who described Westover as just "a plain country school." Instead of Victorian pretension, there was plainness for the most part. Walls were painted white and subdued colors, and the woodwork was stained dark, creating the impression of understated beauty. Bedrooms had mahogany bedsteads with white cotton bedspreads, and there were window seats and large closets with shelves for big hat boxes. The solid wooden furniture—including high-backed benches and long dining tables—was also designed by the architect. Many years later, Lucy Pratt wrote to her friend Theodate Pope that she was "living a lifetime in the midst of beauty you somehow, somehow knew the way to create."

Outside, a formal garden was laid out, where brick walkways were edged with clipped boxwood in the English style. Beyond the Sally Port were a hockey field, tennis and basketball courts, and meadows and woodlands for picnicking and walking. Part of the farmhouse moved to make way for the school was named Crossways and used for cooking classes and parties. In 1916, two years after alumna Virginia Burns died in an automobile accident the summer after graduation, Virginia House was given by her grandfather in her memory; built on the far side of the hockey field, it was designed by Theodate for art and music studios. Around 1912 the architect had brought in noted landscape designer Beatrix Farrand, a niece of Edith Wharton who was in her twenties an original member of the American Society of Landscape Architects. Known for the restraint and refinement in her work, Farrand did a drawing for foundation plantings of woody and flowering shrubs, some of which were to be trained to grow against walls. The plant list has been lost, but her herringbone-patterned brick walkways and little garden house remain.

Miss Hillard emphasized the healthiness of the hilltop site in the catalog, explaining that "there is abundance of light, each room having sunshine for some portion of the day, and the air is kept pure by the most modern methods." The Waterbury newspaperman who visited in 1908 noted that Middlebury was high enough for "pure air" but sheltered from winds by tall elms. He marveled at the school's ultramodern steam plant, sewerage system, and entirely electric kitchen. Despite his fascination with the gadgets, he failed to mention the built-in vacuum cleaning system, but he did describe the clothes chute to the basement laundry and the little elevator for carrying cleaned and ironed clothes upstairs. Even though he raved about the supply of spring water and the raised water tank for automatic sprinklers and fire hydrants, he was unaware that there was not enough water. He also overlooked on exterior walls the stucco that had already begun to crack and crumble.

In the first full school year, 1909–10, about a hundred girls attended Westover including twenty-eight seniors. In the following years, the headmistress was so successful at recruitment that the size of the graduating class grew annually until it doubled to fifty-six in 1914. From the beginning, pupils came from as far away as California, Cuba, and Hawaii. When Katharine Talbott of Dayton, Ohio, visited the East, her friend Theodate Pope took her to meet Mary Hillard. Family lore has it that she was so impressed with Miss Hillard that she said if the school was in a tent or a tree house, she would send all her seven daughters to it. All but her eldest went to Westover, graduating in classes from 1909 to 1924. In gratitude, the family gave the school the Seven Sisters fieldstone fireplace in 1921, which was built in a meadow on the hillside behind the school.

Like Miss Porter, Mary Hillard sought "the right kind of girls," daughters of industrialists, political leaders, and prominent families with inherited fortunes. A number of girls bore the surnames of well-known businessmen: Ford, Rockefeller, Singer, Underwood, DuPont, Goodyear, and Gillette. Some were even thought to be royalty. Jessica Baylis, a member of the class of 1912, wrote her parents that a younger girl, Agnes Irwin, was the daughter of a Japanese princess and an American father. When a Roman Catholic father wrote about enrolling his daughters, Miss Hillard discouraged him, saying the girls would have to go to Mass in an unventilated church in Waterbury overcrowded with what she called "the laboring class"; her underlying concern was undoubtedly the danger of diseases like tuberculosis. It is curious that she did not mention the little cobblestone St. John of the Cross Catholic Church in Middlebury next door, unless her letter was written before its construction was completed, or unless she thought it had one of the "poorly educated priests" of whom she expressed disapproval in the letter. She went on to call Westover "entirely undenominational, and we welcome girls of the Catholic faith, should they wish to come to us."

"Westover is no place to enter your daughter unless you are thoroughly arrived," reported *Fortune* magazine at the end of Mary Hillard's reign. "When Miss Hillard takes Mid-Westerners, they are at least Mid-Westerners with an air: Lolita Armour; the Big Four—Ginevra King, Edith Cummings, Peg Carry, and Courtney Letts—who ruled the younger Chicagoans a few years back." The four gave themselves this name because one social season they were the leading debutantes of Chicago. One wonders whether Miss Hillard had any regrets about what she regarded as the right kind of girl after a troubling incident with young Ginevra. She was the dark-eyed sixteen-year-old with whom nineteen-year-old F. Scott Fitzgerald fell in love when he was at Princeton. They wrote long letters to each other, and one weekend he traveled from New Jersey to Connecticut to see her. When he arrived at Westover, the teenagers chatted in what she had warned him was a "glass cage," meaning a visiting room with glass panes in the doors. He never forgot the way the lovely brunette looked in her prim white evening uniform, and this image and others like it found their way into his fiction for years to come.

The night of the senior dance in the spring of 1916, a Yale boy threw a paste jar through Ginevra and her roommate's open dorm window, and they and others leaned out to talk to the boys. When Miss Hillard heard about this, she flew into a rage and called Ginevra and two others to her office. "Well, she told us we were 'bold, bad hussies'—'adventuresses'—'honey-combed with deceit' etc etc—that 'our honour was stained,' 'rep. ruined,' 'disgrace to school' and the rest of her usual line and a lot more—But that was all very well—as we had done a foolish (*not* however disgraceful), thing and of course we had to take our punishment," Ginevra wrote to Scott. The headmistress, however, went on and then asked them to leave school.

Ginevra telephoned her father, who was in New York on business, and he soon arrived. Miss Hillard had evidently reconsidered the expulsion and was "sweet as sugar to Father, even if he did tell her a few plain truths about herself—You wouldn't have known her for the same woman," the letter continued. Nevertheless, Mr. King insisted that Ginevra leave with him the next morning. After Miss Hillard sent him a letter "flattering me to the skies," Ginevra wrote Scott, her father replied, accusing the head-mistress of "unjustness—unfairness and partiality," and telling her that with her temper she should not be head of a school. Ginevra was so despondent about the incident with Miss Hillard, whom she called "a demon" in the letter, that she lost seven pounds. Her father refused to allow her to return to Westover for her fourth and final year, and she spent her senior year at a school called Miss McFee's on West 72nd Street in New York City.

Ginevra later haughtily rejected her suitor, but Fitzgerald never forgot his first love. She was his model for the beautiful but unattainable girl he often wrote about, like Daisy Buchanan in *The Great Gatsby*. Ginevra as well as Westover appear lightly disguised in a number of other works. His short story "A Woman With a Past," for example, describes an incident in which a headmistress of a girls' school finds a laughing girl lying in the arms of an embarrassed young man after accidentally falling down steep chapel steps. "Unexpectedly, monstrously, just as it had begun to mean something, her school life was over," the story goes, but not without adding that the prim and hysterical headmistress should really have been running a reform school.

Like Ginevra, most students came from homes with servants, but at Westover they were expected to make their beds and do other chores. Miss Hillard believed that wealth came with responsibility, and she was on a crusade to build character. In 1911 she noted with satisfaction that a girl from "an elaborate and luxurious home" was distributing clean laundry. A member of the class of 1914 remembered a classmate crying in frustration because her long hair had become tangled and matted, so her friend showed her how to brush it out herself and wind it back up on her head. Although tuition was one thousand dollars plus extra fees (Miss Hillard hoped, unrealistically as it turned out, to eventually reduce it after the school's loans were repaid), the headmistress proposed that ten thousand dollars be set aside each year for scholarships. In her effort to instill down-to-earth values and interests in her pupils, she wanted to enroll daughters of professors, clergymen, and other middle class professionals. Her girls were told all the time that she expected them to use their privileges and expanding opportunities for the betterment of all. She was impressed by the way English boys' schools produced pupils with high principles, who settled throughout the world like missionaries. "It is our aim to send graduates out to support civilization," she would say to parents. "It is our hope to send them out into Vanity Fair *fortified.*"

No one knew which girls were on scholarship, and a rule banning jewelry and mandating uniforms tended to hide differences in wealth. In the fall of 1909 a tailor from the Abercrombie & Fitch department store in Manhattan arrived in Middlebury to measure for the uniforms that Miss Pope had designed. For classes there were khaki cotton dresses with detachable white starched linen collars and black silk Windsor ties along with brass buttons with the same Tudor rose as in the emblem over the front

Girls in evening uniforms and capes leaving chapel.
WESTOVER SCHOOL ARCHIVE.

door; the day uniforms also had black patent leather belts with brass buckles stamped with the school seal and containing the motto. For afternoon walks there were tan corduroy skirts and camel hair polo coats with black beaver hats. Full bloomers made of nine yards of black pleated wool, worn with black stockings, white blouses, and gray sweaters were put on for sports. And for dinner in the evening the girls were to wear embroidered white voile dresses that went almost to the ground with soft wool capes in one of many different colors. "I think the freedom our handsome uniforms gave in their anonymity was symbolic. I can still feel the shock of Sunday, when for a few hours we reverted to our own clothes and a whole dreary world of complex gradations in taste, income, and social background suddenly sprang up only to vanish as we resumed our innocent and kindly round of uniformed school life," recalled a pupil at the time.

The importance of feminine values was emphasized in a 1909 issue of *The Lantern*, the school literary magazine, when it linked each letter in the name of the school with a virtue—womanliness, earnestness, sweetness, truthfulness, orderliness, vigor, enthusiasm, and righteousness. By adhering to these ideals, girls would learn "the very great art of living," the editors earnestly explained in a high-minded way. Living in an idealistic community "creates mental responsiveness, stimulates liveliness of mind, and makes possible that interchange of humor, wit, and sentiment that makes the best fertilizer for the garden soil of civilized life," Miss Hillard would write in an essay in her late sixties. She eventually established at Westover an honor system, which was explained in the initial issue of *The Lantern* every year. Perhaps it was instituted because of persistent misbehavior. Rebellions against rules and restrictions often took the form of eating forbidden foods in the big closets at night. When Elsie Talbott was class president in 1913, she failed to report that her roommate had hidden contraband chocolates in the covered chamber pot in their room. The honor system valued honesty, studiousness, neatness, loyalty, kindness, and consideration of others. Its existence meant that there were relatively few rules, even though every September Miss Hillard gave incoming students a long lecture about them. Decades later an alumna called it "a code of honor and an idealism which a little at a time I came to accept so joyously that I believed the most complete happiness I could possibly know would be if my life could in some way fulfill [it]."

School traditions were intended to endorse this idealism. The first year Miss Hillard introduced a number of ceremonies and songs including the school anthem, "Raise Now to Westover." The autumn day when everyone was given a lantern to carry outside in the evenings soon became a lantern ceremony in the spring, a picnic with a big bonfire, games, and singing, when the headmistress lit a girl's lantern from hers and whispered a few words of warning or encouragement about the strength of her metaphorical flame. The chapel was decorated with pine wreaths and boughs at Christmas and with white chrysanthemums and lilies at Easter. Repeating familiar rituals every year was a way to enforce loyalty to enlightened values, the headmistress believed. "Creation and presentation of beauty for its own sake is a constant enrichment of school life," she would later write. Furthermore, she believed that such beauty would lead to "a life of harmony, proportion, sincerity, and happiness."

In 1912 Mary Hillard had turned fifty, and as she lost her youthful slenderness, she gained a greater sense of presence. "Instead of any hurry in her walk there was balance and power, [and] at times she seemed to sweep along through the corridor or across Red Hall as if without effort," recalled an observer. She spoke or read poetry in her lilting voice to girls in the chapel, the dining room, the schoolroom, and her sitting room. She greeted each girl as she arrived for breakfast in the morning, said good night after evening chapel, greeted them or said goodbye when they returned or departed for vacations; one year as she stood by the door in her cape before Christmas vacation, a girl nervously said "Merry Hillard, Miss Christmas," and everyone burst into laughter. In her sitting room after dinner, Miss Hillard even talked one evening "in a wonderful way" about making less noise, Jessica Baylis wrote in her diary. Prettiness, the headmistress liked to say, has value only because of the pleasure it gives. And happiness has nothing to do with the pursuit of pleasure but with sacrifice of self and loyalty to high ideals. "Miss Hillard talked to us as she alone can, and as no one ever forgets," wrote another girl in *The Lantern* in 1911.

That year the headmistress described in a letter to Theodate a morning, in which her pride in the school was palpable on the page. Before eight o'clock two girls were playing "the handle rolls of a Beethoven trio" in the gymnasium, as they did every day, she wrote. Others were polishing their shoes and tying black ribbons under their white collars in their tidied bedrooms, or reading in the library, or studying in the schoolroom, or crocheting in Red Hall. When the eight o'clock bell rang, "they all came streaming to prayers, to lift their clear young voices in the heavenly notes that fill our chapel and rise on high morning by morning," she wrote. She felt warmth toward the young girls in her care and admired their "loveliness, spontaneity, and steadiness." As she aged, "the solemnity [went] out of her face and in its place [was] a tenderness which often assumed a look of motherliness," her young minister friend, John Dallas, observed. Eliza Talbott remembered that "she seemed to enfold us in a caring that was the real heart of our Westover experience."

It was not always that way. Among "the triumvirate" that ran Westover—Mary Hillard, Lucy Pratt, and Helen LaMonte—it was Helen LaMonte who was called the balance wheel. A small, erect, slender person, she looked fragile but actually emanated force. When Miss Hillard flew off on tangents, it was she who gave her old friend a steadying hand. With her gentle and delicious sense of humor, Miss LaMonte would quietly calm everyone down with "bits of humor and wisdom scattered about," a pupil remembered. One time the headmistress chose a few girls with flyaway curls for a club for those with fuzzy hair; she decided that its involuntary members would have to recite aloud Kipling's poem "Fuzzy Wuzzy" as a form of penance. After Miss LaMonte heard about this, she told the girls to disband "because she had just returned from the Fiji Islands and feels quite at home among our 'fuzzy heads,'" as one of the editors of *The Lantern* explained in the autumn of 1921. In her great enthusiasm and eagerness for adventure, the teacher had gone with a former student to the South Pacific, where they made sure to visit the grave of Robert Louis Stevenson. They had left New York on an old British India cargo freighter, "Lake of the Flowers," with a few other passengers, including a screen writer and a man from Australia along with his performing dogs. There were "long days of good books and invented games and sleepy long, long thoughts," remembered the former Betty Choate.

As assistant headmistress, Miss LaMonte did the administrative work she disliked in her small office to the right of the front door in Miss Hillard's absence. Like other teachers at Westover, she, a Smith graduate, was among the first generation of graduates of most women's colleges. Hired prior to 1900 at St. Margaret's School, she was a widely read intellectual who loved to teach. In the classroom, Miss LaMonte's method was one of "enticement" into the fascinating world of ideas. Her "attitude was that we were her equals come together for instruction and enjoyment, [and] it would be a breech of manners to behave ill in her class. Still, it did sometimes happen, if the playing fields were being mowed or the apple trees [were] in blossom, that someone was inattentive. This girl was asked quietly to depart and told she might wait in the corridor." When necessary she pointed out errors with gentle humor and exquisite restraint. "What I remember most about Miss LaMonte was her way of expressing the necessary thing without being harsh or causing humiliation," observed a graduate.

Dark-haired with a long nose and a penetrating look, she had very definite opinions. It was said that she had once marched down Fifth Avenue in a suffragette parade. She seemed to embody the highest ethics, indicating a slight air of scorn for what she regarded as inferior. Outspoken in a quiet way, she told girls, "when in doubt—don't," and urged them to be unafraid. With her twinkling eyes and wry smile, she drew to her those who were homesick, needed advice, or wanted permissions. She allowed a girl to use her office for a visit with a beau when the visiting rooms were taken, and at another time let her go to a Yale football game with him without a chaperone because his father was a well-known minister. "We opened our hearts to Miss LaMonte and adored to be near her. We could tell her our secrets and little problems, and she would always make us feel comfortable and happy. She radiated warmth and understanding and would always greet us with a smile and a word that made us feel adequate and at ease. She gave us a feeling of security and of being worthwhile," recalled an early graduate. "And most of the time we were her heroines," remembered Betty Choate Spykman. Miss LaMonte never thought girls did anything wrong, "and if we had a real success, whatever it might be, she rolled her eyes and clasped her hands in rapture."

After her school had opened, Mary Hillard took more time for her private life. In fact, it was necessary for her to withdraw from time to time. It was on a Sunday in August of 1907 that she first met New York art connoisseur Augustus Jaccaci at Hill-Stead, when he was working on a book about private art collections. Mary described him in a letter to her sister, Emily, as "an Italian of aristocratic birth . . . very cosmopolitan, very brilliant, and with a rare simplicity and sweetness of nature which makes him one of the most delightful companions." She soon asked him to make five hundred editions of Westover's first catalog with gilt edges and a silk-lined slip jacket. She and the darkly handsome European she came to call "Jac" became dear friends. After he returned from a trip to Europe, she wrote him that "New York is a better place when you are in it," and she sent him a share of stock in the Westover Corporation as thanks for his work. On her visits to New York during 1909 and 1910, they often dined and went to the theater together. "Our beloved (though sometimes misguided) principal returned from New York Saturday morning in excellent health and spirits," observed Lucy Pratt. "She had been to concerts to her heart's content by night and by day she had done more things than my pen knows how to write."

Mary Hillard's more than thirty surviving letters to Jaccaci have all the warmth, informality, and intimacy as those to her closest relatives and friends. "Dear Jac, you were such a deep comfort to me last night," she wrote in one of them, saying how much she needed his friendship. Their closeness is indicated by her revelation of an important secret to him. "It was wonderful I could tell you what I did last night. You would know it is something I can hardly speak of—never do speak of—but I *wanted* to tell you Jac. For I want everything that makes you and me closer to each other. We each can help the other, we both need help. We are both generous, and generous people have especially human sympathy and affection, for they give out so much. Dear Jac, I'm so grateful to you, and I'm so grateful for what you were and meant to me last night."

In the summer of 1910 she wrote to him in the most intimate manner, revealing that she enjoyed his manliness and felt he appreciated her womanliness. Writing from a vacation cottage in the woods, she alluded to the demands of what she called her "big 'job,'" and asked him to imagine "what, under those circumstances, the brilliancy and cultivation of your mental powers is to me—the joy of having that in a companionship!" After he referred to her as "Mother Mary," she rhapsodized that "you read my heart." She went on: "You need me and I am here, and motherliness is measureless. You may be what you will—glad, grave, weary, troubled—It is all the same. It makes no dif-ference to the great deep understanding that knows *you* and cares. No one else could understand. But we do. We are both so simple. We both need companionship, comfort, healing, in this pathway of life which is so hard for each . . . you need the tenderness and the cherishing that wells in a woman's heart. And I need the strength and courage that lives in high manhood."

A few months later, in early January of 1911, when the man she had called her truest of friends suggested bringing visitors to Westover on a Sunday, she charmingly turned him away. "What a nice party you suggest! And how inhospitable not to say '*Do* come.' But—dear Jac—the work we have to do here is something tremendous. It calls for all one's wisdom to know *how* strength and vitality and powers of the mind can be so safeguarded as to be equal to the demands of schoolwork—and be fresh for it, and full of the joy of working. (My new secretary says, 'I am so enjoying working here. This is such a *happy* place. Everyone is so happy. I love the work here.') I have seen clearly that our hope lies in our quiet winters. Spring and Fall our friends come in great companies. We love to have them; we welcome them. Our safety lies in absolutely quiet Sundays, and in this blessedly quiet winter term. I have no right *ever* to go against my *judgement* in these things. You understand fully. So tempting as your attractive party is I know I am doing my bounden duty to Westover in asking you to wait over the Spring term. I shall love to have you all come up some day in May [if] you care to."

She continued: "And as guests must be at times excluded from the home, so that these beautiful, living vital influences of the home may have freedom to gather and express themselves, just as flame springs from the log, and transforms the grey cold fireplace into a source of light and warmth, so the same conditions must be maintained in the life of such a kind of school as this is, that here may be that mysterious warmth and light and intimacy that comes in separation from the outer world, when the vitality within us, not taxed with social demands, may turn to the intimate daily life and the joy of that fellowship. That is what this beautiful snowbound winter term is to us. We protect it. Should we not? Even if it sometimes, as now, [it] becomes suddenly difficult to do so because one would rather not?"

After so firmly putting the mood of her beloved school above their relationship, either her letters to him ended or he no longer saved them. She continued to turn to him at times, to make memorial books for John Whittemore and Alfred Pope, for instance. After war broke out in Europe, Jaccaci returned to Paris, where he helped French and Flemish refugees. In the winter of 1915 he wrote to her with thanks for getting "the whole of Westover" involved in his cause, for which the King of Belgium later honored him. After the armistice he returned to Middlebury one more time, in 1919, when he signed the handsome leather-and-gilt school guest register he had designed many years before.

Mary had confided to "dear Jac" about her difficulties with Theodate, a member of the school's board of trustees, who, she wrote, seemed "troubled and tremulous at the slightest suggestion of anything connected with Westover." After the school had opened, tensions had arisen between the two strong-willed women. "Genius, and she has it, *needs* the kind of love somewhere that childhood needs. I give it to Theo very imperfectly because I think of myself too much (partly because the demands of daily life attack one so fiercely)," Mary wrote to him after Theo had sailed to Europe without saying goodbye. Photographs of Westover were included in an exhibit of the Architectural League of New York in 1910, and Cass Gilbert, president of the American Institute of Architects, later praised the structure as more "beautifully" designed than any girls' school in the country. The two came up with the idea of giving her a gold medal inscribed "Theodate Pope, architect, 1910" in a leather case to help "dissolve that intangible something—we do not know what—that has seemed to send a frost through her thoughts of me." (Theodate would finally be elected to the American Institute of Architects in 1918 and licensed to practice architecture in Connecticut in 1933.)

Problems had arisen between the two friends, because Theodate Pope would unexpectedly descend on Middlebury with a group of people to show them "her" school and receive a cool reception from Mary, who was fiercely protective of the school routine. "I think this attitude of not welcoming guests at all and every time hurts my dear Theo. I am placed in a dreadfully hard situation. But Westover does not exist as a monument to her genius, any more than it exists as an excuse for social pleasure for me. It belongs to its pupils. It was built for that. It is theirs," she wrote to Jaccaci. It is for this reason that Mary established a surprise holiday when Theo was gladly welcomed back. In 1911, the year when Alfred Pope became president of the board, Theodate's Holiday was announced by his daughter herself at breakfast on the last day of May. Despite tensions between the two women, Mary defended her former pupil and old friend whenever she ruffled feathers, as she frequently did. In a letter to Theo's old beau, Harris Whittemore, she described a moment when "Theo took my hand most intimately, looked straight into my eyes and said, 'You *are* my old Mary, are not you. Yes, you are my old real friend' with entire trust. You will understand, with me, why we must all stand by her."

In the spring of 1915, Theodate impulsively sailed to England on the luxurious *Lusitania* for a meeting of the Psychical Research Society in London, despite warnings about German submarines. After it was reported that the passenger ship had been torpedoed and quickly gone down, Mary rushed to Mrs. Pope's side in New York as they anxiously awaited word of Theo's fate. As Theo clung to an oar and thought she was going to drown, she counted the buildings she had designed, she later wrote to her mother. After hours in the ocean, she was pulled out and left for dead before someone noticed her eyelids flickering. Almost a year to the day after her rescue, Theodate's Holiday had to be renamed Mrs. Riddle's Holiday, after suddenly, at the age of forty-nine, she married John W. Riddle, a tall, thin American diplomat with a large handlebar mustache. Mary slyly suggested in a letter to a sister that it was fortunate that Mr. Riddle had a lot of diplomatic experience. Still, Theo's former teacher was one of the few guests invited to the small wedding in Farmington, where the bride wore pale blue and carried a silver-tipped walking stick. She soon fulfilled her girlhood dream about raising orphaned children in the country.

While Theo was trying to adjust to married life, Mary was attempting to perfect her community of girls and women. She was well aware that in any group a hierarchy develops, particularly among young girls. Some liked each other too little, the headmistress thought, and others liked each other too much. Pupils were often warned about the problems. In the May 1920 issue of *The Lantern*, an editor cautioned classmates about finding fault with each other. "We are terribly critical here, of each other, and we have no right to be. If anyone outside of the school asked you what the girls of Westover were like, you'd have the nicest things possible to say, and they'd be perfectly true. Why, then, when we're here together do we let criticism play so large a part in conversation?" The following year the December issue addressed the problem of exclusionary cliques. "It is always natural that one should see more of certain people than of others . . . But does no one feel that at times we let ourselves become so intimate with a certain group of girls, that we lose entire sight of many others? . . . The result proves to be that we are often, perhaps unconsciously, hard, hasty, and unkind."

Miss Hillard discouraged cliquishness by encouraging girls to follow their interests in school publications and in dramatic, language, and other clubs. "She wanted everyone to be friends with everyone else," a pupil recalled. When a group of ten or so girls formed a secret society in the 1920s, they knew that if the headmistress found out, she would be furious and forbid it. It was also assumed that she would look unkindly on requests to change roommates. The influence of cliques varied from class to class, of course, but it was an excellent sign that pupils were mindful of the attitude against them and addressed the issue openly. So is the fact that some graduates remember no unfriendliness at all. "I can remember little meanness and no cruelty," recalled a student long after graduation, only "a simple, generous, and harmonious atmosphere." Certainly Mary Hillard had a high regard for friendship. As she had written to Augustus Jaccaci, friendship is "much deeper than [the] exchange of thought, that is part of it, and a beautiful and stimulating part, but exchange of sympathies, and of courage, and of comfort may all be silent yet how tremendous is the difference it makes to have them. Such exchange is nothing short of spiritual."

While she encouraged female friendships, she was wary of what she called "exaggerated friendship." This was one of the topics that she talked to her girls about. In the December 1911 issue of *The Lantern,* an editor mentioned that "Miss Hillard's annual talk on crushes came the other day," but she did not elaborate on what the headmistress had said. When "crush" became a forbidden word, girls used other words like "want" and "tra-la" for it. Nevertheless, the adolescents exchanged valentines and flowers, made dates for going to chapel and concerts together, and slept in each other's rooms and even in their beds. Younger girls who idolized older ones would go into a senior's bedroom in the morning to shut her window or make her bed. This was natural and appears to have been much more emotional than erotic. Jessica Baylis confided to her diary that she had a crush on a senior named Polly, and she carefully kept count of the number of times—eight—that she had slept in her room. In her case, it was innocent enough: "I can safely say that I never learned to love any girl so much in so short a time. The most I did was to tell her that she was a dear and give her a bear hug."

Such infatuations are commonplace in an isolated and sequestered female community. Besides being way out in the country, Westover was surrounded by a seven-foot fieldstone wall. Within the school, it was forbidden to read newspapers that reported scandals. In this atmosphere, Miss Hillard gave sensible advice about health: she warned girls about smoking, too much dieting, and about drinking more than one cocktail at a time. Other more benign behavior was under scrutiny. Besides being marked on room tidiness, girls were graded for their posture. If someone yearned to be alone for a while, she could place a sacrosanct sign that read "Please Excuse" on her bedroom door or on a pile of books asking respect for her privacy or possessions. The cure for low spirits was considered to be going on a long walk or doing something for someone else.

An outsider's eye offers another perspective, so it is fascinating to read the description of a visit to Westover in February of 1925 by a Russian political exile named Vladimir Zenzinoff. Mary Hillard had an intense interest in the Russian Revolution, and she invited him to Middlebury to give a talk. Undoubtedly eager for the generous lecture fee, he agreed and was met at the Waterbury train station by a teacher and driver in a luxurious automobile with a fur throw. They drove over the snowy, wooded, hilly landscape to the three-and-a-half-story school, which Zenzinoff described as "an enormous and elegant stone house." Middlebury in winter vividly reminded him of his village in Russia, and his descriptions are reminiscent of Charlotte Perkins Gilman's imaginary Herland, too. "It seemed to me as if I were in a fairy tale," he remembered, and his three days at Westover would turn out to be "unquestionably . . . the most pleasant, cheerful days [and] the most interesting" of his four months in America. His guest room "had a distinctly maidenish atmosphere about it . . . purity, immaculateness, a naive simplicity [with a] . . . snow-white, comfortable bed near the window." But in some ways—the electricity everywhere and telephone in his room—the school did not remind him of his native land at all.

After being told that dinner would be in half an hour, the visitor, who spoke French but little English, admitted to himself that "still I did not know what sort of a school it was, where I was, nor who would compose my audience." A group of teachers met him in the small dining room along with Mary Hillard, "who in her majestic bearing reminded one of Catharine the Great." Through the door to the adjoining main dining hall, he heard the sound of "gay" young voices and tried to look inside, but all he could see were "rapidly moving white silhouettes." Then he understood. "It appeared that I was in a school for—girls! Fear seized me, but soon this gave way to the courage of despair!" After dinner Miss Hillard led him to her sitting room, which was softly lit and warmed by a fire. He noticed a Russian samovar, which had been electrified to boil water more quickly. There were bookcases and upholstered furniture, as well as a piano and a large round table covered with books and magazines. "Seldom had I seen surroundings more comfortable, more attractive, more cultivated," he wrote in his memoir.

Soon his hostess was called away, and Zenzinoff realized that what he called an "enormous, magnificent" room—Red Hall—was filling up. "Girls' voices coupled with laughter became more and more audible, then suddenly silence reigned and I heard Miss Hillard's voice." She entered the sitting room where he waited and asked him to follow her, which he did with trepidation. In the big room "broad rows of chairs [were] densely covered with white figures," he remembered. "On this white background only the faces [stood] out, blonde and chestnut heads, and an ocean of young, eager, radiant eyes. The entire audience was composed of girls of the most charming age—fifteen to eighteen." Then the headmistress turned to the visitor and asked him a question: "We women listen and understand better when we have our hands busy—will that bother you, Mr. Zenzinoff?" He replied that it would not, and to his astonishment the girls pulled out their needlework. When he began to talk in halting English about the hardships of the Russian people under the Bolsheviks, he saw "sad amazement" on their faces. "To them, who had been accustomed to democracy, to an atmosphere of independence from childhood, all this seemed to be the height of insanity and violence. And wherever it was necessary, the dear girls laughed or were indignant. Wherever it was possible, they applauded. And at the end they recompensed me with prolonged applause, which seemed to me quite an ovation."

During the next few days, the Russian observed daily life at the school for girls. Each morning as a breakfast tray was brought to his room, "somewhere near—as if having just waited for this moment—a delicate feminine voice would start to sing and some- one's hesitating fingers would play on the piano. Evi-

A view of the front of the school and the headmistress's apartment from the chapel. SVEN MARTSON.

dently the mysterious singer was practicing some hymns." After lunch he was taken to watch pupils play ice hockey on the frozen pond. All day, he noticed, there was "animated conversation, laughter, gayety [sic]. Childishness, combined with maiden- ish gracefulness, but without even a shade of coquetry." He had exactly the same experience as the fictional young men who stumbled on Herland: "Meeting me, the girls smiled in a friendly way, but without a trace of accentuated curiosity, not to speak of bashfulness—my greetings were answered with friendly words, and open, clear eyes." He attended a play one evening and, after reluctantly saying good night, he immediately regretted refusing to go tobogganing in the moonlight with a group of teachers.

After his visit, the Russian revolutionary's hope for a joyous new kind of existence began to seem real. "I think that those who have spent the years of their girlhood in the school of Miss Hillard must keep for life the wonderful sensation of the possibility of such marvelous fullness of life," he wrote. "Does not here lie the inmost, the most important aim of education—to awaken in the young conscience for the rest of her life a longing for what in youth had already seemed half attained, as if in a dream?" He added that, contrary to the morning prayer of the Jews about not being born a woman, "I would have been glad to have changed for a month into a girl of eighteen and to spend that month in the school of Miss Hillard." It is, he concluded, "a real girls' republic."

3

The Art of Living:
A Balanced Life

MARY HILLARD HAD ALWAYS WANTED HER SCHOOL TO BE A place devoted to the wholesome values of her girlhood, the same ones that had shaped the grandmothers of most of her pupils. Life at Westover would be "simple, sincere, and natural," she had written in the school's first catalog. Her own childhood had consisted of "an education which brought her soul in touch with God, her mind in contact with the great thinkers of the past and present, [and] her body in contact with nature in all her aspects among the hills of Connecticut," in the words of a her minister friend in Waterbury, John Dallas. As she structured a way of life for her young charges—one she envisioned as a balanced existence—she hoped that they would adopt it as their own after graduation. Some activities and traditions were similar to those in other girls' schools, and others were unique to Westover. Mornings were for classes, afternoons were for exercise, and evenings were for studying in the schoolroom, or dancing in the gym, or attending events in Red Hall, or listening to the headmistress read aloud in her sitting room.

The first Westover yearbook, for the 1911–1912 school year, indicates the way the days made up a routine, marked by traditions, in a rhythm that would be repeated for years. On many Saturday nights there were "germans" (a word meaning little plays), parties with songs, favors, costumes, and skits put on by the seniors, athletic teams, and others. From the first year there was the performance of a nativity play in the style of an old English pageant before Christmas vacation. Early on Easter mornings the seniors surprised the new girls by awakening them while walking down their bedroom corridors singing hymns. For a few years there was also a May Day dance with a queen and maidens, along with singing, dancing, and the winding of a Maypole.

As always, there was the emphasis on building strength of character. Echoing Mary Wollstonecraft, an early Westover catalog stated that the goal of academic work was to train the mind to reason and to control the emotions. The importance of thought was underscored by the motto on everyone's brass belt buckle, "To Think, To Do, To Be." Learning, Miss Hillard believed, should also stimulate originality and inventiveness: "A person of liberal education should radiate life and joy and color by passing everything through the prism of the imagination," she liked to say. Freshman year studies were intended to develop concentration, while subsequent years were planned to inform and train pupils' tastes in art and literature. All this education reached an epitome in the senior year. "The studies of the Senior Year, which the thirty odd other lovely girls who will make up our Senior Class next year are to have, are of an especially cultivating character," Miss Hillard wrote persuasively to the mother of a prospective student who had spent the previous year in Europe.

Besides offering classes in art and literature, the school had many others in European and American history as well as a few in psychology, mathematics, astronomy, geology, physiology, and botany. The learning of languages, including Latin and Greek, was stressed, and plays were performed in German and French. Although the headmistress did not emphasize academics to the exclusion of everything else, she did, unlike Sarah Porter, put pressure on pupils by ranking them academically and reading aloud the list from highest to lowest on a day that was dubbed "Black Monday," a practice modeled on boys' schools. She also scolded poor performers. When freshman Marianna Talbott got the lowest grades in the school, Miss Hillard "gave me plain hell in front of the whole school," the girl wrote in her diary. To encourage good grades, the principal

Mary Hillard (left), Helen LaMonte, and Lucy Pratt.
WESTOVER SCHOOL ARCHIVE.

established a policy that allowed a new girl who got over ninety in every lesson in a week to read in the library instead of going to study hall in the evenings.

Many graduates spoke glowingly all their lives about the brilliant teaching of Helen LaMonte, who was born the youngest of five children in 1872 on a farm in Owego, New York. It was the quality of her intellect that impressed them as much as her extensive knowledge. In her History of Painting class, which she taught in a large wood-paneled room, she asked pupils to research paintings and then paste reproductions of them in notebooks. "She was a magnificent teacher," recalled a former student, who credited her with all she knew about art. Many others never forgot what she had said about particular paintings, and when they got to the Louvre and the other museums in Europe (sometimes with their notebooks in tow), they headed for those works of art. Miss LaMonte also taught Literature of the Nineteenth Century, the study of English prose and poetry. One alumna remembered thinking as she entered the class that "'this is going to be good'—and it always was." Not only was the teacher's imagination a delight, but she also explained poems clearly. Another graduate, who wanted to stay at Westover until she had taken every course that Miss LaMonte taught, recalled gratefully that "it was she who opened my eyes to art and my ears and mind to poetry and literature."

Part of a well-rounded life, in Mary Hillard's opinion, was to experience the beauty of nature. Early on she had bought seventy acres and a small nineteenth-century farmhouse in the nearby village of Woodbury. While there is evidence that she acquired the property by borrowing money from friends, she had long believed that principals of profitable schools have the right "to share liberally in the earnings of the school," and she apparently earned an excellent salary. The farm was her personal retreat as well as what she called "a holiday house" for student picnics, parties, and overnight stays with teachers and without any help from maids. She had adored picnics ever since her father had taken his children picnicking, and as headmistress she organized outings often at the farm, where everyone, herself included, cooked outdoors, cleaned up, and sometimes played baseball, and then took the trolley or walked through the woods at night back to Middlebury.

One of the most enthusiastic people about the outdoors was Lucy Pratt, a redhead with a plain face and a prominent nose, who loved the long walk from Middlebury, past Lake Quassapaug, to Woodbury and back. She also liked to lead girls on back roads all the way to St. John's Church in Waterbury for services on Sunday mornings. Along with art teacher Helen Andrews, a quiet painter and etcher who had studied art in New York and Paris, she loved searching for and spreading the seeds of wildflowers they discovered in the woods. Trained as an elementary school teacher, she also loved to give parties for village children in the little white clapboard house near the Methodist meeting house, which the youngsters liked so much that they called it "paradise." Miss Pratt, who worked at a standup desk in a little downstairs office with a fireplace, was responsible for business matters, housekeeping, and upkeep of the grounds. She was so soft-spoken and kindly toward the maids and maintenance men that they nicknamed her St. Lucy. Among the threesome who ran the school, it was she who was eminently practical and meticulous about details, and over the years she was school secretary, treasurer, and an assistant headmistress.

A self-effacing person from a large New England family, Lucy Pratt was also down-to-earth and possessed of a lively sense of humor, a firm ethical nature, and a strong dislike of pomposity. Like Helen LaMonte, she was devoted to Mary Hillard, but she could also deflate the headmistress when necessary, like the time she jokingly referring to her as "the Wise Woman" in a letter to Theodate Pope. When a girl was in danger of being expelled, Miss Pratt believed that if she would admit her mistake in breaking a rule she could stay, but if she would not or was untrustworthy, then she had no place at Westover. She was also dauntless: once when some seniors spotted a Peeping Tom outside the schoolroom, it was she who got into an automobile (along with, according to a rumor among the students, three men with pistols) to chase him away.

Exercise was an important part of a wholesome life, in Mary Hillard's view, and an important reason for a school to be in the countryside. After a childhood of outdoor activities, she was convinced that young ladies suffered from too little exertion. The need for physical education for women was a relatively new idea at the time, and she was one of its ardent defenders. During Westover's first year, girls were divided into athletic teams—Wests, Overs, and Seniors—for tennis, field hockey, and basketball games, and the three apple trees within the quadrangle were named for each team. The headmistress herself selected who would be Wests or Overs and read off the names in the dining room at the beginning of each year. Also, girls were encouraged to take cross-country walks or jogs for three or four miles in groups of at least four. In the winter there was tobogganing, snowshoeing, and ice skating on the school's pond. For an extra fee girls could go horseback riding.

Miss Hillard had a way of getting girls to both go outside and learn poems by heart. If a girl failed to exercise and cross her name off what was called "the walking list," she might be called on to recite at dinnertime the poem that everyone had to memorize each week. The poems were by Emily Dickinson and Emily Brontë as well as by Milton, Yeats, Tennyson, Blake, Stevenson, Keats, and by living poets who gave readings at the school like John Masefield and Walter de la Mare. On beautiful spring days, Miss Hillard, who adored poetry, might take English classes outside and read poetry to them as they sat on the grass. On other days she might suddenly appear in the schoolroom, put on her pince-nez spectacles, read a poem by Shelley or Wordsworth, and then quietly leave. The threat of being asked to recite a poem aloud, however, was a penalty that made some girls resent poetry and even dislike public speaking for the rest of their lives.

The first issue of *The Lantern* noted that a balanced way of life was not one of "solemn priggishness" but one that also "smacks of fun" for students and adults alike. For a Halloween german, Mary Hillard dressed up in a school uniform and a mask and passed around a box of chocolates until the girls realized who the tall, mysterious figure really was. At least once Lucy Pratt dressed up like an opera singer and sang an aria, while Helen LaMonte accompanied her on a violin. Julia Whittemore, the widow of John H. Whittemore, used to invite the seniors to a picnic with lobsters every autumn. On winter nights, all the girls were from time to time loaded onto seven or eight sleighs pulled by horses with bells in their harnesses for moonlit rides and hot chocolate afterward. One spring evening early on, the hockey field was illuminated with lanterns while girls danced minuets. Throughout the years there were many teas and dinners and birthday parties at the little cottage near the school called Crossways. When seniors in the class of 1919 got up their courage to invite Miss Hillard to dinner there, their dignified headmistress surprised them by being "very affable," one of them recalled. There was also what was called the tea bureau on Saturday afternoons in the rented basement of the Methodist meeting house, where girls played the Victrola and sold tea, hot chocolate, and little cakes to earn money for charity.

Social events with young men were also part of a well-balanced life. Girls regularly went in chaperoned groups to the Yale-Harvard and Yale-Princeton football games. There were teas and dances with the students of Taft School, a boys' preparatory school only six miles away in Watertown. Taft's headmaster, Horace D. Taft, was a very tall, warm, quiet man and a good friend of Miss Hillard's. He had become a widower the year Westover opened its doors, and, although girls liked to imagine that there was a romance between the two of them, Mr. Taft had vowed never to marry again. There were also dances at Westover, and the headmistress gave a dancing prize of a Tiffany clock to the escort of a member of the class of 1910. Even though her girls wanted to learn the latest dances, it's unclear what kind of dancing took place since waltzing had shocked Mary Hillard as a child, and in adulthood she was still opposed to what she called "contact dancing."

By that time Mary Hillard was an impressive woman in her fifties with poise and power, a person who wore handsome day dresses and lovely dinner gowns, many made in Paris. Her usual daytime outfit was a well-tailored dark blue suit or dress of heavy navy silk with an organdy collar or other trim. Her dresses were often made in the same patterns and with a ruffle below the waist covering a pocket for a handkerchief. Graduates never forgot her evening gowns of pale gray chiffon, of white Swiss polka dots with an embroidered square collar, and many others. Some always remembered her beautiful shoes with silver buckles. In 1918, after years of raising money, her portrait was painted by the acclaimed portraitist of the American upper class, Lydia Field Emmet, who was a friend of Theodate Pope's. The artist, who had studied with the famous William Merritt Chase, came from a family of accomplished women painters. In the large portrait, the founder's dark eyes look out from under graying hair in an unusually pensive way. And instead of wearing one of her elegant gowns, she posed in the black academic robe she had received the previous year when awarded a Doctor of Humane Letters from the University of Vermont.

Over the years, Mary Hillard spoke about spiritual values so often that it was as if she were a minister or a missionary instead of an educator. There could be no balance in a life without them, she fervently believed, and she felt that her greatest responsibility was to instill religious ideals in younger generations. "True schools are not founded on theories of education," she liked to say. In fact, like earlier women educators—Sarah Pierce, Catharine Beecher, Emma Willard, Sarah Porter, and others—she was a believer in moral education. "Without this there may be training of mind and development of aptitudes but no true education," she remarked at more than one Westover graduation. In this way she sounded like a disciple of Thomas à Kempis, whose work she knew well. "Intellectuals like to appear learned and be called wise," he wrote in *Imitation of Christ.* "Yet there are many things the knowledge of which does little or no good to the soul." She also said on many occasions that the essence of an education at her school was learning about what she called the "Everlasting Reality—of Truth, Justice, Love, Mercy, Honor, Pity, Courage." She would go on to explain that "it is the aim of this school to develop this combination of imagination, disciplined will, and effective power of resolution" by exposing young girls to religion as well as to literature, art, music, and what she simply called "beauty."

As the headmistress devoted herself to her pupils' spiritual development, it was evident to her and to everyone else that she understood adolescents very well. Little eluded her. As girls walked into the dining room for breakfast two by two, she stood at the doorway and looked them over intently. If she let a girl pass, the girl felt reassured; if she noticed that someone looked disheveled, tired, or troubled, she would call her aside and talk with her. This happened a few times with Polly Willcox, a member of the class of 1918. The only daughter in a close-knit family in Ithaca, New York, she felt "exiled from heaven" after she first arrived in Middlebury during World War I, a feeling exacerbated by entering in the middle of the school year after her classmates had already made friends. When Miss Hillard took Polly aside, she comforted her by saying, in effect, "don't ever forget that I'm here," and by reassuring her that she would get over her homesickness. Their talks made the girl feel special, safe, and secure because the headmistress "recognized my need," as she remembered more than eight decades later, when she was a hundred years old.

Polly Willcox also described Miss Hillard's manner as one of "formality over deep empathy." She elaborated: "She drew people to her in spite of her formality. There was no feeling of forbiddingness. She was very open and warm. And *extremely* perceptive. You felt transparent in her view." The headmistress's insight was a trait that was also noticed by pupils at Miss Porter's in the 1880s, as well as by members of the last graduating class she knew at Westover in the early 1930s. When she stood outside the chapel after evening vespers services to say good night to each pupil, every girl felt as if she was looking right through them. (Some teenagers found this so disconcerting that they tried to make their minds blank when they walked by.) Polly went on: "So many of her talks and lectures were so helpful. They made you realize what was the right thing to do and always put you on the right track."

Many girls found that being away from home was a way to discover themselves. An editor of *The Lantern* wrote in 1924 that the purpose of boarding school was to find where one's abilities lay—whether they were intellectual, athletic, artistic, or as leaders—and to develop them, with the effort being more important than the achievement. As their headmistress created an enriched environment by continually quoting Heraclites, Aristotle, Plato, Moses, and Shakespeare, as well as theologians, poets, and novelists, pupils also felt that they were part of something greater than themselves. Life at Westover had a feeling of "great dignity," in the words of Polly Willcox. It was "formidable, imposing, benign, friendly, supportive," she added. "I think it was a splendid school, and I loved it very much after the first year." (Not everyone had her attitude and adaptability, however, and a classmate, who stayed only one year, disliked the aura of "Victorian sentimentality that made me not only figuratively but actually sick.")

There was nothing unintentional about what Mary Hillard was trying to do: she wanted the young girls placed under her wing to mature emotionally. She talked again and again about the need for them to develop what she called spontaneity—the ability of a teenager to shed self-consciousness and to become herself. It was the way French diplomat Alexis de Tocqueville had described the surprisingly frank voice of the American girl in the 1830s: she "has scarcely ceased to be a child when she already thinks for herself, speaks with freedom, and acts on her own impulse," he wrote in *Democracy in America*. The headmistress believed it was a matter of reawakening an earlier naturalness before inhibition set in, the same phenomenon among adolescent girls that Harvard psychologist Carol Gilligan would describe many decades later in her book *In a Different Voice*. It was, in fact, a pivotal part of Mary Hillard's educational philosophy that adults should create the conditions for youths to heal and, in other words, "to be trained by us to be free." This process of personality development could only happen in a small caring community like Westover, she believed, a place that celebrated familiar traditions and provided new experiences.

Among the girls the headmistress understood very well was her niece, Phyllis

Fenn, the daughter of her younger sister Emily. Aunt Mary had "many times been the guardian angel of the family," according to their older sister, Martha, by taking a strong interest in Phyllis and in Martha's daughter, Ishbel MacLeish, as well as in her numerous nephews. After Phyllis's first year at Westover in 1920, however, her mother wrote a worried letter to her sister saying that her only child was no longer lighthearted. In her reply, Mary said that at school Phyllis was "bubbling over with interests and fun," and that it was a "tremendous" transition to go from school to home in the summer. She also elaborated on her theory about female development, writing that the maturity of girls depended on "shattering their self consciousness" by using their minds. In her letter, she wrote that Phyllis should think "how someone she dislikes would act in [a] situation—for she is *free* of *self* in thinking of someone she dislikes and how she would act. It is all a matter of using one's brains and recollecting how little other people are *ever* thinking of those about them—any more than we are thinking of those about *us*." She reassured her sister that it was natural for teenagers to be moody and melancholy, and she predicted that Phyllis would go through many other stages. All adults can do is to create wholesome conditions for them, her aunt wrote, and then "let them grow! Mother Nature is wiser than we are. Leave it to her. The flower too goes through many phases before arriving at bloom and fruitage." She added: "If you could hear how every mother with her first daughter is astounded, dismayed, perplexed and discouraged you would take comfort."

A year and a half later, Phyllis's aunt decided that her niece was ready for a glamorous evening gown and a more sophisticated social life. "Aunt Mary has given me a *new party dress*!!!!!" Phyllis wrote to her mother. "It is a heavenly shade of blue with silver on it. It is rather of a turquoise blue and is chiffon with ends floating from it all around!!!" The aunt and niece then planned to go together to New York City to a Westover friend's debutante dance at the Metropolitan Club. "Aunt Mary said she didn't know whether I would have a good time, but it would add to my experience anyway," the girl confessed to her mother.

Miss Hillard also freely gave advice to other parents about how to bring up their daughters. In a letter to the father of young Betty Choate, she first praised the girl's personality, but then politely stated that she was immature and needed to spend a year in Europe. The headmistress also bluntly said that he and his wife should spend more time with their daughter. Many times, in fact, she advised parents to become less distant dominating figures and be better friends with their children. Speaking of all young people, she rhetorically posed a question to parents on Visitor's Day in 1923: "How can you help them?" And then she gave the answer: "Give up authority—that was only to protect them. Substitute companionship," she said, and "enter into their troubles and their ambitions."

While the principal preached to parents, she also scolded pupils from time to time. She was strict about decorum, especially in the dining room, and girls rarely tried to defend themselves. When a spider dropped down the front of a new girl's dress during

Girls encircling the West apple tree inside the Quad. WESTOVER SCHOOL ARCHIVE.

dinner one time, she let out a cry. Everyone in the dining room became silent, and Miss Hillard told her to go to her sitting room after dinner, where the girl was informed about the time a mouse ran up another girl's leg in chapel, but she remained silent and held onto it until the service was over. When the headmistress was dismayed by what she perceived as a diminishment in the spirit of the school, she would start what were called "reigns of terror" that lasted for days. In February of 1912, for instance, she went to the schoolroom "with trouble written all over her face" to talk about a prank the day before, when girls had dressed up a dummy in a uniform to fool a new teacher. Miss Hillard told the assembled school that the joke had, in the words of a student, "hurt her pride in the girls so [much] that she kept from breaking down before us only with the most heroic effort," Jessica Baylis wrote to her parents. Then the headmistress asked those involved to stand up, and when they did, she spoke to them sternly.

A troubling aspect of Miss Hillard's personality was her tendency to favor some girls over others. She evidently liked leaders and well-rounded students, partly because they were excellent examples to others. She begged the mother of Rachel Latta to send her daughter back to Westover after a year abroad, and when she did, Miss Hillard wrote that "I am glad for Rachel, and deeply glad for the school." Rachel had impressed the principal during her sophomore year, and as a senior she fulfilled her promise and was named by the other pupils as the most studious and athletic student and the second best all-around girl in the school. She and another girl were also ranked the most attractive. Miss Hillard's favoritism had its limits, however. Even though Rachel was a favorite, she lost her good conduct medal after sitting in front of the fireplace in the Common Room for an hour one night after lights out.

Although girls were not allowed to go away on weekends until senior year, when Theodate Pope Riddle invited her younger twin cousins for a weekend at Hill-Stead, Miss Hillard let them go, explaining that she was granting the favor to Mrs. Riddle, not to the girls. In another case, when Margaret Bush was a new girl and asked her headmistress if she could change roommates, she replied, "Margaret, I have never made a mistake in the kind of a girl I've admitted to Westover, but I see that I have made one in you." Margaret felt crushed, but when the term was over Miss Hillard changed her mind and let her do it. (She declined.) The young woman turned out to be a leader who was elected president of the senior class, but in her opinion she and her sister were given special privileges only because their headmistress was so fond of their father. "Not everyone liked Miss Hillard because she had favorites," admitted another student. "I liked her because I was one of her favorites."

Although Mary Hillard knew that it was often difficult "for a girl to leave home and learn to stand on her feet," as she put it to her sister Emily, she was not always sympathetic toward homesickness. "The shock and surprise and excitement of it often make a young girl really ill even though she may be really enjoying it," she theorized.

This attitude is evident in the case of Jeannette Rich, who spent most of her first months at Westover in the infirmary suffering from psychosomatic aliments caused by extreme homesickness. One day when she saw Miss Hillard in the hallway on her way to New York, she timidly asked if she could go home a few days early for Christmas vacation. The headmistress snapped at the girl that she could go home and stay home because she was physically, mentally, and morally weak. The girl burst into tears and rushed off to find Helen LaMonte, who comforted her throughout the rest of the day, until Miss Hillard telephoned and softened her harsh words. Later that year, when Jeannette was in the infirmary with a sports injury, the headmistress stopped in to see her, remarking that she was glad for the accident because it gave the girl a chance "to exercise fortitude." Although shocked by her words at the time, Jeannette never forgot them and afterward even found them helpful.

While Miss Hillard's discipline was often erratic, either too strict or too permissive, it was sometimes relieved by her sense of humor. In the late 1920s, she used to board the bus of girls going to Taft for a tea dance to make sure no one was wearing lipstick or rouge. Once when she ordered a pink-cheeked blonde to rub the rouge off her face, the petrified girl denied that she that she was wearing any. The headmistress, the girl remembered, "stared at me for a breathless second, and then with that twinkle that occasionally appeared, she said, 'My dear, I congratulate you.'" Another time when a student took a dare to sleep in the headmistress's bed when she was away and was discovered upon her early return, Miss Hillard was again amused.

Her way with girls, however, did not work as well with boys, at least with her nephew, Archibald MacLeish, a son of her sister Martha. When, at Mary's urging, Archie was sent from his home near Chicago to Hotchkiss School, a boys' preparatory school about forty miles from Middlebury, she became as close to him as she had been to her deceased younger brother John. "I have a new young nephew come East to school," she wrote happily to a friend. "He spent Sunday with me and kept me inwardly smiling [because] he was so dear and unconscious and so funny." That autumn her youngest nephews were christened in Westover's chapel with Archie and a cousin acting as godfathers and Aunt Mary as godmother. The moving service, attended by relatives, friends, students, and staff (including the handyman, maids from the West Indies, and laundresses from Ireland), made her weep. A few weeks later she described the "chapel full of those lovely girls with their angelic reverent young voices chanting the hymns," an experience that "makes one's heart rise up to one's throat." After the christening, a few girls were invited to join the older boys in the headmistress's sitting room, where she read Romanian and Irish folk stories aloud until the bedtime bell.

One spring evening when Archie was eating at the head table on a raised platform in the dining room, a senior asked the very pretty Ada Hitchcock to fill an empty seat. Eighteen-year-old Archie was immediately infatuated with Ada, but, after learning that he was writing her every day, his aunt tried to discourage the match. She thought he was too young to be in love, but there is another less benign interpretation. Ada was the daughter of a self-made merchant in Farmington, and Mary, according to family lore, wanted her nephew to marry a girl from a more prominent family, like Esther Cleveland, the daughter of a former President. The MacLeishes welcomed Ada warmly, however, and the pair planned to eventually marry after Archie's graduation from Yale, where he was class poet. After his stint in the army and enrollment in Harvard Law School, a wedding date was set in June of 1916. Aunt Mary slowly came around, but in such a dominating way that Archie half resented her giving a dance for them, taking over the wedding rehearsal, and putting them up at Crossways the night before their honeymoon in Bermuda. (His sister, Ishbel, graduated from Westover that spring as president of her class and winner of the John H. Whittemore award for "Faithfulness, Justice, Truth, Humility," then followed in her mother's footsteps to Vassar.)

Miss Hillard thought her nephew would make a brilliant lawyer, perhaps fulfilling the promise of her beloved brother John, so she also opposed Archie's growing interest in becoming a poet. When he turned down a partnership in a Boston law firm to move to Paris and write poetry, she furiously tried to talk him out of what she regarded as a bohemian way of life. During a bitter argument, she called him a Bolshevik and he responded by calling her a reactionary. Since she had always adored poetry and had introduced him to John Masefield, whom he regarded as the greatest living English poet, Aunt Mary was in a precarious position. "I do not think even she would argue that the law as a career is more desirable than letters," Archie wrote to his mother. Again his parents backed him, and the young couple and their child moved to Paris.

It was one of the times when Mary Hillard was wrong about what was right for a young person. Many years later the Rev. John Dallas wrote about her tendency to be willful and wrongheaded. "There was a majesty and almost a fury in her love," he observed. She "never knew or understood how she wounded," but afterward would try "to put together again what she felt she had broken." And, he went on, what often looked like possessiveness was her ability to see another's potential. "It was not to superimpose her own will upon another that made her love seem a fury. Rather it was a desire deep within her intelligence and will . . . to compel the recognition of the vision which consumed her soul . . . Fire burns. The result often hurts." Mary was well aware of this character flaw. "I too give pain without knowing I do when if I could exercise more imagination and restraint I would not do so for anything," she admitted to her friend Harris Whittemore. In retrospect, it appears that much of the advice she gave her girls over the years was learned from her own excruciating experiences.

MacLeish's anger deepened after his aunt wrote him in France that she disliked his poetry and so did the editors she showed it to. After she refused to read a published book of his poetry, Archie wrote his mother that "I have definitely, and, I am afraid, not very regretfully, broken with Aunt Mary." He asked his aunt to stop writing and trying to see him. Nonetheless, his feelings remained ambivalent and while still abroad the couple named their newborn daughter Mary Hillard MacLeish. When they returned to the United States, Archie made a tenuous peace with his aunt, but his anger lingered. When she asked him to read his poetry at Westover the year before her unexpected death, he refused. After winning the Pulitzer Prize for poetry in 1933 a year later, he did give a reading at the school, and Ada gave a performance of French songs she had learned in Paris. He returned to Westover again a decade later when his daughter was unhappily enrolled, when he gave a dramatic and disturbing talk about his youthful falling out with the woman he later called his "intelligent and experienced and lovely" aunt. It gave him a feeling of release, but he still did not understand her devastating opposition to him as a young poet.

As a result of her love of poetry and the other arts, Mary Hillard also believed that a balanced life was a cultured life. Over the years, she invited a wide variety of excellent performers and lecturers to Middlebury to excite her students' minds as well as to arouse their sensibilities and to train their tastes. Many of the visitors were men and women she had met or heard about during her travels and active social life. She was a member of many prestigious and exclusive clubs in America and abroad (including the

Waterbury Club, the Chilton Club in Boston, the Colony Club and the Cosmopolitan Club in Manhattan, and the Ladies Imperial Club in London), where she enjoyed talking with interesting and informed people and associating with prominent ones. The year she turned fifty, for instance, she wrote her sister Emily from the Colony Club that she was glad to be meeting "so many people of distinction."

Even earlier, while she was at St. Margaret's School, she had drawn social worker Jane Addams of Hull House in Chicago and Professor Woodrow Wilson of Princeton as speakers. During Westover's first full year, she took pupils to hear African-American educator Booker T. Washington in Waterbury and then invited him to speak in the school chapel. The next spring of 1911 her friend Theodate brought a house guest at Hill-Stead, writer Henry James, to Middlebury to see her handsome school. The girls, waiting for the well-known novelist in Red Hall, applauded when he arrived, but when he was taken to the schoolroom to speak to them, he smiled and bowed but said very little. "My mind has been undermined," was about all he could say, according to Helen LaMonte. "On he went from there felicitating us upon the felicity of dwelling so felicitously in this felicitous setting. More applause. Much waving of hand and hat as he departed, his last sentence unfinished, so great a vocabulary that the choice of the right word was too difficult." The next year a Yale professor lectured about the pleasures of reading, a talk that interested Jessica Baylis so much that she quoted him in her diary as saying that "the happiest people are those that [sic] have the most interesting thoughts."

Although Miss Hillard was not musical herself, she loved music and encouraged a great deal of it at Westover. Singing began in morning chapel and ended with evening vespers. Everyone was given a voice placement test on arrival at school so she could sing her part in all the hymns, ballads, and school songs. Besides offering instruction in singing, piano, and violin, the school had a superb Glee Club under the direction of Isaac Clark, who was at Westover for years. "You are a delightful girl to remember your old man coach," he wrote to a former student. "Such a glee club. I don't believe there ever was such an one anywhere—my heart aches as I think of the future, the standard is so high—how can it be kept up—Certainly we do not want it to fall below this year . . . When one has looked forward to beautiful things all his life and has found them as I have with my work at Westover—and only there—perhaps you can realize what it all means to me . . . It is the one shining spot in my life—You are one of the few that know it."

Besides singing, there was a great deal of listening. Music of the highest quality was performed in Red Hall every year, where a grand piano was stored in a large closet behind the wide landing on the staircase. The Budapest String Quartet started its season there for many years; the Stradivarius Quartet also performed as did members of the New York, Philadelphia, and other symphony orchestras. The list of individual musicians is long: in the fall of 1909, for example, a pianist gave a talk on Bach and then performed the master's music, in 1917 the Tuskegee Singers sang Negro spirituals, and in 1924 the renowned Wanda Landowska played the harpsichord.

Miss Hillard, whose older sister, Helen, a nurse who had worked at the Henry Street Settlement House in New York, also wanted to expose her students to problems in society. In her belief that privilege brings responsibility, she had the reformer Jacob Riis lecture about the terrible living and working conditions of immigrants in American cities; in fact, the year that Westover was founded, thousands of members of the International Ladies' Garment Workers had a strike in New York. Then in 1914 Max Eastman, the editor of the leftist magazine *The Masses*, arrived from Manhattan to lecture without wearing a tie; after one was put together for him from shoelaces, he spoke about slang, to everyone's surprise. "There has been much speculation as to whether Miss Hillard knew what he was going to say," wrote an editor of *The Lantern* afterward. "Anyway, she spent an hour in the schoolroom the next morning counteracting the effect."

When school let out for the summer, the headmistress and her colleagues usually left for a few months in Europe. These trips were interrupted after the summer of 1914, when she and Lucy Pratt were in England as World War I broke out. A few years before in England, Mary Hillard had met poet John Masefield, who then visited Middlebury while in America on a lecture tour, and the two corresponded during the war. She asked him questions about the hostilities that he could only answer philosophically if at all, explaining that after being on the battleground for several months he had "no certainty of our purpose here." In a letter written in April of 1917, he went on: "Now the biggest battle that ever was fought is raging, and I have been watching it from a hole in the ground in the biggest roar and racket that ever troubled the earth. It is not possible to describe it, except that there is over the earth, an angel of wrath, that is all angry and dark, a sort of threat or menace, not a night, nor a dust, nor even a smoke, but something made of all these, and reddish and rather threatening and all shot with blinks of very terrible fire, and it is like the very Devil of Hell sitting in the air enthroned . . . Up above, there are aeroplanes droning and casting glitters, and shells bursting (and larks singing) and a sky all blue with the spring."

"I often think of Westover in these places of death and ruin and awful blasted horror," he continued in his letter. "Westover is a very beautiful and a very happy memory to me, all kindness and happiness and bright dazzling winter weather, and a happy place to come to out of the cold and the night." His vivid words from the trenches, which Miss Hillard read to her pupils, no doubt influenced her later devotion to the cause of world peace, as did the death in 1918 of Martha's son, Kenneth MacLeish, a pilot with the Royal Air Force.

After America entered the war, pupils marched in military drills on the hockey field and participated in patriotic parades and events in Waterbury, including a pageant in St. John's Church, when the girls waved the flags of the Allies and sang their national anthems. They also worked for the war effort by knitting clothes, making bandages, organizing a nursing course, and raising money for orphans. A red banner with the names of those in the school community who were most involved in the war effort was hung in the chapel. When the armistice was announced early in the morning of November 11, 1918, girls gathered in their nightclothes in Red Hall to listen to Miss Hillard, wearing a pink bathrobe and her hair still hanging in a braid down her back. She lead everyone in patriotic songs before they entered the chapel for an impromptu service. Later, students rang the bell in the tower until its rope fell off, and a large celebratory bonfire burned on the village green.

That year John Masefield returned to Middlebury to read his poetry and preside over what would become a yearly writing contest for seniors. The poet, who was later named poet laureate of England, gave the winner, Polly Willcox, a beautifully bound book as a prize for her short story about circus camels. Poets were always high on Miss Hillard's wish list of visitors, and Walter de la Mare, another of the most famous poets of the day, also read his poetry there. A few years later William Butler Yeats arrived from Waterbury by sleigh after a snowstorm had made the roads impassable by automobile. Other lecturers during those years included a bishop from Kyoto who spoke about the position of women in Japan, a female scholar from Oxford University who talked about novelist Jane Austen, and a son of Leo Tolstoy who spoke about his famous novelist father.

Reformers and radicals continued to arrive in Middlebury to talk to the girls. Among them was gray-haired Catherine Breshkovsky, a member of the Russian intelligentsia, whose sympathy for the plight of the peasants in her country had led to her imprisonment and exile. Miss Hillard became aware of her plight and arranged for this woman, called Baboushka or "the little grandmother of the Russian Revolution," to visit in March of 1919. When the visitor in a white headscarf and coarse brown robe glimpsed the West Indian maids, she rushed over to embrace them, calling them "dear children, not long from slavedom." More fluent in German and French than in English, she dined with pupils at the French table, where she expressed displeasure at maids waiting on table and approval on hearing that girls made their own beds. One time while singing Russian folk songs to students, she spontaneously started doing folk steps under an apple tree in the Quad before suddenly turning serious again. "She seemed as she moved amongst us to create a wonderful atmosphere of heroism and eternal hope," remembered French teacher Henriette Coffin.

Although Miss Coffin remembered that Baboushka had wondered whether the girls in "this house of so many riches" could comprehend the troubles in Russia, they raised money for her causes for years. In 1927 she sent an embroidered dresser cover to the girls of Westover along with a plea to help a young Russian woman scientist. "The letter was an appeal from a poor country to a rich one," wrote an editor of *The Lantern* in the March issue. "But it was more than that," she continued. "Written by a great woman, whose life had been spent, in every sense of that word, for her oppressed people, and who at her present age of eighty-three years has not the remotest intention of quitting her post, it contained an expression, in rather broken English, of the courage, enthusiasm, interest, hope, and appreciation of a very remarkable personality" whose "outlook on life is broad, varied, and alive, excluding only despair and defeat." Baboushka's countryman, Vladimir Zenzinoff, was touched by the way the old lady was remembered at Westover—"her name here is surrounded by a sort of halo"—and he noted in his memoir that photographs of her visit "are reverently kept by Miss Hillard as relics." He observed that "time and again did she speak of the Grandmother and her life to her pupils, and these stories evidently formed a part of her educational system."

Indeed, in Mary Hillard's effort to teach the importance of philanthropy, she established the Dorcas Society, named for a Biblical woman known for her good works. Members of Dorcas sewed and knit clothes for the needy and undertook charitable work in the community. Every pupil was expected to give up dessert during Lent; as she left for church on Easter morning, she was given a gold coin she had earned for the donation plate. Girls also hosted a Christmas party for neighborhood children every year complete with a Santa Claus and gifts. After Miss Hillard took students to Waterbury to hear a talk by Sir Wilfred Grenfell, a quiet English doctor who ran a humanitarian mission in Labrador, they began to raise money for him as well. The headmistress also established a charitable Mary Hillard Society, which over the years gave away thousands of dollars to many causes, including churches, visiting nurses, girls' clubs, crippled children, and missionaries in China.

Miss Hillard's wide sympathies and worldly interests created a well-rounded life of her own, especially after the war when she was able to travel to Europe again. In 1928 she offered to take Ursula Van Wagenen Ferguson on her first trip to Europe. Ursula had been the admired president of St. Margaret School's class of 1908, and after her graduation she was a chaperone at Westover for a while before her marriage. When she moved to Middlebury with her husband and young son and daughter, she renewed her friendships with the Misses Hillard, Pratt, and LaMonte. She became deeply involved in the life of the school and was eventually hired to oversee the Dorcas Society. During the summers when not in Europe, Miss Hillard liked to have the Sunday midday meal served outside in the Quad for whomever was around—her nieces and nephews, teachers and friends, as well as members of the Ferguson family—when "she would always try to stimulate the conversation to some interesting topic," recalled the Fergusons' son, John.

The women's trip to Europe typified the busy, purposeful, and even grand way in which Mary Hillard traveled. Before their ship left New York, gifts of books and magazines, baskets of fruit, bouquets of flowers, and boxes of nuts and candies arrived in the stateroom. Perhaps it was on that trip when she gathered all the fresh flowers in her arms and dropped them into the sea right after the ship left port. "A withered flower is the size of a withered soul," she liked to say. "She could not bear to think of so much beauty left to fade and decay—nor of such expressions of love and friendship allowed to wither and to be neglected," explained a friend. Miss Hillard, Ursula wrote in wonderment to her husband, had seven pieces of luggage, including a hat box, a bundle of rugs, a box of books (including a three-volume history of England), and a tin box for picnic lunches. When the two arrived in Paris, they met up with Helen LaMonte (who was traveling with young Gertrude Whittemore and a school friend) as well as a number of acquaintances (including Vladimir Zenzinoff) for sightseeing and social, sporting, and cultural events. In England the two toured the countryside in a chauffeur-driven automobile, meeting up with Theodate, John Masefield, and a Westover alumna or two. Mary had many appointments in London, including a luncheon with Lady Astor at her home, and a meeting with two Englishwomen, a Miss Low and a Miss Michello, who would both teach at Westover the next year.

As a result of all that Mary Hillard brought to her community of females in Connecticut, attending Westover was much more than simply getting an education from books. The year the school opened, a girl perceived that she was learning the art of living, and others throughout the years would echo her words. Accordingly, it was at graduation near the end of her reign when the headmistress proclaimed that "your diplomas are precious to you because they are sign and emblem not alone of mastery of courses of study successfully completed. They are sign and emblem of more than that—the hidden and secret message running through them . . . [of] your loyalty to radiant, glorious, immortal, unchanging spiritual values with their 'power to quicken, quell, irradiate, and through ruinous floods uplift' the souls of men." The years under her tutelage had taught Bidda Blakeley, for one, "about beauty and honor and all the wonderful qualities of life," she remembered. "And *thank heaven* I went there."

4

The Spirit of the School: Engaging Youthful Idealism

LIKE HER FATHER WITH HIS MINISTRY AND HER MOTHER WITH her streak of religious fervor, Mary Hillard was deeply grounded in her Protestant faith. "It has been a long time since I have really been afraid of *anything* in life," she wrote to her old friend Harris Whittemore, now president of Westover's board of directors, because of the solace she took in the words of the Twenty-Third Psalm. "The Lord is my Shepherd, I shall not want," the ancient psalm begins, before going on to affirm a deep reliance on a benevolent God. "That beautifully expresses what I have become, through much suffering of many kinds," she wrote to him in middle age. If God "leads us 'into the paths of righteousness' nothing else matters." But religion was much more than reassurance to her; it was also revelation. One of her close friends, the Rev. John Dallas, believed that "she had a great deal of the passion of the Mystic and even moments of illumination which often helped her to decisions." As she got older, she often spoke of the spiritual world as the realm in which she most genuinely existed. The soul, she once elaborated, was a place where good and evil struggle like "winged steeds and a charioteer," where one horse aspires upward toward heaven and the other attempts to plunge downward toward the earth.

As she looked back, she was extremely pleased that her school was in Middlebury. Not only were her girls able to enjoy the peaceful countryside, but the little village had remained devoted to religious traditions. Believing as she did that "true education" must be built on spiritual values, she had always insisted that the practice of religion be part of daily life at Westover. It was at St. Margaret's School that she got to know the Rev. John N. Lewis, its chaplain and a school trustee, whose friendship and diplomacy had helped her leave Waterbury in the face of strenuous opposition. (He was so fair-minded, in fact, that he would be chaplain of both St. Margaret's and Westover for the rest of his life.) The kindly Dr. Lewis had graduated from Williams College and divinity school in Middletown, Connecticut, before becoming pastor of St. John's Episcopal Church in downtown Waterbury, where he presided for almost forty years. The headmistress and the minister had a warm and jocular friendship; perhaps in recognition of her greater age or forcefulness, he affectionately called her "the chief" or "the captain." Although she was raised a Congregationalist, they generally agreed about religion because he was considered "a low churchman." Impatient with overemphasis on ritual and theological debates, he was more interested in advocating religious tolerance and doing good deeds, like sheltering homeless men in the old parish house behind his church.

Soon Mary Hillard decided that the minister needed a horse so he could get to Middlebury more easily than by the trolley that left the Waterbury green every half hour. The morning after the so-called Clerical Horse Upkeeping Society of Westover School presented him with a bay with a white foot and several gaits, a group of girls waited excitedly for him to ride into sight up the hill. Perhaps because his only children, twin daughters, had died in early childhood, he developed a devotion to all the young girls under his tutelage. Certainly generations of graduates remembered him fondly, noting the way his presence brightened a room. A short, energetic person with round blue eyes and a moustache with a black Scotch terrier often at his side, he was cheerful, humorous, direct, and informal, a man who liked to camp in the woods of northern Maine during the summers. In the confirmation classes he taught at Westover every year, he encouraged girls to raise all their theological questions, and they gratefully recalled his open-mindedness many years later. He was also insightful. Polly Willcox's father was a minister's son who had rejected religion and forbidden her to go to church; when she got to Westover, she felt a sense of "terror" in the chapel, but Dr. Lewis, she always gratefully remembered, "heard my hunger" for the spiritual and gently helped her get over her fear of religion.

The small Gothic chapel, where so many pupils were confirmed in the Episcopalian faith, was also a place where alumnae were married and their babies were baptized. Chapel services were held for the entire school twice a day on weekdays, often led by the chaplain in the morning and by the headmistress in the evening. During processional and recessional hymns in the mornings, there was what was called the chapel line. In preparation, pupils lined up with hymnals in hand on both sides of the long downstairs hallway from Red Hall to the chapel. As the organ in the chapel began to sound, its notes were echoed by a little portable pump organ (called "the grasshopper" after the person playing it, who had to pedal vigorously with her knees flying up in the air) down the hall near the rope to the bell tower. Then the heads of the Glee Club waiting in Red Hall would begin to sing the hymn and walk toward the chapel, while the others fell into line behind them also singing. The lead singers would sit in the front rows of the chapel and direct the rest of the singing with their heads. With its little balcony, terracotta tile floor, carved woodwork, and arched window over the altar, the chapel was a place for many moments of beauty. Mary Hillard rapturously recalled a vespers service in the spring with the shadowy figures of girls in "diaphanous white dresses, the long sunlight and shadows falling in through windows and open door, the evening light and sounds without" along with the singing of old hymns within.

From the beginning there were other religious traditions at Westover as well. Continuing one Miss Hillard had started at St. Margaret's, each autumn she handed new girls a copy of St. Paul's Letter to the Corinthians (I, xiii) for memorization. She also often recited it to the girls in such a dramatic way that a member of the class of 1910, Adelia Brownell, said that no one ever forgot it. In the first year of the school's existence, the headmistress also read a sermon to the Bible class, "The Greatest Thing in the World," by a nineteenth-century Scottish theologian, the Rev. Henry Drummond. It is an explication of this New Testament epistle about the importance of what the St. James edition of the Bible calls the practice of "love," an enveloping form of loving kindness. At Christmastime there was a candlelight service in the chapel, and on Good Friday or the Saturday before Easter, she would read for hours the lengthy life of Christ from the Gospel of St. Luke. On Easter morning, after upperclassmen surprised younger girls by singing "Jesus Christ is Risen Today" at dawn, everyone attended St. John's in Waterbury or in the Congregational or Catholic churches on the Middlebury green, followed by a festive meal in the dining room decorated with daffodils, tulips, and other spring flowers.

Chapel was the central event of the day for many girls over the generations—the expression of the spirit of the school, which itself was a carefully constructed trilogy of tradition, beauty, and idealism. In the essay Mary Hillard wrote in the late 1920s for the book *The Education of the Modern Girl*, she explained her philosophy and her purpose. She began by describing the susceptibility to spirituality of impressionable girls, writing that "the most fascinating aspect of work with the young is the constant re-emergence, with a freshness and novelty like that of a new discovery, of the sensitiveness of youth to 'real existence, colorless, formless, intangible, visible only to the intelligence that sits at the helm of the soul,'" quoting the words of Plato.

In her talks in chapel and elsewhere, she quoted with panache from a wide range of philosophers and poets, particularly from the best translations of Plato and the Greek dramatists. When she entered the schoolroom in the morning to recite a poem or say a few inspiring words, it was always "an exciting event," said Helen Ferguson, a pupil during Miss Hillard's final years as headmistress. Her voice was "the most amazing and the most unforgettable that I have ever heard," she continued, like Eleanor Roosevelt's. "It was soft, never harsh or grating, but vibrant and penetrating, high, and clear. It was almost as if her whole soul rejoiced in the fullness of what she was saying." In her essay, the headmistress also described the experience of a young girl discovering her spirituality as essential as that of a baby beginning to breathe and see. She also wrote that a school can either reinforce a girl's spirit—"fuse it into tempered steel"—or destroy it, depending on the strength of the spirit of the school.

While Mary Hillard gave much of her attention to strengthening this spirit, important developments were happening in the world around Westover. As the movement to win women's right to vote gained momentum, the old argument went on about whether the female role was to morally influence male voters or to be educated to vote for herself. It also addressed whether indirect private influence or direct public action was more effective or appropriate for wives and professional women. In February of 1912, a suffrage meeting advocating the vote for women was held in the Middlebury town hall across the village green from the school. Its impact on the young girls is unknown. An editor of *The Lantern* reported that only three of them attended the meeting, and she published nothing about it or the suffrage cause itself. There's little indication in the written or verbal record of Mary Hillard's attitude toward the meeting or the movement, except for a hint in a letter to her sister Emily written a few months later. "This vote for women is just a minor matter and trivial compared to our real grievances," she wrote elliptically.

Undoubtedly one of her "real grievances" was the fact that controversy still raged about the education of women. In the eighteenth and nineteenth centuries, female literacy was encouraged because it was believed that mothers and teachers would pass on their erudition to children. By the early years of the twentieth century, however, President Theodore Roosevelt and other Republicans were expressing disappointment that college women were less likely to marry or have large families than other women (especially immigrants, who, they feared, were giving birth to many future Democrats). Finally, the Nineteenth Amendment giving women the vote was ratified in 1919, and it is evident that Mary Hillard took a great deal of satisfaction in it. In 1924, preceding the first presidential election in which she could vote, she had current events taught and mock elections held at Westover. Most of her pupils reflected the positions of their parents and supported the Republican, Calvin Coolidge, against the Democrat, John W. Davis. The headmistress refused to say how she would vote until the evening of a torch-lit political parade around the Middlebury green when, right at the end, she suddenly donned a donkey's mask.

Educators were also debating whether to educate young women for lives inside or outside the home or for both. As she aged, Mary Hillard, like her elderly mentor Sarah Porter, said that even highly educated wives should devote themselves first to their families. "Man is responsible for initiative and achievements and woman for nurturing, sensitivity, selflessness," she told a generation or two of Westover girls. In this way she differed from nineteenth-century feminist Elizabeth Cady Stanton, who had emphasized similarities instead of differences between men and women, and from other women educators, who stressed the preparation of young women for the professions. So when Ada Hitchcock MacLeish wanted to study voice in Paris after her marriage to Miss Hillard's nephew, her former headmistress worried that the young wife and mother's aspirations would undermine her marriage.

The heart is the source of life, Mary Hillard said at graduation in 1926, and it is the woman who is responsible "for keeping the life of her own emotions strong, deep, restrained, and true—and so a fountain of living water." She repeatedly cautioned her

Mary Hillard a few years after the opening of Westover School. WESTOVER SCHOOL ARCHIVE.

girls against what she called excessive "self love," and over the years she repeatedly urged them again and again to be "patient, obedient, reverent, submissive, loving, brave," virtues, she must have known, that were more appropriate for wives than for headmistresses. Evidently, she had one set of rules for the majority of her graduates who married and another for the few who did not. Her exhortations seldom took into account the qualities of accomplished women like herself with the inspiration, intelligence, ability, ambition, and even aggression to create a community like Westover. Even so, there are indications that she had private misgivings about the institution of marriage. "Give me a legislature that will abolish this change from butterfly to cocoon," she wrote to her sister in May of 1912, suggesting that, despite all her advice to her pupils over the years, she regretted seeing spirited girls retreat into the role of subdued wives, echoing an observation of French diplomat Alexis de Tocqueville more than a century earlier.

It was well known that Westover's headmistress would hold a girl back from graduating to avoid an early debut. Likewise, she worried about what she regarded as unwise engagements. In the same way that she had warned Miss Porter's pupils in the 1880s about romantic love, she constantly urged Westover students not to idealize marriage but to view it as merely the bedrock of family life. At graduation in 1917, she urged the seniors to be realistic about marriage partners and to ask themselves: "Are you willing to have your children have that man for their helper, their protector, their guide?" The next year she told the graduates that "attraction is a secondary meaning of love. Never forget that. The deepest, oldest, richest meaning of love is holding dear which you can *promise* to maintain." Once she suggested that a student see her young naval officer without his handsome uniform to better make up her mind about him. Another time, when a pupil named Brenda Hedstrom told her that a beau was arriving to propose marriage, Miss Hillard kindly offered them her sitting room instead of one of the reception rooms with glass doors. Then, unable to resist delivering a dose of reality, she asked Brenda if she wanted to watch her beau eat soft-boiled eggs every morning for the rest of her life. "That settled the question, and I said 'no' to the young man," the girl remembered.

Regardless of her personal views about marriage, Mary Hillard did not openly advocate or really explain her own decision not to marry. She never married, she told people, because she did not have time for marriage, but when she was young a middle-class woman had to choose between marriage and the professions. Her graduates' weddings were of intense interest to her, and throughout her more than two decades at Westover's helm, she carefully kept a handwritten list of how many alumnae had and had not married. Not marrying had nothing to do with her feelings for children. After tending her younger sisters and brothers during her childhood, she understood youngsters well. In her sitting room she kept a cupboard full of fascinating gadgets and toys for them that they never forgot. She knew very well, as she explained at a graduation ceremony, that "we can be mothers in soul without being mothers in body." Near the end of her life she expressed mild regret at not being a grandmother, but there is no earlier evidence that she had any sorrow about remaining single and not having children of her own.

Times were changing, and it was becoming increasingly clear that Westover's college preparatory program needed improvement. Ever since the establishment of women's colleges in the nineteenth century, academic standards of finishing schools had risen, but not quickly or high enough to get many of their graduates into college. After women won the vote, more young women wanted additional education, putting pressure on girls' schools to prepare them for College Board examinations. Criticized at times for her lack of emphasis on higher education, Mary Hillard felt misunderstood. Not a college graduate herself, she believed that women could make valuable contributions to society without a college or university degree. Helen LaMonte, a Smith graduate, agreed, calling her good friend Mary a "genius" in her own way. The headmistress often asked incoming girls whether they wanted to go to college, and she aided and encouraged those who did including her niece Phyllis, who went to Radcliffe. "The need of the occasional girl who wishes to prepare for college is . . . met," she had written in an early catalog, and she "holds the right to send pupils into college on certificate," meaning that she was able to get college administrators to waive some requirements for her graduates. Undoubtedly she was influenced by her assumption that most of her alumnae would never want or need to work or earn a living, so over the years she had been more intent about imparting culture than about preparing them for careers. In fact, one of the reasons for newly prosperous families to put a daughter under Miss Hillard's tutelage was to instill in them traditional womanly values, a parental impulse that continued without much challenge until the onset of the Depression.

Westover was still intentionally a school where mediocre students could flourish. In 1928, when Adeline Simonds arrived from Providence at the age of fourteen, she was young for her age, messy, and such a poor speller that she was asked if she had ever been to school before. When her father worriedly wrote Miss Hillard about his daughter's loss of weight and struggles with French, she reassured him. "We are very accustomed to having young girls in their first year find themselves a little at sea in the first few weeks and we are equally familiar with seeing everything straighten out happily after a while," Miss Hillard replied. "I am keeping a watchful eye on Adeline. I do not want to lighten her work as it will be such an advantage to her to keep up with all of the subjects she is carrying and I feel sure she will swing into doing so presently." The girl's C average was one of the lowest in the school that term, but by spring Miss Hillard reported to her father the "awakening of her interest in work and greater concentration and effort." Since she was getting A's in algebra while doing poorly in other classes, it's likely that she had an unnoticed learning disability. Adeline, or Lally as she was called, managed to pass French, but she had to repeat Ancient History the next year. Making a valiant effort, she started getting up at six in the morning to study. "They sure are rushing us in our studies," she wrote her father. Another time she admitted that "I've been working awfully hard lately, but not to very good results much to my distress."

After Christmas of her junior year, she managed to become a B student but lacked enough credits to graduate with her class. At first she wanted to leave Westover, but then she decided to stay but declined to return for a fifth year. Still, all her life she had pleasant memories of her years of boarding school. Right away she made many friends, and in her sophomore year two older girls invited her to room with them after a roommate left. During her senior year, she made Glee Club as a second alto and was chosen as head of the Over hockey team. She loved field hockey, even though in winter she had to practice outdoors in the cold before seven in the morning, at recess, and then again in the afternoon. She wrote her parents about the exhilaration of playing an informal game in the November dusk, when "we just tore around like wild people." Most important of all, at Westover she fell in love with reading. All her life she brightened at the memory of discovering the novels of writers like Thomas Hardy and John Galsworthy, even though she had read them instead of doing her homework.

Most of the studious minority at Westover who took advanced classes with Helen

LaMonte's older sister, Susan, and other teachers were usually the daughters of well-educated professionals or were exceptional or gifted in some way. Polly Willcox, the daughter of a Cornell University professor, was among the three out of forty-five who went on to college from the class of 1918. Polly always remembered gratefully the way Miss Hillard had helped her get into the honors English program at Cornell and her principal's desire to have more pupils enter the college preparatory program. But Miss Hillard was battling a strain of disinterest and anti-intellectualism among students as well as their parents. In 1925, for instance, she urged the *Lantern* editor to apply to college, but the student decided to go to Europe and take classes in Rome and at Oxford University instead. Even into the early 1930s, many girls regarded their college-bound classmates as not "the usual Westover types," in the words of a member of the class of 1934, the former Louise Mead. Nevertheless, since almost half the students in American colleges and universities were by then women, Miss Hillard began visiting Eastern women's colleges to learn how to better enable her graduates to get into them.

In her sixties, Mary Hillard was more than ever an imposing and impressive figure with an aura of queenly dignity as she presided over the life of her school. In the black-and-white photograph of herself that she gave to every graduate, a bespectacled elderly woman with a fine bone structure looks out with a sense of gravity and power. "Her white hair [was] arranged with dazzling precision, the study of which lightened many a dull chapel hour as I tried in my mind to unweave it and fathom its architecture," said a student at the time. The headmistress had become hard of hearing, but she didn't mind because "whenever anyone had anything important to say, they usually said it so that everyone could hear them," she used to say. Still, there were difficulties. Miss Hillard is "quite deaf," Adeline Simonds told her parents. "She asked me if my name is pronounced Ader-lin or Adeline. I said Adeline—and she said oh, Aderlin."

In recognition of the passage of time as the headmistress approached the age of seventy, she began to think about the necessity of retiring and finding a replacement for herself. Although Helen LaMonte was capable of taking her place, she was also nearing retirement age. Understanding that Westover must become primarily a college preparatory school, Miss Hillard wrote to the presidents of the women's colleges she had visited for names of possible candidates with strong academic credentials. Many years earlier, she had called hiring excellent teachers "the most difficult thing in the world," so she must have known that finding a new principal would not be easy. It was Helen Taft Manning, a historian and dean of Bryn Mawr College, who highly recommended Louise Dillingham in 1930, a young scholar who was in her third year as assistant director of a junior year abroad program for American college students in France.

In February of 1931, Mary Hillard sailed for England with her usual many pieces of luggage to see an exhibition of Persian art in London and to meet the promising young woman with the Ph.D. from Bryn Mawr. From the Ladies Imperial Club in London where she was staying, she wrote a large number of ecstatic and extremely long letters to Helen LaMonte and Lucy Pratt about minutiae of her days; she described, for example, wearing a plum-colored crepe dress under a matching Parisian coat with a black Persian lamb collar, along with a rose-and-black scarf and a purple hat with ostrich feathers. She also described going to the Cavendish Hotel at five o'clock one afternoon to greet Louise Dillingham after her arrival from Paris on Saturday, February 27. "A perfectly delightful person presently walked in," she wrote the next day to her friends back in Middlebury. She whisked the younger woman off for tea at her club before a glowing coal fire. Then the Misses Hillard and Dillingham dined at the English Speaking Union and went to see George Bernard Shaw's play "Arms and the Man" at the Old Vic Theatre. "Miss Dillingham and I shook with laughter all through that funny, funny play and would gladly have shouted our approval too had not the men's strong voices done it so adequately," her letter continued. After the curtain went down, they took a taxi to an open post office so Miss Hillard could send a cable. The next day they attended church together and then spent the rest of Sunday motoring to Cambridge and Oxford Universities. The day after that, Miss Hillard saw off young Miss Dillingham before she flew back to Paris.

After Mary Hillard's return to Middlebury in March and a meeting with Westover's board of directors, the young woman was offered a position, which she immediately accepted. The headmistress felt that she had found someone to whom she could entrust the spirit of her school, who was also a scholar with a fine mind who would improve the academic program. That spring the inevitability of change was on her mind. At graduation, she talked about all the technological changes that had happened during her lifetime—the invention and development of the telegraph, telephone, and radio, as well as trolley cars, automobiles, and airplanes. And then she spoke again about the values she believed to be eternal. "If Westover stands for anything, it stands for changelessness of Spiritual Reality," she said. "Truth. Justice. Mercy. Love. Selflessness. Fortitude. Patience. Courage. Integrity. Honor."

The following September, thirty-four-year-old Louise Dillingham arrived in Middlebury to observe and be observed. Miss Hillard had asked her to teach Psychology as well as to study ways to improve the curriculum, especially its deficiencies in science. The plan was for her to spend two years at the school, and if all went well, Miss Hillard would retire in June of 1933 and her new assistant would take her place. It was soon evident that the Bryn Mawr graduate was working out well and, along with the Misses LaMonte and Pratt, she became another assistant headmistress.

Miss Hillard had already made other plans for her beloved school to go on without her. Most of the three thousand shares of stock in the Westover School Corporation were still owned by the original investors or their heirs. She wanted the stock to be held by the alumnae under the aegis of the Mary Hillard Society, so Westover's board of trustees would have control over the school as the years went on. Accordingly, rules governing the charitable society were changed, and the headmistress turned over her own stock to it. Other stockholders were asked to gradually offer their shares at the original price so the school could afford to buy them, and most agreed; by 1932 almost fifty thousand dollars worth of stock had been bought back by the school.

After the onset of the Depression in the autumn of 1929, economies were necessary as families struggled to pay the school's high tuition. Miss Hillard stressed at graduation in June of 1932 the importance of being optimistic, since hard times in the past had been followed by more prosperity than ever. As the country lost confidence in capitalism and began to change in many ways, she repeated ritualistically, like a litany, that moral values never change. "Loyalty to them demands the putting forth, to the utmost power of resolution and exercise of will," she told assembled students and their parents. Then everyone sang one of her favorite old hymns beginning with the words: "Fight the good fight with all thy might, Christ is thy strength and Christ thy right, Lay hold of Life, and it shall be, Thy joy and crown eternally."

Soon afterward, on June 14, she had her seventieth birthday. There was a story told a few years later, by a young alumna from Middlebury who knew her well, that she celebrated by inviting young people to a big party on the roof garden of a New York

City hotel. Around the time of her birthday, she also bought a colonial house on Good Hill Road in Woodbury. She intended to live there in the summer and in an apartment on North Street in Middlebury in the winter after her retirement the following June. She talked about inviting friends for teas and meals and doing all the things she had never had time for before. On July 2 she signed a new will, leaving most of her property to her sister Emily's husband, Jerry Lincoln Fenn, a Hartford lawyer and executor of her estate. He was to dispose of her possessions according to wishes that "I may indicate verbally or in writing," except for the house in Woodbury, which she wanted her old friend Helen LaMonte to use as long as she wanted.

A few weeks later she sent out lighthearted invitations to a picnic on a hillside in Woodbury on a Sunday afternoon, July 10, followed by a visit to her new home. She also attended a banquet of the Unico Club in Waterbury, when its annual Mary Hillard Awards were given to Italian-American high school graduates. She was intensely busy that summer, more than usual. "She had the most fertile mind and imagination. She always had ideas, she always had projects, and she kept things going all the time," said Ursula Ferguson's fifteen-year-old son John. The Rev. John Dallas remembered that her small, strong hands with their short fingernails were always in motion, revising "a list of things to be done, people to see, picnics to be planned, letters to write, a picture to be visited, a list that never came to an end because it was added to, day by day throughout the years." He added: "No one can look at the eyes which are in every picture of Mary Hillard without realizing that she was a dreamer, that she saw beyond the moment, [and] that plans were in the making deep within."

That summer of 1932 during the Depression, she organized John, his younger sister Helen, and nine other teenagers to do chores around the school one day a week for twenty-five cents an hour, followed by lunch, tennis, and swimming. In the humorous contract she drew up, she offered a five dollar bonus to anyone who could lure away a man she nicknamed "San Christophero" for a holiday to Vermont or the Great Lakes. This man was Dr.

The view over the playing field and hillside from the Sally Port.

William F. Verdi, a skillful and dedicated surgeon who specialized in chest surgery at St. Raphael's Hospital in New Haven. It's probable that she got to know him when he performed the mastectomy she was said to have undergone. For years, rumors among pupils had romantically linked their headmistress and this gentle, handsome bachelor. Certainly she was always inviting him to her picnics and parties. A few years earlier, when planning her trip to Europe with Ursula Ferguson, she had even invited him and Ursula's husband to join them in England. But William Verdi was said to be "married to his profession," and he rarely accepted her invitations.

In August, Mary Hillard took the teenagers in two automobiles to Vermont for a few days. They left without Dr. Verdi, but with some of the doctor's sisters and nephews and nieces, including Rose Angela Pelliccia and Rosemary Pallotti, who, along with Helen Ferguson, would graduate from Westover in the class of 1935. It was an extraordinary trip because of the energized and exuberant mood of Miss Hillard, as Helen described it three years later: "Every day was a miniature of her life, and every little act was merely a representation of the big acts in her life." When the group passed a circus, the automobiles stopped while she bought all the balloons from an astonished vendor. And when they paused at a drug store, she invented a soda concoction called "the Italian special." During dinner in a little Vermont inn, she asked the boys to call her Aunt Mary, but she told the girls that they would have to wait until after they had graduated from Westover. Helen later sadly said, "I never called her Aunt Mary."

Then on the first day of October the headmistress was quietly admitted to the Avery Convalescent Hospital in Hartford. Ten days later, on the morning of October 10, Helen LaMonte received a telephone call informing her that Mary Hillard was dead. She went to find Lucy Pratt and Louise Dillingham to tell them the shocking news, and then said to them: "Ask no questions. It will be easier for you that way." It was Visitor's Day for parents of new girls, and the assistant headmistresses agreed not to change the day's plans. After the guests had left and the faculty was informed, Miss LaMonte and Dr. Lewis entered the schoolroom during evening study hall. The chaplain "talked to us simply for a while, and then, first asking all of us not to flicker an eyelash, he told us quietly that Miss Hillard had died early that morning," Helen Ferguson said. Everything would go on as always, he told them. There was absolute silence for a moment, and then everyone resumed doing her homework, or, at Miss

LaMonte's suggestion, wrote to tell their parents. "Dear Mother and Father—This will be very short because I don't feel like writing very much. Dr. Lewis told us that Miss Hillard passed away this morning," Lally Simonds wrote, adding that Dr. Lewis had told them that the headmistress had been staying with her sister, who was recovering from an operation. After study hall, many of the girls stayed up late after the last bell, sitting on their beds and window seats together talking and trying to absorb the news of their sudden loss of the majestic Mary Hillard.

The next morning, a memorial service was held in the chapel. On Sunday, Ursula Ferguson, who noted in her diary that it was her daughter Helen's birthday, picked the last of the fall flowers from her garden to bring to the burial service in the Plymouth cemetery, where the ashes would be buried near the tombstones of Mary Hillard's mother and father, her older sister Helen, three younger brothers, including her adored brother John, and other relatives. That afternoon there was a large service at St. John's Episcopal Church for Westover trustees, teachers, pupils, alumnae, colleagues of the deceased, and her many relatives and friends. It is evident that Dr. Lewis, in his choice of readings and hymns, was well aware that his good friend Mary was finally released from an intolerable weight, what he called "the shadow of this world."

The following day, a rainy Monday, a week to the day after the headmistress's death, the Westover trustees met and elected Louise Bulkley Dillingham, who was a few weeks short of her thirty-sixth birthday, as principal. At the meeting, Theodate Pope Riddle resigned from the board, and Helen LaMonte was elected to it.

Everyone was stunned by Mary Hillard's sudden death. Horace Taft of Taft School remarked with wonderment that his friend had seemed in excellent health the last time he saw her. Older Hillard family members told the younger ones that their aunt had died in her sleep. *The Waterbury Republican*, published by Miss Hillard's longtime friend E. Robert Stevenson, whose daughter Sylvia had just entered Westover, reported in the paper that after catching a severe cold on an automobile trip to see a recently bereaved old girl in western New York, the headmistress had undergone "an unexpected change for the worse" in the convalescent home. When Helen Ferguson later told her brother that she had heard from her mother that Miss Hillard had committed suicide, it seemed very out of character to him. But, in fact, a physician stated on her death certificate that Mary Robbins Hillard had "Melancholia" and had died by her own hand at nine o'clock in the morning after drinking carbolic acid, a substance that was used as a disinfectant at the time.

Helen LaMonte and Lucy Pratt remained in a state of shock, as if they could not explain the death to themselves, and they were too distraught to discuss it with others. Ursula Ferguson, who along with Miss Pratt returned in the rain to the cemetery a few days later to remove faded flowers from the grave, at first had refused to say anything, either. Everyone was "absolutely devastated by her death," her son John recalled, and "they couldn't cope with it." Their way of going on was to hide what had happened. Miss LaMonte ended up burning her own diaries, and anyone else who knew or suspected what had happened kept silent. At a time when mental illness was not well understood, everyone was deeply worried about the effect of what really happened on the girls and graduates of Westover. Although they were afraid of telling the truth about her terrible death, they also believed that without it eventually being known, her life would never be fully understood.

Those who suspected the melancholia, or depression, offered some possible explanations for it. "Old age and inactivity were not for her," wrote Mr. Stevenson in an editorial in *The Waterbury Republican* the day after her death, suggesting that the prospect of retirement had been more difficult for her than anyone had imagined. Those who knew about her mastectomy may have wondered if the cancer had returned. Perhaps there was another private sorrow. It was finally John Dallas, by then the Episcopal bishop of New Hampshire, who offered insights about Mary Hillard's mental state in a memoir about her written about a decade after her death. In it, he indicated that the woman he had known for two decades had experienced times of deep despair throughout her life, pointing to "bereavement, financial strain, misunderstanding, the loss of friendships, hatred, and the loneliness of one in command." He was grateful that she had endured as headmistress of Westover for so many years. "How she was able to live so long as she did after she had put her dream into action is a marvel," he wrote, which suggests that in hindsight her suicide was not so surprising to him.

It's evident that throughout her life, Mary Hillard had secretly and almost successfully battled the emotional illness that shadowed her family. An aunt was mentally disturbed, as well as a younger sister Fanny. Some, including a member of the class of 1919, the former Helen Church, had heard that Miss Hillard had never married in order to avoid passing on the inherited disease. Her most intimate friends had known for years that when the times of depletion arrived, it was necessary for her to go away to rest and recover. At other times she possessed superabundant energy, especially during the last summer of her life. "There is something akin to a Greek tragedy in this side of Mary Hillard's life," reflected Bishop Dallas. "It shows in the expression of her eyes in most of her pictures—a meeting of the elements of life and death but without fear."

What remains troubling is the way Mary Hillard finally allowed the metaphorical "winged steed" she spoke about to at last plunge to earth so violently. Over the years she had bravely attempted to regard her dark moods in a positive light. In a 1910 letter to August Jaccaci that suggested a shared knowledge of mental distress, she philosophized about what she called the radiance behind the anguish. Three years later she wrote to a brother-in-law: "I have learned to know well that my periods of anxiety and physical or mental stress are the soil out of which anything strong in my soul has had its birth and by which it is still nourished." Faith would strengthen people in their darkest hours, she had often told Westover's classes. She repeatedly said that the greatest challenge in life was to uphold the values on which the spirit of the school rested, so few thought that she would fail at this herself. Only weeks before she took her life, she encouraged a sister to act "nobly, willingly, courageously, and patiently" and risk an operation. On reflection, it is clear that when telling others the importance of remembering in the night what is seen in the light, she was also speaking to herself.

Whatever the reason for her final depression and death, Mary Hillard made a big success of her small school. The year before she died, *Fortune* magazine reported that Westover School was among the top ten of the 1,200 girls' schools in the United States. Academic standards had risen, and she managed to get the school accredited in 1931 by the New England Association of Schools and Colleges. And, in her selection of a successor in Louise Dillingham, she had brought the school into a new era. Westover's founder was respected as an educator and admired as a person. "Miss Hillard created a great school out of her own mind, realizing her idea and her ideal," said her friend William Lyon Phelps, a professor at Yale University. During almost half a century, she had touched the lives of more than a thousand young women, including many "girls of girls," daughters of alumnae. "I can see her now, standing tall behind the desk (it seemed as if she never sat down) with head high, covered with snowy hair pulled straight back," remembered Helen Ferguson. She was the greatest woman young Helen had ever known, and the only woman who "could have been president of the United States and have made an excellent job of it." Westover was more than a school: it was, she added, "a world apart, but a precious world that gives one a lasting yearning for what is good and true and fine in life." And due to Mary Hillard's periods of despair, her accomplishment was even greater than most people ever realized.

5

Louise Bulkley Dillingham:
Becoming Miss D

A YEAR BEFORE THE UNEXPECTED DEATH OF THE HIGHLY ES-
teemed Miss Hillard, the youthful Louise Dillingham led Westover chapel services,
helped with admissions, taught psychology and advanced French classes, all the while
getting to know the students, the teachers, and the nature of the school by "observing
and absorbing its life and traditions," she later wrote. A pupil at the time recalled that
she "kept a low profile" and was "very pleasant." A black-and-white snapshot taken of
her at the time shows a sturdy, stocky young woman with a wide generous smile and a
very intense gaze, her dark hair combed back in a no-nonsense manner and gathered at
the nape of her neck. She was remembered as a firm but kind teacher with a twinkle in
her eye, who spoke French so rapidly and in such a soft voice that she was very difficult
to understand. She was also an innovative instructor: one of her psychology pupils never
forgot that she asked them to create an index for an imaginary psychology textbook.

Miss Dillingham observed the school under what she would later describe as "the
benevolent guidance" of the other assistant headmistresses, Helen LaMonte and Lucy
Pratt, who had been there since the beginning. "In no time she had investigated every
nook and cranny from bell tower to underground passage . . . Long before the end
of the year she knew us all and every department and we felt she could break the
bank of Monte Carlo if she cared to, such confidence and devotion had she roused
in every one," Miss LaMonte remembered. "After Miss Hillard suddenly died, there
was Miss Dillingham, a tower of strength and everybody's friend, ready to carry on

with no interruption, ready also to start the changes and growth due to follow." Five months after the founder's death, Miss LaMonte wrote to the alumnae that the new headmistress had "great sympathy" with Westover traditions. "I always like to think that Miss Dillingham is Miss Hillard's choice, a person whom she both admired and loved." Miss LaMonte was speaking from a point of view that, unfortunately, was not prevalent among the pupils.

When Louise Dillingham had arrived as heir apparent, "none of us were too pleased," recalled a member of the class of 1933. The thirty-six-year-old administrator seemed to the adolescents both older than her years and without the charisma of her predecessor, to whom the seniors dedicated their 1932–33 yearbook. The founder of the school "was an extraordinary woman who really loved the girls, and I never had that feeling about Miss Dillingham," said another alumna, who graduated in 1934. "It was hard because everybody loved and respected Miss Hillard so much." The students had also heard that this outsider was going to turn Westover into a college preparatory school, and undoubtedly there was some apprehension about it. And whereas Miss Hillard had melodiously addressed them as, "Now, girls," the younger headmistress began with a brisk, "Now students," recalled another pupil, who, nevertheless, liked the unassuming manner of the person she called "Dilly" behind her back. "Miss Dillingham seemed very cold and aloof to us and also very, very academic," yet another graduate remembered. A few liked nothing about her at all. "She was very shy, and very red, and very fat," remembered the class president in 1935. It is true that the snapshot of her also shows a young woman with a double chin, piano legs, and an overall fleshiness that made her appear to be without neck, wrists, or ankles.

President Franklin D. Roosevelt had been elected a few weeks after she was elected headmistress, and the country was experiencing enormous cultural and political shifts. As capitalism came under attack in the face of widespread unemployment, the appeal of socialism and communism was growing. After the President closed the banks to avoid a panic in 1933, spring vacation was cancelled at Westover because no currency was available to pay for transportation. Nonetheless, Miss Dillingham elaborated upon her educational philosophy with more hope and idealism than she ever would do again. In it, she made the assumption that her young students would be able to learn something called "the Truth." She also wanted them to believe that change always meant "progression," and even that society's "present falseness, ugliness and evil" did not necessarily have to lower personal standards.

During her first years as headmistress, Miss Dillingham often consulted with the senior class officers. She made few adjustments, well aware that she must tread gently and not appear disloyal to her revered predecessor. The new administrator embraced Miss Hillard's practice of having every girl memorize the passage from St. Paul's Letter to the Corinthians. Returning alumnae were glad to see that everything seemed the same. One of the modifications the headmistress ventured was to allow comic strips to remain in *The New York Herald Tribune* on Sundays. Another was the abolishment of the terrifying "Black Monday," when grades were read out loud. She kindly decided to read the honor roll instead.

Events arranged by Miss Hillard went on as planned. Biologist Julian Huxley spoke about evolution, while writers Vita Sackville-West and Harold Nicholson discussed changes in English social life. A maharajah opposed to Mahatma Gandhi explained the view of the upper classes in India. Miss Dillingham, for her part, urged speakers to address the students at the level of college freshmen or sophomores. Concerts were given by the usual groups, and by guitarist Andrés Segovia, the English Madrigal singers, and the Hampton Singers, an African-American quartet. The rising bell still rang at quarter of seven in the morning, and breakfast was followed by chapel. There were the three classes, a break for cocoa or bullion and sweet buns at eleven o'clock, and then three more classes before lunch at a quarter after one. Next there were the walks on country roads or sports like field hockey outside or volleyball and basketball in the small upstairs gymnasium or on the outdoor wooden platform near Virginia House. Study hall in the late afternoon was followed by dinner, vespers, and club meetings until lights were ordered out at nine-thirty in the evening.

Graduation requirements remained a year of rhetoric, mathematics, mythology, and psychology; two years of Greek or Latin as well as English literature; three years of French; and five years of history, including the history of art. Colleges, however, were beginning to want students with less knowledge of dead languages and with more understanding of economics, current events, and the sciences. This was thoroughly understandable to Miss Dillingham, who, when she had written down her educational philosophy, had explained that a learner needs "intellectual honesty, emotional control,

The Dillingham family around 1908. From left: Tom, Sherbourne,
Mrs. Dillingham, Dorothy, Hope, Louise, and Helena.
COURTESY OF DOROTHY D. GOODWIN.

mental discipline, and the understanding of scientific method."

In regard to her latter concern, she had a physics laboratory installed in the southwest corner of the basement of the main building in 1933. The next year she hired Adela Prentiss of Middlebury, who had graduated with honors from Wellesley College in 1921, to teach psychology, physiology, biology, and chemistry. As one of the few married women and mothers working at the school, she would also teach what was called "Personal Living" and the facts of reproductive life in her classes. During her three decades at Westover, she would start a science club, let psychology students get practical experience by volunteering in the community, and take physics students on field trips to places like the telephone company's central exchange in Waterbury.

Five years after becoming headmistress, Miss Dillingham told an alumna that there was "a very much larger proportion" of girls going to college than ever before. One of the reasons was that college entrance requirements were lowered during the Depression, and another was that more of the teenagers realized that they would eventually have to find jobs. In the fall of 1933, Rebecca Love, a senior taking the general non-college course, walked into the headmistress's office and announced that she wanted to go to Bryn Mawr. "I knew the dimensions of the Parthenon, the floor plan of St. Paul's cathedral (and many others), I had read English literature from Beowulf to 1900 at a college level, I knew how Mantegna contributed to the evolution of art, and I was well on my way to a speaking acquaintance with the piano repertory—but I had had no mathematics in four years, no French or Latin in three," she remembered. Miss Dillingham informed her that getting into Bryn Mawr would be impossible but suggested Vassar because of its music department. On her College Board examinations, Rebecca failed Latin, barely passed French, and did superbly in English, but, despite her uneven academic achievements, Miss Dillingham managed to get her accepted ("when I consider the factors on her part which went into moving that particular mountain, I still react with disbelief," the girl later said), where she won the Vassar piano prize and then went on to become a physician. By 1936 about a third of the seniors were going on to college, more than in most other girls' boarding schools at the time.

Nonetheless, that year when Louise Dillingham turned forty, she failed to impress a young novelist from New York City, who was on assignment from *Fortune Magazine* to write an article about fashionable girls' boarding schools. "Westover is a negative phenomenon among boarding schools where, after all, girls who are cooped up for eight months of the year are apt to get some very strong impressions to carry away with them," went the unsigned article in the April 1936 issue. "It is a school virtually without personality. Miss Hillard had a personality, and old Westover girls at least remember how she could spout their genealogies to guests, but in 1931 [sic] Miss Hillard went wherever headmistresses go when they die. Now there is Miss Dillingham, who has a bland Bryn Mawr manner." The writer, who had gone to a girl's school in Boston and worked for *Vogue* and *Vanity Fair*, went on to state that Westover's traditions "are not enough to give color to a school. Even the uniform is a somewhat *au lait* shade of khaki." Evidently she interviewed some absent-minded alumnae, since she also wrote that "for numbers of Westover graduates there is also the rather weird feeling of having no clear memories of their alma mater."

A month later, the editor-in-chief of *The Lantern*, Jean Baker, responded. Identifying the writer as Nancy Hale, the senior accused her of writing in a pseudo-complimentary way that was difficult to counter. Nevertheless, in her editorial the student strongly objected to the description of Westover as lacking character and being forgettable. Instead of defending Miss Dillingham, however, she described the school's traditions as representing "an ideal" created by the legendary founder of the school, whom she had never known. "Certainly such an ideal could not escape having personality!" she wrote.

The senior wrote nothing about the claim in the *Fortune* article about pupils being blondes ("or on the light side of brown"). Or that they were from the wealthiest families in the country, who could pay tuition of two thousand dollars a year, a fortune during the 1930s. Or the writer's description of the ecclesiastical look of the school, or at least that of Red Hall, with "a clean, bare, New England aspect to the interior, where all upholstery is in a shade of pew-bench red that is rarely seen outside churches." Nancy

Hale did report that Westover girls seemed to take life seriously. Some seniors told her that "if they do make their debuts, it shall be only in order to learn more about people," she wrote. "Westover, which used to be a finishing school, has become definitely serious-minded." She also noted that the headmistress had told her that the girls were much busier and more realistic than in earlier years, as indicated by their strong interests in psychology, sociology, modern history, and current events. She also said that they were marrying later. Certainly Miss Dillingham encouraged their interests by, for instance, allowing economics and civics classes to attend a mock trial with women jurors sponsored by the League of Women Voters in Waterbury.

When Louise Dillingham had visited Westover in the summer of 1932 before beginning to work there, it was not the first time she had been in Middlebury. During the early years of her childhood, her family had spent summers on the island of Nantucket before buying a summer house in Woodbury, which was closer to her father's corporate law office in Manhattan. As a young girl, she used to explore on horseback the dirt roads around the old villages in the area. Her first glimpse of Westover may have been on horseback or from the window of an automobile on the way to Waterbury.

Both her parents had been born in New York City, raised in New Jersey, and descended from New England ancestors—the Dillinghams were from Maine and the Bulkleys were from Connecticut. Frank Ayer Dillingham, a graduate of Yale and Columbia Law School, had married his childhood friend, Louise Gregory Bulkley, on January 23, 1896. The couple's first child, Louise Bulkley, was born nine months later on the first day of November. Winthrop (known as Tom) was born three years later, followed quickly by Dorothy, Helena, Hope, and Sherburne. The Dillinghams lived in a big, handsome old house in Summit, New Jersey, with a servant's wing for the cook and the upstairs and downstairs maids; there was also a chauffeur, as well as farm workers to tend the horses and other animals, and a governess to take care of the six children.

The children's mother, the elder Louise Bulkley Dillingham, had gone to the all-girl Masters School in Dobbs Ferry, New York, and all her life she remained a reader with a great deal of intellectual curiosity. She was also an invalid for most of that time. After her youngest child was born on Nantucket, she had contracted tuberculosis. Instead of going to a sanitarium, she spent her days on a screened sun porch that her husband had built for her. It was where she rested in the fresh air apart from her children, so they would not catch the highly contagious disease. "I think at a really crucial point in their lives, they needed mothering that they didn't get," speculated Dorothy's daughter about her mother, aunts, and uncles. She remembered hearing that when the youngest, Sherburne, was about two years old, he had begged his mother for an embrace, and when she demurred, the child promised not to tell anyone. It was very painful for both of them, since Mrs. Dillingham was a very loving person. Her enforced seclusion was an experience that marked them all deeply, leaving her children with a legacy of difficulty in expressing emotions. On weekends it was their father who taught them to sail, garden, and ride horses. Louise kept an eye on her younger sisters and brothers, and they looked up to her for most of their lives.

Louise was first taught at home and then at the private Short Hills School, with the exception of a winter spent studying on Nantucket with a Miss Gulielma Folger, a ship captain's daughter, who lived in a little house full of books. When Louise reached the age for boarding school (her parents were considering the all-girls Rosemary Hall in Greenwich, Connecticut), it was discovered that she already knew enough to go to college, so she was enrolled in Bryn Mawr instead. Bryn Mawr was on a par with Harvard University, and its entrance examinations were as rigorous as well. Its faculty was excellent and, alone among all the women's colleges in the country, it had a Ph.D. program. When three days before the start of the semester it was learned that Louise lacked knowledge of algebra, the story goes, her father gave her a crash course in it. Presumably she passed with flying colors, since at the end of that academic year, 1912–13, she was honored as the second "Bryn Mawr Matriculation Scholar for New York, New Jersey, and Delaware."

When she had entered Bryn Mawr in 1912, she was not yet sixteen and was among the youngest girls ever to enroll. Its president, Martha Carey Thomas, had earned her Ph.D. summa cum laude at the University of Zurich, since there was no way for a female to get the degree in the United States at the time. Influenced by Charlotte Perkins Gilman, M. Carey Thomas, as she liked to be called, spent her life rebelling against the prevailing belief that higher learning for women was unladylike. In 1899, the portrait painter John Singer Sargent had portrayed the college president enveloped in a black academic robe and as if sitting on a throne; her pale hands and face were emphasized against the dark background, while her straightforward gaze was made regal, serene, and self-assured. She urged her graduates to become academics, and she liked to give fellowships to the best of them, even those who were married. It was she who famously said, "our failures only marry." Like Mrs. Gilman, she fervently advocated what she called "the woman's point of view," meaning the need for more womanly or humanistic values to permeate American culture. Louise Dillingham later called President Thomas as impressive as another woman who had profoundly influenced her, Mary Robbins Hillard.

Even as a young Bryn Mawr undergraduate, Louise was a student leader who was elected vice-president and treasurer of her class. In 1916, at the age of nineteen, she graduated magna cum laude with majors in both French and German literature. The following year she did graduate work in French and Spanish at Columbia University, where she also worked as a secretary at her father's law firm, Rounds, Dillingham, Mead & Neagle. One of her father's friends remembered Louise at twenty as an attractive and very bright young woman with a taste for martinis.

Frank Dillingham had helped found a sugar company in Ensenada, Puerto Rico, of which he was president and chairman of the board. During Louise's second year out of college, she moved to the island to be an assistant secretary in the general manager's and comptroller's offices of the firm, the South Puerto Rican Sugar Company. For the next five years she lived in a woman's club on the large sugar plantation, which had, besides a refinery and sugar cane fields, churches and houses for workers as well as schools for their children. It was during this time in her life that Louise Dillingham's heart was broken. On one of her visits back to New Jersey, she confided to a sister that it is very difficult when the man you love marries your best friend. This sister, Dorothy, observed to her daughter that afterward her eldest sister no longer tried to be an attractive woman.

In late September of 1921, Louise received a telegram from President Thomas offering her a fellowship at Bryn Mawr, where, along with work in a residence hall and in the dean's office, she could study for a graduate degree. That autumn she declined the offer, but after it was proposed again in June right before President Thomas's retirement, she accepted it. During the next two years, she worked for a master's degree in French and social psychology, which she earned in 1924. She also won the M. Carey Thomas graduate fellowship for study abroad, so the next year she studied for a Ph.D.

at the Sorbonne. During the 1920s many American artists, writers, and intellectuals were living in Paris, including Archibald MacLeish, Gertrude Stein, Scott Fitzgerald, and Ernest Hemingway. After her year abroad, she returned to Bryn Mawr to head a residence hall and finish her dissertation, "The Creative Imagination of Théophile Gautier: A Study in Literary Psychology." This work about a nineteenth-century French writer and art critic, who believed in art for art's sake, won her a Ph.D. in 1926. She then remained at her alma mater for another year as a student advisor as well as a teacher of modern French literature, old French philology, social psychology, and other subjects.

The following academic year, 1927–28, she became an assistant professor of French at Wellesley College in Massachusetts. Eager to get back to the excitement of Paris, she took a leave of absence and returned with the junior year abroad program run by the University of Delaware, where she advised and arranged housing for women students. She extended her stay in Paris, continuing her study of French literature and collecting sixteenth- and seventeenth-century books in the language. It was in February of 1931 when she took an airplane to London to meet the headmistress of Westover School, who ended up asking this eminently qualified young woman to be her heir apparent. "Why Miss Dillingham ever considered coming to Westover in the first place will always be a mystery," Helen LaMonte reflected many years later, "but to our great good fortune come she did, having fallen under Miss Hillard's gifts of persuasion." Although the young scholar was qualified to take a position at a college or university, she was willing to leave Paris and work with younger pupils. Perhaps it was because of her admiration for Mary Hillard, or her desire to be in charge of a school, or her memory of central Connecticut, or a combination of these reasons as well as others.

When she had lived in Paris she had traveled throughout Europe, but her years in Puerto Rico left a stronger mark on her, and it was to Hispanic cultures that she would gravitate for the rest of her life. In her era, the sitting room in the headmistress's apartment at Westover had silver cigarette boxes from Peru and Brazil, piles of old Spanish manuscripts, and rare books about the exploration and settlement of Latin America. On summer vacations she liked to pack a set of oil paints and travel to Mexico, Guatemala, South America, or the American Southwest; she visited Argentina and Paraguay when her youngest brother was posted in those countries with the diplomatic corps. She also traveled to the lost city of the Incas in Peru, Machu Picchu, which a Yale classmate of her father's had discovered and excavated. For a while she held a Pan American day at Westover for girls studying Spanish, and at least once a Mexican dinner was followed by dancing to recorded tango music in Red Hall.

The school had always wanted to buy the old Methodist church next door, and it eventually did so in 1923, then used its main floor as an assembly hall. Years earlier, Mary Hillard had talked the congregation into moving its church building to make room for her girls' school. She wrote to Harris Whittemore about the negotiations: "My own first association with the Methodist Church of Middlebury was when I sat in the front room of Deacon Abbott's sweet home down by the mill while the Methodist brethren retired and sat in the kitchen while they discussed for just how much they could squeeze the Westover Corporation for permission to move their parsonage a bit and put our chapel on its original location." She added that she was glad the churchmen had not known that the Westover chapel would hold Episcopal services, because then they might have demanded a higher price.

Helen LaMonte had told Mary Hillard that the school needed a librarian, so Esther Millett, a graduate of Simmons College, was hired. When she arrived in the fall of 1929, there was no real library at all. The Common Room behind Red Hall had been the original library, but it was outgrown long ago, and books were shelved here and there in offices and classrooms. After Miss Hillard's death, Miss LaMonte began to turn the meeting house into a library in memory of her old friend. An architect was hired, and names of contributors were entered in gold letters in a handsome book. As renovations got underway, pews were removed, the pulpit was replaced by a fireplace, and bookshelves for seven thousand books were built from the basement to the balcony. A large brass chandelier was hung, and upholstered furniture was moved in, along with a big table to display newspapers and magazines. Then the large portrait of Miss Hillard was brought over from the wood-paneled room where Miss LaMonte taught to the place of honor over the fireplace in the new Mary Robbins Hillard Memorial Library.

The pupils were impressed that the lofty space, where daylight flooded in through tall arched windows, had the ambience of a comfortable living room. "It is perfectly unbelievable, with deep wine-red rugs that sink for miles under your feet, and real sofas

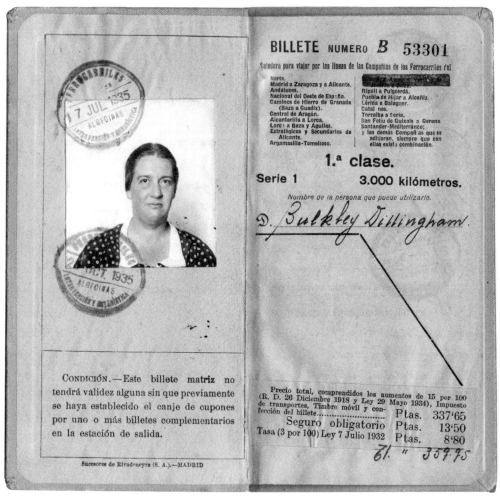

BILLETE NUMERO **B 53301**

Valedero para viajar por las líneas de las Compañias de los Ferrocarriles del

Norte.
Madrid a Zaragoza y a Alicante.
Andaluces.
Nacional del Oeste de España.
Caminos de Hierro de Granada
   (Baza a Guadix).
Central de Aragón.
Alcantarilla a Lorca.
Lorca a Baza y Águilas.
Estratégicos y Secundarios de
   Alicante.
Argamasilla-Tomelloso.

Ripoll a Puigcerdá.
Puebla de Híjar a Alcañiz.
Lérida a Balaguer.
Catal nes.
Torralba a Soria.
San Feliu de Guixols a Gerona.
Santander-Mediterráneo;
y las demás Compañ as que se
   adhieran, siempre que con
   ellas exista combinación.

1.ª clase.

Serie 1   3.000 kilómetros.

Nombre de la persona que puede utilizarlo.

D. *Bulkley Dillingham*.

CONDICIÓN.—Este billete matriz no tendrá validez alguna sin que previamente se haya establecido el canje de cupones por uno o más billetes complementarios en la estación de salida.

Precio total, comprendidos los aumentos de 15 por 100 (R. D. 26 Diciembre 1918 y Ley 29 Mayo 1934), Impuesto de transportes, Timbre móvil y confección del billete........................ Ptas. 337'65
   Seguro obligatorio   Ptas.   13'50
Tasa (3 por 100) Ley 7 Julio 1932   Ptas.   8'80
        61 " 359.75

Sucesores de Rivadeneyra (S. A.).—MADRID

Louise Dillingham's visa photo, 1935. WESTOVER SCHOOL ARCHIVE.

that aren't deceiving like the ones in the old library. After three weeks we still come to it, only to sit and gaze in stupefaction; even the weekly fights for *Time* have ceased," observed a girl in the November 1935 issue of *The Lantern.* Instead of just being able to borrow books on Sunday afternoons, they could now be taken out for two weeks and then renewed. Miss Dillingham noted that the beautiful new library had stimulated the students' interest in reading, and she later called Westover a reading school, while other educators noted that the girls are constantly "reminded that reading is a pleasurable experience." Before long Miss Millett was publishing extensive summer reading lists and organizing autumn book sales. As girls returned from church on a Sunday every autumn, they found Red Hall transformed into a bookstore with a thousand titles that could be ordered from the Scribner book store in New York City. The library was a fitting memorial to the founder, at least one senior thought. "The last Senior class to know Miss Hillard is gone, but to those of us who have been denied her friendship has been left the privilege of having the library which has been built in her memory," wrote Jean Baker for the following issue of *The Lantern*. "Surely, in a place as lovely as this, we can . . . feel that we, too, have known Miss Hillard."

It is interesting to note that a member of the class of 1914, who had known Helen LaMonte for years, felt that the library was actually more reminiscent of her than of Mary Hillard. Both Miss LaMonte's neat, book-filled office and her sitting room evoked feelings of "quiet liberation," she said. "This library has not only the same feeling of ease and freedom that was felt in Miss LaMonte's own rooms; it is a mature, satisfying place." Miss LaMonte, who was by then in her early sixties, was quietly planning to retire after the opening of the library. At the end of the 1935–36 school year, she and her sister Susan departed to open a bookstore, "The Bookroom," in a brownstone in the Georgetown section of Washington, D.C. She "never said goodbye to us when she left," recalled a senior that year. "How could she?" Students who had waited to take her course in the history of art were deeply disappointed, but all they and others could do was dedicate an issue of *The Lantern* to her. "It is so difficult to get used to Westover without her, and no one can ever really take her place," another girl wrote despondently in the issue. At least Miss LaMonte used to write letters full of wisdom to her former pupils in her tiny and tidy black script, a practice she kept up all her life. When she returned to Middlebury the following June, she greeted the girls warmly and gave them a first edition of Nathaniel Hawthorne's *The House of the Seven Gables*.

Most of the well-educated women whom Miss Hillard had hired remained under the new regime. Many of them had been forced by the Depression and gender discrimination to teach in a preparatory school rather than a college or university. These unmarried teachers formed a close circle, and on Saturday nights they put on evening dresses for buffet dinners in the faculty lounge of Virginia House. Among them was Leslie Clark, a graduate of Bryn Mawr who had taught at Westover since 1913, whom

Miss Dillingham named assistant headmistress in 1936. Like the other accomplished and versatile teachers, she was able to teach a number of subjects, including the French language and English history. She was "diminutive, spare of build, steely-eyed, and demanding," remembered a former student, and "she presided with dignity and fairness over the schoolroom, dining room, and chapel." Another teacher who stayed was Elizabeth Kellogg, who had been a student of Miss Hillard's at St. Margaret's School; another alumna of Bryn Mawr, she had begun teaching history and English literature at Westover in 1925.

Emma Hibshman, the tall, stately daughter of a Lutheran minister, had arrived the autumn when Miss Hillard died. Born in Pennsylvania, she was educated in Tennessee before going to Vassar and getting a master's degree in English literature at Yale. She had first seen Westover in the late 1920s, when accompanying a group of students from another school to a meeting on international affairs in Red Hall. She was impressed by the handsome room and even more so by Mary Hillard, and afterward she wrote to the principal repeatedly until she was allowed to join the staff, even though there was no opening. Throughout her many years at Westover, she taught several subjects, too, from Latin to English. A colleague called her a Mona Lisa personality because of her enigmatic and aloof persona. A wandering eye made listeners wonder if she was looking at them or not, and it contributed to the sense of elusiveness about her. It was in the classroom, including Miss LaMonte's former course in nineteenth century English literature, that she revealed her warmth, sense of humor, and sharp wit.

Among those whom Miss Dillingham hired was Elizabeth Cushman, a classical scholar she had known as a Bryn Mawr underclassman, to teach Latin and a class about the worlds of the Romans and Greeks. She also hired her own sister, Helena, who had dropped out of Bryn Mawr before graduating from Vassar, to teach art history before she married and moved to Wyoming. In 1935 the headmistress rehired Madame Julie McLintock, a red-haired Frenchwoman who had studied at the Sorbonne and at Oxford. She had taught French at Westover in the 1920s before marrying a British mining engineer, but the marriage didn't last. She was full of *joie de vivre* and was thought by the girls to be an intriguing older woman "who had really lived," in the words of one of them. Evelyn Merrimon was also rehired during the Depression; she was "a red-headed aesthete" influenced by Isadora Duncan, who had studied music in New York and liked to spend her summers in Italy. She played the organ in chapel, taught piano and music history, and presided over the recorded classical music concerts during quiet time on Sunday afternoons in Red Hall. "She was a fine and demanding musician, a romantic who did not suffer fools gladly or indeed at all," remembered the former Rebecca Love, especially the "effete" fellow pianist and music teacher Bruce Simonds, who also taught at the Yale School of Music.

Every few years the faculty and staff put on a satirical Saturday night skit for the students. One year it was the spoof of a radio talent show. The master of ceremonies was Charlotte Low, a tall Scotswoman and graduate of Cambridge University, whom Miss Hillard had hired in 1928 to teach English literature and medieval history and to direct plays. That evening she had her colleagues reporting news flashes, clicking castanets, juggling, turning cartwheels, and sword-swallowing. "The highlight of the evening was a duet and a waltz by Miss Dillingham and Miss Millett, whose performance registered the most applause on the electrical machine, which must have recorded a deafening tumult of shouts and screams," *The Lantern* reported in May of 1935. In other years the headmistress clowned it up in a gay nineties bathing suit and in a cowgirl outfit.

Despite the frivolity, Miss Dillingham knew that teachers gossiped about the girls, so she gave the faculty as little personal information about the pupils as possible. Instead of holding meetings, she invited teachers to her sitting room on Tuesdays after dinner for demitasse cups of coffee. During the rather formal gatherings it was difficult for some of them to approach her chair and make small talk, but others, like Elizabeth Fry, didn't mind at all, knowing there would be other times for serious discussion. Miss Fry was shy and soft-spoken, one of her pupils remembered, as well as a "splendid" teacher of modern history, who was "eager to fan any spark of interest" in her students. She had been a Bryn Mawr student when Miss Dillingham was in charge of a residence hall there, and Miss Fry had not thought highly of her then. It was only at Westover, after she arrived in 1938 to teach literature, too, that she realized how "remarkable" a woman Louise Dillingham really was. She was a person who gave her teachers a great deal of freedom in the classroom, but "we were always aware that she expected very high standards," Miss Fry said. "Westover was a delightful place to work, and I feel privileged to have been there for six years with Louise Dillingham."

She was "definitely but somehow unobtrusively" in command, Elizabeth Fry also observed. Even before the young headmistress turned forty, she exuded a sense of authority. A pupil noted that "her crisp, definite, explicit way of speaking to us left no doubt that she was completely in charge." It was a "very final way of speaking," another would say in later years, describing the way the headmistress spoke rapidly while clamping her jaw shut after enunciating each word. It was intimidating the way her unsmiling mouth made a long straight line across her face. It was also unnerving the way she would suddenly emerge from her sitting room and sweep with a straight back through Red Hall, requiring girls to rise suddenly to their feet, as they were expected to do when an adult entered a room. "When she passed you in Red Hall or the corridors—which wasn't often—she would never stop and chat. It would be a nod, a brief smile, and she would keep going. On looking back, I'm sure it was shyness," observed an alumna many years later. Her aura, however, led to observations at the time about social ineptness or even forbidding unfriendliness. She looked regal in her hooded black Ph.D. robe that she wore for chapel and in the evening dresses she wore on Saturday nights, but she seemed remote as she sat on the raised dais in the dining room and presided over the pupils at the long refectory tables. "She was like a god overseeing our little Westover world—not the Old Testament one of wrath, but rather a powerful benevolent, if austere, deity, whose all-seeing eyes noted all misdemeanors and rule infractions of her awe-struck charges," remembered yet another one.

Although Miss Dillingham appeared remote, she actually had an encyclopedic knowledge of her pupils. Every September she used to stand at the front door of the school and give every new and returning girl a firm handshake, and in a few days she learned the names of all the new girls, an undertaking that took others a few weeks. Undoubtedly aided by her study of psychology, she had insights into girls she rarely talked with, often to their astonishment, when they later read letters she had written to their parents. She knew instantly who the student leaders were, for example. Her intuition, instinct, and intelligence were always at work, to say nothing of her growing experience. She could look across the dining room and immediately tell a girl's mood by her posture. One time after an irritated mother met with her, the mother emerged from the headmistress's sitting room and exclaimed that Miss Dillingham had told her more about her daughter in a few minutes than the parent had learned during fourteen years. When a pupil in the class of 1938 dutifully asked for permission to go to a dance, Miss Dillingham observed her closely and asked if she really wanted to go; when the girl equivocated, the headmistress said no with big smile on her face. "My abiding memory of Miss D was the feeling I had, when I was with her, that she could see right through me, into the very core of my being. There was no doubt in my mind that my every thought, wish, impulse, every brain wave was perfectly manifest to her. I felt like a little fly in the lap of a God who was gazing at me and guiding me in unspoken ways," said a former student many years later.

Miss Dillingham's reserve also concealed another reality—that she actually felt very warmly toward the young girls in her care. She deliberately kept her distance for a number of reasons. For one thing, it was said that she did not want to have favorites the way her predecessor did. For another, she wanted the adolescents to mature without adult interference. Only without adult involvement would they do so, she believed. The 1935–36 catalog explained that students under the guidance of seniors were allowed to help run the school as a way to learn a sense of responsibility, to set goals, and to carry them out. "Here at Westover we do try to realize in studies and in daily living at least one phase of true education: the thorough, original execution of any task undertaken," the headmistress said. She used to tell the students repeatedly that "you are here to become strong, self-reliant women." She later elaborated about the importance of training the intellect, telling an alumna that "our whole attempt is to have all the members of the school think as clearly and unemotionally as possible about the questions which arise in their daily school life and which are necessarily prototypes of the problems which they will meet later on."

When the headmistress perceived or heard about a personal problem of some kind or another, she would quietly consult with teachers or student leaders about it. Sometimes this approach worked, but often it did not. Some girls from broken families found stability in the school routine, but often those with serious emotional difficulties did not. A pupil in the class of 1938 thought that the headmistress lacked "understanding and compassion" with "several very troubled" girls. Yet another time, when a new girl became so depressed that she stayed in bed instead of going to class, Miss Dillingham went to her room to talk with her. "She may have been strict, but this showed her softer side," the student said. The headmistress told another distressed girl to come to see her any time, day or night. "I wouldn't call her my friend, but I would say she was an emotional support for me. I'll always be grateful to her and also for my education," she later said.

As a disciplinarian, she was lenient or harsh depending on her understanding of a situation. After her autombile passed a few new girls who were walking out of bounds by mistake, she called them into her office and kindly reminded the terrified girls of the rules. Another time, after a girl named Mary Hilliard and a friend went on a walk and deliberately met up with some boys from Choate School (including the young John F. Kennedy) in a fancy convertible and smoked some cigarettes with them, they were almost expelled. "Miss Pratt was enraged and told me—often—that I was unworthy of my heritage" as a daughter of one of the seven Talbott sisters, whose parents had given the school its fieldstone fireplace. Afterward Mary's mail ended up on Miss Pratt's desk, where it was opened with the excuse that it might be intended for the former headmistress. When Mary complained to Miss Dillingham, the two had what she remembered as "a long inspiring conversation, and never again did I receive an opened letter."

It was evident from the headmistress's talks to pupils on Sunday nights in her sitting room, in chapel on Monday nights, and at other times that she "had high standards and expected everyone to do their best," remembered a student in the 1930s. "She was fair, understanding and insightful, but did not relax on the rules." When she knew about infractions, that is. After a new girl asked permission to listen to Edward VIII's abdication speech in December of 1936, Miss Dillingham replied, "cer⁄ tainly not." (Radios were only allowed to be played on rainy Saturday afternoons.) Nevertheless, the teenager could not resist, and she and her classmates took radios into their big walk-in closets to secretly listen, reasoning that if they all did it, the entire class would not be expelled.

Over the years, pupils who had never known Mary Hillard had more praise for her successor. It would be Louise Dillingham's intelligence, kindness, and force of personality that they always talked about, especially those who knew her best. She was "the only heavy set person I've ever known who seemed light as a feather because of her quick wit, keen mind, and great disposition," said a student who became head of school. The mother and aunts of another girl, who had arrived the fall that the founder died, told her that while Miss Hillard was "brilliant and fascinating," her excitable personality gave "an emotional intensity to her regime." In later years, this alumna had no doubt that the new headmistress had been her "ideal successor." Miss Dillingham was "an anchor and someone I could talk with quietly and easily and [who] seemed calm and interested." She added that "with her doctorate in psychology and strong rationality, she did a lot to temper the hot-house atmosphere in a girls' boarding school." Rebecca Love had entered Westover at the age of twelve as the youngest girl in the school. An only child, she later called herself "totally unequipped to deal with my peer group, intellectually precocious and an emotional retardate." When she later discovered two bundles of old letters to her parents, one from the first headmistress and the other from the second one, she saw that the former praised her progress in piano but ignored her immaturity, while observations by the latter were "perceptive and more qualified." Years later she described Louise Dillingham as "a woman among the best of women, shy, witty, non-conforming, strong."

The headmistress was among the first to reach a girl who had fallen and broken her leg while rushing for the mail. Immediately sizing up the situation, she knelt down and relieved the pain by holding the leg just right. "Never again was I somewhat terrified of that stout, impressive person. I *adored* her," the girl later said. Miss Dillingham calmed down another student upset by a school election by making her understand what had happened. "She was a truly remarkable and wise woman," the student would say many years later. While the principal's outward severity masked a shyness that could produce a hot, red blush, she also had a way of "throwing her head back in laughter" that put pupils at ease. A senior class president who spent time alone with her found that "I could talk with her freely, and she responded with wisdom and humor," she recalled. "I like to feel that we were the first class to call her 'Miss D' in public (although everyone had been doing it privately)."

Soon after being named headmistress, she had bought from the estate of Miss Hillard her eighteenth-century farmhouse in Woodbury, where she used to spend a day a week. "During these times *nobody* dreamed of troubling her except in the case of the direst emergency," recalled Elizabeth Fry. Furnished with New England antiques and artifacts from her travels, it was where students saw another side of their headmistress. When alumnae were staying at the school in 1938, the freshmen who were put up at her house were surprised that they had so much fun. "She really seemed to enjoy us, and much of our awe was dissipated," one of them remembered. And after a Glee Club concert and dance with all-boys Deerfield Academy was cancelled after an outbreak of scarlet fever in 1939, she invited the disappointed singers to dinner, where they performed the concert while sitting on her living room floor in front of a big stone fireplace.

"I think I can say that on the whole the girls have a very good time," Miss Dillingham wrote in her formal manner to an alumna five years after becoming headmistress. "They enjoy the responsibilities which they have and work hard in their studies, plays, music, etc., but they seem to feel free to hold conversations with their friends, to go on picnics, etc. At the moment their great concern is the acquiring of sunburn and while we sometimes wish they were less vigorous about this and perhaps quieter in the dining-room, we should, after all, dislike very much to have them unduly restrained and unnatural in their interests and pastimes."

Plenty of testimony supports her point of view. Many years later an alumna still relished her memory of Westover at the time. "It allowed you to have a childhood" and "simple girlish fun," she said. "On the other hand, the intellectual part of it was extremely unusual and good," and, she added, "we certainly learned all the things about being kind and decent to other people." In June of 1939, an editorial written by a senior in *The Lantern* noted that during the class's years in Middlebury, they had made friends, acquired abilities, and experienced beauty. "The routine of our life here has given us all self-control and a new sense of order; the keeping of the unwritten rules has increased our sense of honor and our regard for others; the constant contact with natures differing from our own has developed tact and tolerance; the stimulus of different organizations may have disclosed a talent hitherto unknown, besides teaching leadership and cooperation; finally, the very work itself has given us a desire to know,

Members of the class of 1936 during graduation.
WESTOVER SCHOOL ARCHIVE.

and an all-important ability to plan and use our time. We have learned too the value of Sincerity—of feeling deeply, and speaking and acting genuinely." Many years later, Mary McCreath, who along with two sisters had attended on scholarships in the 1930s, said that at Westover she had learned "to put first things first [and] to never take no for an answer."

6

Encouraging Independence:
Democracy and Honor

THE NEWS OF THE BOMBING OF PEARL HARBOR REACHED WEST-over at the end of the Sunday quiet hour on December 7, 1941. One pupil heard about it as she walked from the library into the main building and past Lucy Pratt's downstairs office, where the radio was on. The next day, everyone gathered in Red Hall to listen to President Roosevelt's grave words over the radio announcing his intention to ask Congress to declare war on Japan. In the following months, as beaux, brothers, and brothers-in-law prepared to go to war, Louise Dillingham eased the rules about male visitors. Young men were now allowed to visit at times other than Saturday afternoons. And instead of sitting together in one of the small downstairs rooms with glass-paned doors, girls were allowed to take their callers to the Common Room for Coca-Colas and cookies, to the senior garden, and past the hockey field and up the hill to the Seven Sisters fireplace. Eventually, male guests could stay for dinner, followed by a movie, or dancing in the gym. Occasionally, word came back that a friend or relative had been wounded, and in at least one case, killed.

Even before America declared war, students had been learning first aid and raising money for the British wounded through "starvation" meals and parties selling soft drinks and grab bags and telling fortunes and playing games of chance. The Glee Club gave concerts to benefit the Red Cross, and the French Club sent off food packages to Europe. Members of the Dorcas Society rolled bandages and volunteered at Waterbury Hospital. An editorial in the June 1942 issue of *The Lantern* urged students to volunteer

Members of The Lantern *board in 1939–1940.*
Sitting on ground from left: Avery Rogers, Maria Randall,
Kate Rand; seated, Elysabeth Barbour; standing,
Grace Ewing, Mary Frances Stackpole, and Mimi Schwarz.
WESTOVER SCHOOL ARCHIVE.

for the war effort during summer vacation, and many of them tended victory gardens, sold war bonds, worked on farms, in hospitals, and were airplane spotters and entertainers for the armed forces. Younger teachers like Caroline Lloyd-Jones, a Bryn Mawr graduate who taught French and Spanish and was an assistant headmistress for a year after Leslie Clark retired, left to join the WAACS. When the West Indian maids gravitated to more remunerative wartime work, students began cleaning their rooms and waiting on tables instead. One day when serving the head table, a girl learned that a nod from the headmistress meant that she wished her water glass refilled; the next evening, when she refilled the glass without waiting for the nod, Miss Dillingham said to her approvingly: "To the wise, a word is sufficient."

During the war, gasoline rationing resulted in more of a sense of seclusion at Westover. The weekday ban on listening to the radio and reading newspapers increased sense of isolation. Despite the disruptions within many families, girls felt sheltered and safe because Miss D "provided a haven in the storm," recalled a member of the class of 1945. "She was always there for us. Her door was open as was her heart." A classmate agreed. "She held the school very steady indeed." Her reassuring words and calm demeanor also acted as an anchor for the faculty and staff. After Elizabeth Fry left Westover in the summer of 1943, she returned for a Christmas visit with Esther Millett at her Woodbury home, when they went to the headmistress's Christmas and New Year Eve parties, along with many others from the school including Daisy Bell, Miss Hillard's and now Miss Dillingham's long-time secretary as well as next-door neighbor. The head of the school was "a warm and convivial hostess," Miss Fry remembered, who always served plenty of drinks and delicious food, and who liked to open her door at midnight on New Year's Eve to welcome another year.

As always, Louise Dillingham was a warrior on behalf of higher education for women. There is much testimony about the many ways she stimulated students' interest in going to college and then got them in against long odds. While a third of her pupils headed for college, even more went during the war as male students joined the armed forces. It was a big change, since a student had written only a few years earlier in the June 1939 *Lantern* that "In spite of our present ambitious plans, it is doubtful if many of us [will] ever have careers, and more than likely that our lives will be very like that of our mothers." Going to college was also controversial. In the spring of 1944, members of the Debate Club posed the question of whether women should attend college during wartime; "the result was close, but the judges ruled in favor of it," according to *The Lantern.*

Miss D especially liked getting the best and most serious students into her alma mater, sometimes even sending applications to Bryn Mawr for them. Of graduates in the classes of 1938 through 1940, eight went to Bryn Mawr, the largest number to any one college. (Among those who did not go college, five married, nine went to art school, eighteen undertook "informal" studies, and the others took jobs or did volunteer work.) At the end of one girl's sophomore year, the headmistress called her into her sitting room. "She simply said she wanted to know why, with such a good mind, I did not seem to want to use it. I was floored. No one had ever suggested that I had a mind or that I should use it! Her kindly interest really turned my life around. I owe her not only the discovery of the world of ideas but the fact that I ended up going to Bryn Mawr College, then the hardest to get into, and the college to which Miss D herself and many of the finer teachers in the school had gone," remembered the former Patricia Castles.

After she interviewed one promising young girl applying to Westover interested in composing music, music lessons were suddenly included in her scholarship. When this girl later asked whether she should take Italian or German, the headmistress suggested Italian, even though she was the only one to take it. She was also assured that she would get into Bryn Mawr, and she did. In regard to Miss D's way of encouraging and even pressuring pupils to go her alma mater, some girls called her domineering but another used the word "strong." "She was strongly responsible for my choice of Bryn Mawr, and I am eternally grateful for that guidance," said this member of the class of 1948. Another, whose father as well as the headmistress wanted her to go to Bryn Mawr, was told that "if I got into the best college in the country I should go to it," she remembered. But when those urged to go to her alma mater chose Smith or Vassar instead, Miss D was gracious about it.

There's the story of another student who wanted to go to college, but whose father, a businessman, did not understand why women needed higher education until Miss Dillingham invited him to her sitting room for a talk over a few martinis. This advocacy persisted throughout her more than three decades at Westover, even after university educations became more commonplace. Toward the end of her tenure, when she was talking to Abigail Mason and her mother, an alumna who went to Radcliffe, the mother stated that her daughter should not plan to go on because she had done poorly in grade school. The headmistress then turned to the young girl and asked if she agreed, and she admitted that she did want to go to college. "Then I think you should try the college course," Miss Dillingham replied, astonishing the girl, since no adult had asked her opinion about such a serious subject or even contradicted her domineering mother in front of her before.

In her effort to get girls into college, Miss Dillingham added many courses and doubled the teaching staff, while also making it an eminently qualified one. Teachers used to say with a touch of awe that she could teach any class in an emergency, but in fact, most of them could do it, too. During the 1944–45 school year, four of the twenty-seven teachers held doctoral degrees, and most of the rest had attended graduate schools or had masters' degrees. Lucy Pratt's niece Marjorie, who had studied at Vassar, Radcliffe, and Oxford University, was hired in 1943 to teach history and current events. Not all the faculty credentials were academic, of course. Ethel Swantees, who taught art, was a respected Impressionist painter who had studied and exhibited in New York City. Miss D looked for teachers who had mastery of their subjects as well as teaching skills, or what she called "the ability to awaken enthusiasm for learning."

When the headmistress interviewed Patience Norman in 1943, the two intellectuals had a long, fascinating conversation, the younger woman remembered, and the older educator indicated a disinterest in the applicant's high score on her Connecticut teaching certificate. It was much more important to her that the teacher was an honors graduate of Smith College with a master's degree in history from the University of Minnesota. It was undoubtedly most important of all that the young scholar with the big, bright brown eyes and a wide smile radiated intensity and excitement about ideas. Kind, caring, and encouraging, Miss Norman would teach history, especially the Russian and French revolutions, without conventional textbooks and with verve and a sense of mission. Her travels in Nazi Germany during the 1930s had made her a fierce defender of democracy. Again and again she would tell pupils that it was important to understand the past so it would not become the future. Passionately interested in politics, her sitting room at Westover was crammed with the books and newspapers she read voraciously. She was very proud when a former student, Eunice Strong Groark, was elected lieutenant governor of Connecticut. Miss Norman was very fond and appreciative of Louise Dillingham, explaining that "she was usually unbelievably generous to me—though not in salaries, but in talking to me and considering my aims in teaching." She remained on the staff until her retirement almost four decades later, grateful to be teaching small classes in a tolerant school like Westover because she was hard of hearing.

During the 1940s, Miss Dillingham continued to teach classes in psychology and sociology as well as an ethics seminar for seniors heading to college. The seniors were invited to smoke and drink strong coffee while sitting on the floor of her sitting room for the two-hour class on Sunday afternoons. Then "her shyness gave way to spontaneous humor, and her warmth surrounded us," remembered a student at the time. Another liked the way they were treated as "interesting adults who could discuss serious subjects." Miss D habitually sat with a leg tucked under her amid a cloud of cigarette smoke looking like a cross between "Gertrude Stein and a benevolent Buddha," said another girl. It was her "clear, sparkling, penetrating eyes" that another girl always remembered. Yet another never forgot that the headmistress forbade using the word "thing" in the required research papers. "Any one of you who uses the word 'thing,' anywhere in your work, will fail the course," she warned. Miss D did fail a girl who wrote her paper in a week rather than in months. "She was quite right," the student later admitted. "Things came too easily to me, and she well saw it was not a good thing. So spring vacation was spent writing another one." When the school was later evaluated by a group of educators, they highly praised the ethics class and other electives, saying that they "add dimensions that are truly unique in secondary education."

Although most of the teachers at Westover were women, a few were men. When alumnae later mentioned their most inspiring teachers, they almost always mentioned Joachim "Jock" Schumacher. The son of a prominent Berlin lawyer, he had earned a

Ph.D. in literature from the University of Heidelberg in 1931. Unlike the rest of his family, he was an early and outspoken critic of Adolph Hitler, so he was forced to flee from Germany for Switzerland with his blonde Swiss wife-to-be, Sylvia, a well-trained pianist, whom he had met a decade earlier at the wedding of his sister and her brother. In Switzerland he was a cultural correspondent for a German newspaper, but soon he was also expelled from there because of his political activities, and the couple moved to Paris. Since he had written a fiery anti-fascist, pro-democracy treatise, *Fear of the Chaos*, he still felt endangered, so the Schumachers left for New York in 1937 before its publication. The daughter of a Swiss doctor, Sylvia Schumacher had spoken English at home as a child, so she quickly found a job at the Henry Street Settlement House. Her husband eventually found positions teaching sociology, music history, and other subjects at the City College of New York and at the New School for Social Research. After Sylvia became pregnant with their first child, they wanted to leave the city, especially after they were robbed of their jewelry and finely tailored European clothing. Somehow Louise Dillingham heard about these well-educated émigrés, and after meeting them in Manhattan, she immediately issued them an invitation to visit Middlebury.

In 1938, at the end of a job-hunting trip to colleges throughout New England, Jock Schumacher, thirty-four, arrived at the Waterbury train station. A taxi left him at the arched door near the Westover chapel during a quiet Sunday afternoon. He walked along the empty corridor until he reached Red Hall, where he "stood astounded," he later recalled in a talk in that very place. "I had never seen anywhere a large room or small hall quite like it." He never forgot the sight of the lovely "rare mauve twilight" coming in the large windows and French doors that late afternoon. "Without a person around I felt invited, impersonally welcome." He vividly remembered "total absence of any kind of ostentation, not even that of self-conscious simplicity. A certain gay clarity, at once delicate and firm, [that] pervades the entire room, in which the squared columns (yet how slender) form, along with the double rows of proportioned windows and modest doors, a certain indefinable quality, as do the bar lines in a Mozart score. Not accidentally did I later find that Mozart sounds especially good in Red Hall, since there seems to be not just a structural but spiritual affinity between a particular musical style and the implicit 'music of the edifice.'"

He also described the large, lofty room encircled by a balcony, as "airy, lighthearted, eminently reasonable without being severely rational." After he learned about the building's architectural history, he praised the "colonial *savoir*" of the meeting room created by Theodate Pope Riddle, whom he praised as "entirely free and remarkably gifted." He marveled that an American woman with little architectural training "had something better: a spirited mind [and] very good eyes." He went on, effusively praising the rubescence of Red Hall in its carpeting, draperies, upholstery, and tufted lamp shades, all set off by pale walls and dark woodwork. Its ambience "accommodates, is infinitely flexible without loss of identity, resists pomposity (the red carpet nicely muffles obnoxious noises without causing loss of surprisingly good acoustics for good noises)." He added that despite the regal color of the room, the overall effect was astonishingly "non-pompous," since the ruby rug "resembles a red meadow" more than a royal place. With the reflection of crimson on the ceiling, there is "something potentially festive in Red Hall—a rare quality not often found in architecture either old or new." It may have been the inherent femininity or American essence of the room, but whatever it was, it told him what he wanted to know about the small girls' school. "I still [view] Red Hall as most completely expressing, through deliberate design and proven practice, the Westover spirit," he would say about that room that many alumnae regard as the heart of the school.

The afternoon he had first stood in Red Hall, an elderly lady with fine features had entered the room and asked if he was the new teacher, adding that Miss Dillingham was expecting him. He realized that he was "wanted, perhaps already hired (but never, later, was I told so to my face)." The New England headmistress and the European refugee hit it off very well. Whereas administrators of other schools and colleges had found him without a specialty or too over-educated, she liked the fact that he could teach several subjects in depth. They also had intellectual rapport. While she had written in her education manifesto in 1934 that "it is above

Sylvia and Joachim "Jock" Schumacher after their arrival in America. COURTESY OF MARK SCHUMACHER.

all as a pursuit of the true that I understand education," he fervently believed that art was truth in visible form. They also liked to laugh together, especially about the time a pupil called a classical painting "the virgin on the rocks." Like a few others, he discovered that the headmistress "could laugh at her foibles and, sometimes, she admitted that she had made a mistake."

Due to gasoline rationing, fewer speakers and performers managed to get to Middlebury during the war (with the exception of writer May Sarton, who arrived to read wartime poetry), so musicians and others on the faculty had to step in. The Schumachers gave a series of Sunday lectures on the relationship of music history and art history. Mr. Schumacher also taught a current events class based on the reading of humorous political cartoons. He liked to laugh at himself, especially his heavily accented English. "Because I talked naturally in much Greek and Latin terminology with a German accent and many overstatements," he said later, "the daughter of a highly renowned member of the cabinet burst forth from her door and yelled in the corridor: 'He is divine, [but] I can't understand a damn word!'"

Soon he was teaching the history of art in Helen LaMonte's old wood-paneled room as well as classes from time to time on the history of civilization, musicology, modern art, Italian painting, philosophy, and other topics. The teacher prided himself on not talking down to his teenage pupils, whom he called "ignorant but very intelligent." He did not use textbooks and encouraged the girls to describe their own reactions to the world's great art. "You can't bore them to death with tests and lectures," he would explain to anyone who asked. "I let them discover what is there, and the gifted ones take the others along with them." Miss Dillingham "liked what he taught and how he taught," recalled Sylvia Schumacher, who began teaching piano at Westover after the war.

Mr. Schumacher's intense and animated personality had an amplified effect in the mostly female milieu. Irreverent and witty, he always talked to his pupils in a high-minded and wide-ranging way as if they were interesting people. His Introduction to Philosophy class decades later was, among other things, a seminar on love and marriage. One time he talked about his admiration for Eric Fromm's *The Art of Loving* and elaborated on his belief in traditional courtly and complementary roles of men and women. He told the impressionable young girls in the class that woman is not born to compete intellectually with man but to understand him and bring loveliness and love into life. "A woman who tries to compete loses her superiority," the white-haired man stated, a notion that made at least one of his students hesitant to talk about politics with boys.

At the end of the war, Jock Schumacher turned down an offer to teach in a German university in order to stay in Connecticut. After leaving Westover to teach comparative literature at Sarah Lawrence College for two years and then returning, he said that "it was not easy, but I managed twice not to become a professor." He added: "I owe it to Westover if I eventually learned to be a teacher without ceasing to remain a student." (Before arriving in the mornings, he had arisen early to write poetry and work on a book about Leonardo da Vinci, which was eventually published in Berlin.) He remained at Westover because of the "complete freedom of teaching," as he put it. He also could not imagine "a better place for family, leisure, laughter, and sustained intellectual studies" than in his home on a wooded hilltop in Woodbury. A free spirit who called himself "a sort of Christian-pagan," he liked to make mobiles and play the viola in a chamber music group. As he neared retirement in 1977, he was well aware that his pupils, past and present, were very glad that he had stayed at their school. "It was balm to my soul to read in so many of the letters from you that my style of informal teaching was substantial enough to convey the demands great artists make upon us as our true teachers, rather than those we impose upon them in the easy schemes of so-called art history," he said. One of them remembered that "he taught us to see, and he introduced us to studying and learning for the pure joy of it."

The day after Germany surrendered to the Allies in May of 1946, the head of the Glee Club helped the headmistress put on her black scholar's robe for a chapel service. As she did, Miss D turned to her and said: "Today we sing 'Onward Christian Soldiers,' and we did with unequaled joy," the alumna remembered. Louise Dillingham regarded World War II as a great struggle between dictatorship and democracy, and she came to believe that democratic freedoms demanded individual initiative and equality of opportunity. After the armistice she wanted more than ever to prepare her pupils for self-government, and for what she called "the obligation of leadership." She asserted that "self-knowledge and self-discipline are essential if such responsibility is to be successfully taken." During this time, one of the ongoing debates in American education was over the role of private schools in democracies, or even whether they had any role at all. Aware that Westover and other independent schools were under scrutiny, she defended them as superb training grounds for citizenship. Since democracy was dependent on freedom of speech and the press, a student newspaper, *The Wick*, was started in 1945. *The Lantern* would come out less often and limit itself to poetry, fiction, and prose.

The girls wanted more self-government, too, so a Faculty–Student Council was initiated in 1946, formalizing the informal discussions between the headmistress and the student leaders of earlier years. During the war, the elderly Lucy Pratt was the last of the founders of the school still at Westover. A soft-spoken lady with fading reddish hair and a kindly expression, she finally decided to retire in 1945 and return to her birthplace of South Glastonbury, Connecticut, where she lived until her death a decade later. A Westover alumna named Marion Griswold, a niece of Helen LaMonte's who had been Miss Pratt's secretary since graduating in 1923, was named treasurer in her place. Out of respect for Miss Pratt, Miss Dillingham had been reluctant to make major modifications in the school routine, people thought, and now she felt freer.

Student government, in turn, relied on an honor system that stressed honesty, studiousness, courtesy, orderliness, politeness, kindness, and loyalty. The first issue of *The Lantern* in the fall still reprinted the principles of the honor system simply signed "A Westover Girl." In 1935 an editorial in the magazine had noted that students, especially seniors, "must be made to realize the distinction between what they prefer to do, and honor . . . Though it takes effort to live highly, almost everyone who realized what it means is able and willing to make the effort." These principles led to rules about cheating and plagiarism, visitors and telephone calls, radios and record players, as well as many matters about safety and health. New girls were given a detailed and lengthening list of do's and don'ts, even the requirement to report the first day of a menstruation period to the athletic office. If a student broke a rule or persistently violated a value, she was supposed to admit it. If she did not, seniors were supposed to remind her of the mistake, and if she continued her misbehavior, she should expect to be reported to Miss Dillingham. The system gave students a reassuring sense of order and limits, a number of older alumnae have testified. "The honor code was in the air," explained one of them, who graduated during wartime. "You were on your honor to eat three things at a meal, not run in the corridors, or talk after lights out. It was peer pressure in a very nice way." Eventually the honor system was inscribed on a brass plaque over the fireplace in the Common Room.

Louise Dillingham in her sitting room in the 1950s. WESTOVER SCHOOL ARCHIVE.

Some administrators thought that living by an honor system was more a matter of education than discipline because of the difficulty of the decision about whether or not to report a misbehaving friend. "It is not easy to live by honor," an alumna on the staff later acknowledged, but she said it was an effort worth making. "There have been those this year, last year, and in past recent years who have been able to live up to the rules . . . easily, gracefully and without undue stress, strain or false virtue." In any event, as a student attempted to uphold the honor system, the effort was intended to strengthen her character.

Miss Dillingham continued to want the young girls under her wing to become stronger by working out things for themselves and even standing up to her. If a group came to her without a well-reasoned request, she was likely to turn them down in the hope that they would return with a better one. A "no" from the headmistress didn't necessarily mean no, this staff member used to tell disappointed students, urging them to try again. Miss Dillingham also had an enigmatic saying: "When in doubt do the right thing," which she probably thought granted girls respect and freedom, but actually left many teenagers struggling to make the right decisions. "I sometimes wonder how we all grew up," remarked a pupil at the time. When one class president felt overwhelmed and went to talk to Miss D, the headmistress would ask in a straight-forward manner what had caused a problem, what effect it was having, and how to solve it. "I think you can handle this well," she used to say, "but it is vital that *you* believe that you can."

Since seniors were traditionally responsible for discipline and supposed to set good examples, Miss Dillingham was glad when elected leaders had high principles along with firmness and modesty. Sometimes she shared insights with them. "Whatever the subject matter," said a class officer in the 1940s, "her brown eyes were riveted on mine [and] her sensitivity to personal problems of the students was evident. She could often turn a serious or troubling situation into less of a problem with one quick, amusing observation." Miss D had long talks with one class president, which were "wise about the vagaries of adolescents," the alumna later remembered. Another class officer appreciated her headmistress's "fine, dry sense of humor" as well as "her balance, wisdom and curiosity." She recalled that "while we did not always agree, I found her to be firm and fair minded in what hindsight tells me was an extremely demanding role."

Since the headmistress was convinced that young people must learn by trial and error, she sometimes allowed senior class presidents to make questionable decisions. "The areas for mistakes can be controlled, we hope, to the point where the mistakes made are not dangerous or permanently damaging, but no young girl or boy is going to be truly educated, is going to have a healthy mind, if he or she had not had to exercise judgment, to make decisions, to try to form a permanent sense of values," she believed. Although she wanted to encourage her pupils to become mature and inde-pendent, Louise Dillingham, who was by then in her fifties, was such an imposing and indomitable presence that her small school for girls often seemed less like a democracy than her little kingdom.

Still, visiting educators thought Westover was doing an excellent job of preparing students for living in a democracy. One wonders what they would have thought on a spring evening when new class officers were elected. Governor Chester Bowles of Connecticut was supposed to give a talk to the teachers that day, but his wife arrived instead with a state police escort to talk about women's role in politics. After the votes were counted, the screams of jubilation and the ringing of the bell in the tower made the policemen worry that the school was on fire. As they investigated the grounds and glimpsed young girls lying in circles under the apple trees inside the Quad, one state trooper was overheard by a teacher saying to another that he would never send his daughter to a school where girls screamed like banshees and slept under trees, not that he could afford to, anyway.

Despite displays of girlishness, Miss Dillingham persisted with her agenda. Giving a girl responsibility was a way for the pupil to learn "what she can do and what she must be careful about," Miss D would say. She had a theory that defended this detachment. Although a psychiatrist was always on call, she believed that psychiatry should be practiced at home because it was often the family, not just the daughter, who was troubled. Her belief avoided stigmatizing and scapegoating a girl, but it also denied necessary help at times. This was probably the case in regard to one of Miss D's seven nieces, Louise Garfield, her namesake and the daughter of her youngest sister, Hope. When the ninth grader was unhappily enrolled at Westover in the 1940s, she broke the rule about respecting possessions of others, and her aunt finally had to ask her to leave the school. Miss D addressed the students about the matter in a manner that few ever forgot. "My heart broke for her, as she really had tried to help this girl, but when it became impossible, she treated her as she would have any other student," recalled a pupil at the meeting. A classmate agreed: "She was unflinching and dignified in dealing with the necessary penalty."

A few years later, another niece, Dorothy Smedley, a daughter of Miss D's sister Dorothy, entered Westover. During her childhood, the girl had visited her aunt, who was also her godmother, at her home in Woodbury a few times. Once was during the war when she was around thirteen, when she and her Aunt Louise baked bread and arranged flowers together. "She loved arranging flowers," Dorothy remembered. "Her garden was one of her great pleasures." After Dorothy was enrolled, however, her aunt kept her at arm's length. She was in the school infirmary for a few weeks with pneumonia before Aunt Louise visited her. "After that, I got up," Dorothy said. Although she appreciated the excellent education she had been given, throughout her life she regarded this aunt as an intimidating person without warmth. Dorothy never got over her bad memories of her years at Westover either, although she later reflected that when she was a teenager, she probably would not have been happy anywhere.

Sometimes when the headmistress decided that an adolescent needed and deserved more adult attention, she tried to do something about it. It's likely that she had her favorites. Aware that the parents of a head of Overs were divorcing, Miss D often called Sarita Van Vleck into her sitting room supposedly to discuss rule infringements. It was a new experience for the young girl to have an older woman's full attention, and she relished it. "Never did I suspect until years later that it might have been her way of checking up on me," Sarita said. "She was definitely the wise guide I unknowingly needed at the time, and I shall always be grateful to her generosity of spirit."

At times, of course, girls broke the rules, especially those about smoking cigarettes. Perhaps because the headmistress was a heavy smoker herself, she responded to illegal smoking in idiosyncratic ways. After a group of seniors was caught smoking a few weeks before graduation one year, she punished them by striking the words "meritorious conduct" from their diplomas and not allowing them to stand up at graduation when their names were read. When a girl was caught smoking in her bedroom another time, Miss D, speaking to her amidst a haze of cigarette smoke in her sitting room, reminded the girl that smoking was forbidden in most of the building by the fire laws. If she wanted a cigarette, the headmistress continued, she could come and smoke one with her. Sometimes Miss D appeared puzzled about what the punishment for smoking without permission should be. When two seniors were caught breaking the rule around that time, she called their class together during a Sunday quiet hour and asked them what the penalty should be.

At other times, when the principles of the honor system were violated, the headmistress became enraged. One spring, a group of seniors sunbathing on the outdoor wooden sports platform had rolled up their shorts and sleeves and unbuttoned their blouses. After airplanes from a nearby Air Force base deliberately flew low over them, the entire school was again summoned to a meeting. "Miss D's eyes flashed with the lightening of a fire-and-brimstone preacher. 'Girls, if you are going to act in this disgraceful way you can just (here she spluttered with anger, lost for words) just go back to your beaches!' We were too cowed to giggle," a pupil remembered.

A *Lantern* editorial had stated during the war that although women did men's work during wartime, women's real war work was establishing peace, beginning at Westover "by cooperating with the honor system, by avoiding 'cliques,' and making friends of all kinds." New girls were given little date books listing the evening chapels which upperclassmen filled in, enabling everyone to get to know those in other classes. Evidence of cliquishness or unkindness could turn the principal's face into a mask of anger. One year three seniors, who had discovered a secret space in the back of their big closet, put up satirical drawings of teachers. When the caricatures were discovered, Miss Dillingham became so enraged that she reported the matter to the colleges where the students had applied. Her reaction was a "vindictive and draconian action" in the view of the girls and their parents, who did not understand how flagrantly the cruelty violated the spirit of the honor system in the headmistress's eyes. When one of the girls returned to Vassar for a follow-up interview, the admissions officer laughed off the incident, and all three of them ended up going there.

At other times, the headmistress gladly allowed girls to break the rules when there was a good reason, like appreciating a moment of natural beauty. One winter night after the lights were out, a student went to her window to watch a snowfall. Suddenly a "dazzling display of northern lights began flying across the sky above the snowflakes," she remembered. "Without thinking I cried out the open window, 'northern lights!' then ran out into the corridors yelling 'northern lights!' to any who would hear. Within moments the whole school was watching out all the windows, a joyous recess that lasted until the aurora itself went out, about twenty minutes, as I recall." She continued: "Word reached me before we all went back to bed that Miss D had been seen viewing all the excitement, so I realized that since a rule had been broken, I probably would be disciplined the next day. But as I left the dining room after breakfast, Miss D instead expressed appreciation of the alarm, and concluded, 'wasn't it wonderful!' She then showed me that it had made the front page of *The New York Times*. Needless to say, it was the rarity of the event and her balanced judgment that carried the moment." Another winter night a few years later it was the headmistress herself who spotted the northern lights; the fire alarm was sounded, and everyone went out onto the hockey field, where everyone was "greeted by curtains of color pulsating through the sky."

7

The Desire for Justice:
Admitting Negro Students

WHEN VETERANS RETURNED HOME AFTER THE END OF WORLD War II, it became more difficult for women to get admitted to college or to use their educations in the workplace. Meanwhile, they were encouraged to devote themselves to domesticity. Educators were affected by this anatomy-is-destiny crusade, and many assumed that education should only prepare women for becoming better wives and mothers. "It took intellectual courage to question the premises of 'feminine' education," a historian has noted. A number of older educators resisted these beliefs, and they proposed women's history studies as a way to inspire younger female scholars, but most of them were conflicted or silenced. Bryn Mawr's president, Katharine McBride, a psychologist, believed in separate social roles for men and women but also respected the wide abilities among women. Barnard College's president, Millicent McIntosh, taking a middle path, tried not to either downplay or exalt the traditional female role. Interestingly, it was the male president of Sarah Lawrence College who held that higher education for women was for their own self-fulfillment.

Louise Dillingham had come of age and entered Bryn Mawr at a time of rising aspirations for women, but progress had slowed and then halted in the 1920s and 1930s before going into a decline in the 1950s. Speaking in 1954 as if she and her school were one and the same, she stated that "Westover believes that to acquire an education is to learn a good way of life." It is difficult to believe that this erudite scholar was not disappointed by the lowering expectations among her students, but no one remembers her expressing any bitterness about it. It is evident that she did not expect others to be as exceptional as she. "She could tell what a girl was capable of and would not suggest things outside her range," remembered one of her secretaries. "Miss D accepted people for who they were, while challenging them to be the best that they could be." It was fine with the headmistress if an alumna wanted to stay home and raise children, and "she was delighted if someone was happily married," a teacher said. If a pupil had a good mind and wanted a career, however, Miss Dillingham preferred that she be a teacher instead of a secretary. Most parents during that era expected the single women at Westover to give their daughters fine educations, some polish, and perhaps a little backbone, but certainly not to be models for an unmarried way of life.

Taxes were raised at the beginning of the war, so Westover issued bonds in 1942 to buy back outstanding stock from stockholders and become a tax-exempt institution. With only a miniscule endowment, however, this action did not alleviate the school's financial problems for long. In the inflationary postwar period, costs soared while income from tuition stayed essentially the same. Since Theodate Pope Riddle had designed the main building for a set number of students, it was difficult to increase enrollment. In 1940 an infirmary was built behind the school, and the old infirmary on the second floor of the original building was turned into a few more student bedrooms. After the war, when enrollment was around 160, the headmistress eyed the small upstairs gymnasium as a place for more bedrooms. But instead of being able to afford a new gym to replace it, funds suddenly had to be used to convert the power house from coal to oil. It seemed that all expenses had gone up, except the low salaries of the teachers. From time to time Jock Schumacher, often the only man on the faculty, would be persuaded by his female colleagues to ask Miss Dillingham, usually unsuccessfully, for raises.

Meanwhile, Miss D did not want to sacrifice the scholarship program, since the "abilities and personalities" of the girls who benefited from it contributed enormously to the school, she recog‑

Alumnae Secretary Adele Ervin, member of the class of 1942.
COURTESY OF ADELE Q. ERVIN.

nized, as had Mary Hillard before her. The presence of these studious and promising pupils "has reduced emphasis on material standards by the student body as a whole and brought recognition of other and higher values," she and the president of the board wrote in a fundraising letter, adding that the trustees were also committed to providing scholarships, even it if meant increasing tuition for others. Tuition had recently been raised, in fact, but it still remained difficult to meet rising expenses. A larger endowment was essential to provide better scholarships and salaries for teachers, the headmistress realized.

At this time, she tried to appeal to the growing number of graduates to give money to their old school. In 1947, the initial issue of *The Alumnae Wick* was published, and the first alumnae day was held. The next year the charitable Mary Hillard Society was turned into the Westover Alumnae Association with the headmistress as president. Over martinis at an alumnae gathering around that time, Miss D convinced Adele Ervin, a member of the class of 1942, to return to Middlebury to take the new position as alumnae secretary (and also to coach field hockey, lacrosse, and the dramatic club). During the war Adele had volunteered for the Canadian Red Cross—she was too young for the American branch—and had served with it in London. In the fall of 1948, she was given a sunny upstairs office near the balcony around Red Hall, where she began to pull together an alumnae address book. Tall and attractive, she was remembered for wearing stylish green outfits "to spark her eyes" and "always darting to do something useful or handy for someone."

Meanwhile, Governor Chester Bowles had recently criticized the state's private schools and colleges for discriminating against minorities. An anti-bias bill was introduced into the state legislature, and a new Commission on Interracial Affairs sent out a questionnaire to educational institutions in Connecticut, including Westover. To the question of whether the school had an admission policy based on race, religion, or national origin, Miss Dillingham replied that it did not. She went on to say that only a single Negro student had applied in the past fifteen years, and she stated why this young woman had not been admitted. "While I felt that discrimination, with its attendant evils, was taking place," she would later elaborate, at the time she had explained to the girl's mother in a lengthy correspondence that enrolling only one minority pupil among so many whites would be unfair to her daughter. Then she wrote on the questionnaire:

"The entrance of a small group of properly qualified Negro students would be seriously considered."

When Miss D had pondered the problems of democracy during the war, she had often thought about the issue of integration. The application of the African-American girl had made her realize that the time was coming when schools should take a stand on behalf of "equality of opportunity in a democracy." At the end of the war, she had invited black writer Langston Hughes to lecture in Red Hall about the contribution of the Negro to American literature, and he had talked about Phyllis Wheatley, the young eighteenth-century African slave who had written widely admired lyrical poetry. Then in January of 1949, Eleanor Roosevelt had spoken at Westover about the importance of human rights. That evening she dined with student leaders at the head table in the dining room and had coffee afterward with the faculty in Miss Dillingham's sitting room, then stayed for the night. (The evening was forever etched in everyone's memory because the former first lady and the headmistress wore identical black lace dresses with large turquoise bows on their bosoms.)

A few months later, a newspaper reporter, who had become aware of the head-mistress's answer on the questionnaire, found it unusual enough in an era of widespread segregation to ask for an interview. Miss Dillingham telephoned a few trustees, who agreed that she should talk to him because the topic was "a matter of principle which could not be ignored, however much we might regret the publicity," she explained to the parents of pupils. During the interview, she spoke about Bryn Mawr's recent decision to integrate, as well as her experience of working with people of African heritage in Puerto Rico. "It's as simple as this," she told the newspaperman. "If we profess democracy, we should practice it. The war, which was supposedly fought for democracy, has forced us to think about these things."

Soon an article appeared in *The New York Herald Tribune* under the headline: "Westover School Ready to Take a Small Group of Negro Girls." That same day Adele Ervin wrote to the alumnae, explaining and endorsing Miss Dillingham's decision. "In a small community [like] Westover each student will have the experience of knowing a fine colored girl and that experience cannot help but make each girl feel *personally* conscious and to a degree responsible for the terrible injustice of prejudice," she wrote.

"If Westover can bring home the Negro problem, in all its individual injustices, to its girls, who themselves will command positions of influence in their communities, it will have done its utmost to alleviate one of this country's most bitter problems." An editorial in the New York newspaper a few days later praised Westover for following in the enlightened footsteps of Harvard and Yale. It added that the school's admissions policy would strengthen the hand of other New England educators, many of whom were under attack by Southerners for hypocrisy. "By joining the progressive parade," the editorial went, Westover had enhanced its reputation "as an outstanding college-preparatory school for girls."

When Helen LaMonte read *The Herald Tribune* article on a train to New York, she felt so proud of Westover that, when changing trains in Newark, she sent Miss Dillingham a telegram: "Three long, loud cheers for you and all your Alumnae backers!" Another time, the former teacher noted that Miss Hillard had invited the Negro educator Booker T. Washington as well as the Bishop of Liberia to speak in the chapel and dine afterward in the dining room. "I have always felt she would have gloried in Miss D's courageous stand and would have done exactly the same," Miss LaMonte said. She admitted that she had never known any well-educated African-Americans until she had moved to Washington, D.C., where she and her sister ran their bookshop for eleven years. (After the war, they returned to Owego, in upstate New York, to live with their elderly parents in the family farmhouse alongside a river.) She wrote to a worried alumna that when her own alma mater, Smith, had planned to integrate she had been apprehensive, but she later saw that the college was "still the same place, with a little more liberal, kindlier atmosphere than before." Young women of today, she explained, "want to make the world a better place where people can breathe freely with no race prejudices, no color lines, no class distinctions." She went on: "Think what the Glee Club could be with some young Marion Andersons or what dramatics might become with their genius." Private schools, she continued, "must march ahead or they will be left far behind and become as extinct as the Dodo bird."

Her old friend Louise Dillingham entirely agreed and, furthermore, believed that her pupils did as well. When the newspaper article appeared, ninth grader Roberta West asked in a letter to her mother, who was originally from Oklahoma, if she had been sent to Westover "so that I could mix with people of the same social background. I don't think so but I want it confirmed, yes or no. Today in the Herald Trib an article came out about Westover admitting Negroes. I am very much for it and couldn't be more pleased . . . You wouldn't take me out of here would you. I think I wouldn't leave for 2 reasons. 1. I think Westover is a marvelous school and I now have more feeling toward Miss D. and the school. 2. I would love to be in such a fascinating experiment . . . I hope you feel just the way I do . . . I think it will be interesting to see how many do not come back next year. You know, I think that the ones who don't come back are the ones that the school really doesn't need." Roberta remained at Westover.

Roberta always felt very proud of "this important and—considering the times—courageous, step that Miss Dillingham and the school took," she said many years later. While most pupils or parents in the 1950s did not regard intellectual women as role models, many of them were inspired by the headmistress's strong principles. She "taught us the importance of ethics, of high standards, of service to our fellow men and women," another alumna remembered. "How much I valued her unassuming ways, and the message she gave me at the Lantern ceremony. She spoke of the Bright Light I was to carry into the world." Another recalled "her intense energy, the rapid, clipped pace of her conversation and that giant intellect, far beyond the grasp of a seventeen-year-old whose biggest concern was whether her socks matched. Miss D was truly a giant among women and a profound and lasting influence in my life." And another simply said that "she was a powerful role model for us all."

Initial praise for the admissions policy was followed by an uproar and then a drop in applications, while the headmistress tried to calm everyone down. "We do not wish to 'crusade' here at Westover," she wrote to parents and alumnae. No minority students had yet applied for admission, she said, and it was unlikely that any would be enrolled by the fall. When she heard that Emma Morel, a Southerner from Georgia and a senior the previous year, had written her classmates in alarm, Miss Dillingham wrote her former student a long letter. "I have known from our discussions and from your Ethics paper of last year that personally you and I, with different upbringings, would find it hard ever to agree on the intrinsic merits of the negro [sic] race," she wrote. After strongly stating her beliefs in equality of opportunity and the recognition of individual worth, she acknowledged that "I do not pretend to say that the process of giving opportunity is easy." Even so, the headmistress ended her letter by saying that she hoped that Emma would eventually understand and support her position.

Another fierce opponent was the husband of an alumna, Georgina Miller Bissell, who had graduated in 1939. The couple's niece was at Westover, and they were considering sending their two daughters there, too. A Yale graduate, George Bissell argued that it was a different matter to integrate a university of four thousand students than a small school of a hundred and fifty girls, because large educational institutions allows for more freedom of association. He wrote to Miss Dillingham that he feared integration would somehow "snowball," and it may already have "fostered a Frankenstein no matter how loudly the school may now be applauded by the 'liberal' thinkers." Months later, he expressed his annoyance that the headmistress had not answered his letter, and she wrote the lawyer a brief note pointing out that tax-exempt private schools must respect state antidiscrimination laws. At the time, the state's department of education was interested in licensing independent schools. In response, a number of private school principals had recently formed the Connecticut Association of Independent Schools to set academic standards and head off state regulation.

Louise Dillingham's courageous stand deepened the school's financial struggles, however. Families from the South, with the exception of the Scotts of Richmond, Virginia, withdrew their daughters or declined to enroll them. Enrollment dropped by eight to ten students a year as operating costs continued to rise. The headmistress did not want to raise tuition again; it was already "unfortunate" that it was among the highest of any girls' boarding school, so applications from "desirable students" were fewer than she would have liked, she wrote the alumnae. In the letter, she literally begged the alumnae to find applicants, asking them "to bring to Westover able, responsible and interesting girls, from different economic strata and varied geographic areas, girls with diverse interests and talents but with similar high ideals, who may all contribute to make the School a real training-ground for citizens of a good world." Meanwhile, she held her ground, stating that Westover must also be "a *good* school" where girls "can receive a superior education, in books and in living."

She began traveling every year with Adele Ervin by train or automobile throughout the country to meet with alumnae and talk about the controversy over integration and try to raise money. One year they would take the northern route, and the next year they would take the southern one. The headmistress asked her former student to call her "Louise," but Adele was unable to mouth the word and continued to call her "Miss D." The nature of their mother-and-daughter relationship is suggested by a story about a stop in Cleveland one year to visit Miss D's sister, Hope Garfield. Adele wanted to bring back to Middlebury as a school mascot one of the cocker spaniel puppies that Hope bred, but the older woman refused to hear of it. In any event, on the women's return from their first trip in early 1950, eight of the twelve trustees at the winter board meeting unanimously voted to back Miss Dillingham's stand on integration, despite their fears for the future of the school.

To try to allay their anxieties, the trustees insisted that a public relations firm, Tamblyn and Brown, be hired. In polls, the firm learned that sixteen percent of the alumnae reached by telephone were against the admissions policy and eighty-four percent were for it. Answers on a written questionnaire, however, indicated that a majority disapproved. Many parents, the pollsters found, said they feared that teenage girls were too young and emotional to deal with the issue of race relations, while fewer felt that admitting minority group members would give "a more realistic democratic experience and education than in the past." The firm finally recommended that the trustees retain the admissions policy both to protect the school's tax-exempt status and to avoid greater controversy by abandoning it. Enrollment continued to decline, however, and in 1951–52 it fell to only 138 pupils, an all-time low. Instead of giving teachers raises, Miss Dillingham was forced to ask them to take salary cuts. Weekly wartime minimum meals were instituted again. And Westover was "perilously close to going under," Adele Ervin remembered.

During those years, Adele got to know Helen LaMonte well, going along with her niece, Marion Griswold, to visit her in Owego, writing her often, and sending chrysanthemums on her birthday in September. The elderly woman warmly addressed Adele as "my dear niece-by-choice" and "My Only Adopted Niece, Adelicia," and the younger woman called her "Aunt Helen." Westover "still seems to me the most enchanting place in all the USA," Miss LaMonte wrote, when Adele hinted about leaving her job as alumnae secretary, adding the caveat that the school still needed a good gymnasium and theater. She also counseled the unmarried Adele when the younger woman expressed concern about a future without children and grandchildren. "Grandchildren are very desirable but one can manage very happily without them and think of all the daughters you can soon number. It is already a tidy number and they are most rewarding." When Adele expressed frustration about the difficulties of raising money for Westover, the founder empathized and also expressed her own anger: "The way men toss millions about them like dimes is hard for one to understand when I think how any project for the education of women has to grow dollar by dollar. Once a feminist always one, I guess."

Meanwhile, Louise Dillingham was attempting to admit a group of four to eight African-American girls of different ages. It turned out to be more difficult than she had thought, and in the autumn of

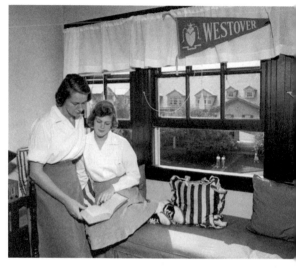

Girls studying at a window seat in a dormitory room.
WESTOVER SCHOOL ARCHIVE.

1950 only two girls of color arrived in Middlebury. One of them, Michelle Baussan, a shy senior with a Russian father and a Haitian mother, had probably met the headmistress the previous summer, when Miss Dillingham had vacationed in Haiti. Although Michele's native language was French, she turned out to be "a very good student," the headmistress thought.

The other girl, a junior, was Miriam DeCosta of South Carolina. She had been highly recommended by Elizabeth Avery, who had attended Westover in 1911 and 1912. A native of Michigan, Elizabeth had moved to the South with her second husband, where she had scandalized Charleston society by divorcing him to marry Judge J. Waties Waring, after he also obtained a divorce. She held enlightened views about race relations, and Judge Waring backed minority voting rights in his court. In January of 1950, after she gave a fiery antisegregation speech that attracted national attention, the Ku Klux Klan burned a cross on the Waring's lawn. Around that time, Elizabeth told a black friend about Westover's new admissions policy, and the friend suggested that Mrs. Waring meet Miriam. The girl's father was the dean of the graduate school of South Carolina State College in Orangeburg, and her mother, also a college graduate with an advanced degree, was a college professor. The Warings invited Miriam and her parents to lunch at their home—another radical action at the time—before writing to Miss Dillingham about her.

Westover was Miriam's first experience of the white world. Miss Dillingham thought her poised and self-assured, and she admired the way she seemed to adapt quickly, easily, and naturally. Classmates remember Miriam as always self-contained and sometimes high-spirited, as well as a good athlete and a great student, but the fact is that she often wept at night. The girls were pleasant enough, she remembered, but there were problems with parents. On New Girl weekend, the only people who spoke to her parents were teachers and the Rev. Charles Ives, the minister of the Congregational Church across the Middlebury green, who had recently delivered a strongly antiseg-regationist sermon. As a result of parents' opposition to Miriam rooming with their daughters, she was only girl in the school without a roommate during her two years at Westover.

To make matters worse, she was also the only African-American in the entire school her senior year, except for members of the household staff, like Minnie Price, who had been the headmistress's maid before working in the school post office. Antici-pating difficulties at Glee Club dances, Miss Dillingham asked her and another girl to be the ones to play records on the Victrola. While the headmistress later recalled that Miriam used to dance all evening at such events, Miriam recalled them as "unpleas-ant." She also disliked the headmistress's awkward attempts at impartiality, what Miss Dillingham called an attempt not to discriminate either "*for* or *against*" a Negro pupil. Well aware of her educational opportunity, Miriam studied diligently and found the teachers "wonderful," especially Spanish teacher Celeste Fernandez. She never forgot Mr. Schumacher's fascinating Ideas and Images elective about northern European and Spanish painting. When she graduated in 1952, it was with the highest grades in the senior class and with the school prizes in art, French, and Spanish.

Despite the school's attempts to integrate and its emphasis on college, the image of Westover stubbornly remained that of a finishing school, a place where families sent their daughters for social polish. A Peter Arno cartoon in the June 23, 1951, issue of *The New Yorker* showed an elderly mariner helping a lovely young lady in a short dress and high heels into a small motor boat with the caption: "You've got to hand it to Westover when it comes to plain know-how," suggesting that its silly graduates knew their way around wealthy older men. Judging from a quotation in *The Wick* a few months later, Louise Dillingham found this cartoon a painful reminder that girls' schools needed to change their images and step up their scholarship programs. Many of the students were from the East and related to alumnae, but the headmistress wanted to find applicants from all walks of life, especially those who were eager to learn. As she struggled to raise money for financial aid and to find deserving students, she decided it was time to hire a director of admissions. In 1952 she offered the position to Rose Dyson, after inviting her to dinner at her Woodbury home. Miss Dyson was a graduate of Smith who had studied French at the Sorbonne. Within a year, Miss Dyson had increased the enrollment to 170 students, and she continued to add a few more in each of the following years.

Despite Miss Dillingham's efforts, when Margo Dean, the daughter of an oral surgeon in Washington, D.C., arrived as a sophomore in the fall of 1952, she was again the only girl of color in the school. Protests by white parents continued, and before the Scotts from Virginia arrived one weekend to visit a daughter, Miss D felt she had to ask Margo to stay out of sight. The following fall Audlyn Higgins entered the sophomore class at the age of thirteen. Her father, a Baltimore surgeon from Jamaica, believed in boarding schools because he had gone to one in England. In May of 1954, during her first school year at Westover, her parents sent her a newspaper clipping with a "jubilant headline" about the Supreme Court outlawing segregation—and the concept of separate but equal—in public schools. However, for a number of reasons, involving both the school and the society around it, Lyn would be the last African-American at Westover for many years. Nonetheless, Miss Dillingham regarded the school's six-year period of integration in the 1950s as "very successful" because the four Negro girls had been liked and respected by everyone at Westover.

Meanwhile, the drive to create an endowment was off to a slow start. A Fathers Association was started in November of 1952, and it raised a little money. Despite the increase in enrollment, expenses continued to exceed income, and only with the help of an annual alumnae fund drive was the budget balanced. During those difficult years, Louise Dillingham became exhausted and "immensely frustrated" because she thought members of the board of trustees did little to help her. The lawyers and businessmen on the board were inactive because of their "awe of her grasp and intelligence," remembered a staff member. The men admired her "good hard common sense" and her "extraor-

English teacher and administrator Elizabeth Newton.
HUGH ROGERS.

dinary objectivity in arriving at judgments," one of them later said. Miss Dillingham liked the company of males and, in fact, she often enjoyed talking more with fathers than with mothers of pupils. "She had no small talk, and she was uncomfortable with fools," explained Adele Ervin. Despite the men's admiration for the headmistress's executive abilities, they blamed her for being a poor fundraiser. "She wasn't naturally outgoing, and it was hard to sell herself to people," said Donald Henry, a lawyer and husband of an alumna, who was on the board for twenty-three years. He also blamed the failure of fundraising on the relatively few number of alumnae of a school that had been founded less than fifty years earlier.

A New York socialite, the former Barbara "Babe" Cushing, president of the class of 1934, became chairman of the Westover development drive in 1952. During that time, she asked New York fashion designer Mainbocher to update the school uniforms. Black blazers had long ago replaced the colorful capes, but little else had changed over the years. Lacy white dresses were still put on for dinner, and black bloomers with black stockings were still put on for field hockey. Day uniforms were beginning to be made out of a brown-and-white pinstripe material, while the tan corduroy skirt, sweater, and camel's hair polo coat stayed the same. That year the seniors were allowed to change the color of their blazers, and they chose an attractive purple. When a *Wick* reporter asked students in 1953 what school uniforms might look like in the year 2000, they offered all kinds of futuristic fantasies, but no one suggested that there would be no uniforms at all.

During the 1950s, women intellectuals often felt isolated, and they found female institutions like Westover a comfortable refuge. Among those drawn to the school was Elizabeth Newton, who had started teaching English there in the autumn of 1951. A member of Vassar's class of 1940, she had a graduate degree in literature from Yale. She never forgot how warmly she had been welcomed by Elizabeth Kellogg, the head of English department. Miss Newton always appeared chic and coiffed and, even though she was given to flamboyance, she exuded a strong sense of willed self-restraint. Master of the acerbic quip, she gave very little praise and very few A's to her pupils, but many of them would later praise her rigorous teaching anyway. In the classroom, she was concerned, above all, with the organization of ideas, the precision of thought, and the discovery of what she called "the controlling abstraction," or the idea behind every piece of poetry and prose. Passionate about Shakespeare, she also aimed to cultivate an aesthetic appreciation of literature in her pupils. When the class of 1959 dedicated its yearbook to her, they described her as an "inspiration, which helped us to produce our best thoughts," and they added that her feisty "spirit . . . gave us strength." A few years later, an accreditation committee would rate the English department and its class discussions as so "splendid" that they asked if its classes could last a little longer.

When later asked why she had remained in the little world of Westover for more than three decades, Miss Newton replied that "the place was so beautiful, so absolutely beautiful." By this she meant the appearance of all the young girls in their uniforms, as well as the architecture, inside and out, from the classical rhythm of arches in the cloister to the regal crimson beauty of Red Hall. She also appreciated her freedom in the classroom and her few obligations outside it. Since the headmistress believed that the adolescents brought each other up, and the school was only responsible for their safety, Miss Newton and the other teachers only had to be present in the dormitory for evening check-in time when they were on duty every other week.

In this milieu of mostly never-married and middle-aged women and a few widows, there was a quiet understanding between the Misses Newton and Dillingham. "One occasionally felt a pleasurable sense of conspiracy, as when [Miss Dillingham] pointed out a framed definition in French of a happy life, ending *'peu d'enfants!'*" Miss Newton remembered. The headmistress encouraged the young scholar in a number of ways, like asking her to initiate and teach an Advanced Placement English class. The teacher also respected and admired the older woman very much. In fact, Louise Dillingham was probably one of the few people in existence who could tell her what to do. "As well as an autocrat, Miss D was an aristocrat, of course," she later said. "She was a great woman—brilliant, idiosyncratic, and unbelievably forceful."

The principal's deep knowledge of the pupils was on display every June, when class schedules were drawn up in her Woodbury home. Gathered around two card tables in front of the fireplace, she, along with Rose Dyson, Emma Hibshman, and others would let down their hair and discuss the abilities of the students very frankly, remembered a secretary, Lee Lort. As Miss Dillingham assigned girls to classes without looking at notes or forgetting a name, "it was a remarkable performance every year," said another observer. A teacher, Polly Bartlett, likened the headmistress to "a living, breathing computer"; she remembered that "after long periods of silence, she would *suddenly* dictate lists of student class sections in each of the various levels of English, math, history, and science," as the others wrote furiously and tried to get it all down on paper. "It was absolutely amazing, and to me quite humbling, to be in the presence of a mind like that."

Afterward, on those and other evenings at her home, Miss Dillingham would organize fierce games of bridge that went on late into the night along with drinks, dinner, and coffee. Over the years, the delicious dinners were cooked by Miss Dillingham's tall West Indian maid, Margaret Stanbuck, or by Sarah "Sadie" Pierce, a small, round, and very nice older member of the house staff, who was regarded as "everybody's grandmother." The headmistress was regarded as good company as well as a considerate card player who was careful to play by the rules. Still, when she asked other players to call her "Louise," it was only with the greatest effort that they were able to do it. She and librarian Esther Millett were the best bridge players, and they often teamed up against Liz Newton and Polly Bartlett, who were close companions and friends.

On Miss Dillingham's summer trips, often with a woman colleague for company, she would put on a large hat, set up her easel outside, and spend a day oil painting. She was modest about her abilities as an artist, and she apparently exhibited her colorful landscapes and still lifes only once, in 1944, at a show of the Society of Independent Artists in New York. She had an affinity for art students, and she used to invite the Art Club to her home in the spring, where everyone would spend an afternoon drawing or painting in her flower garden or by the pond behind her old farmhouse. One young art student, Sherrill Williams, never forgot the way she quickly took her side in an argument with an elderly room inspector, who had called the girl's paint-splattered bureau scarf "dirty." When Sherrill became indignant and went to see the headmistress, Miss D "nodded with great seriousness and then pointed to her own paintings around the room. 'Sherrill,' she said, 'you and I are artists. Not everyone understands. You must indeed keep your bureau scarf white, but I know that there is a big difference between paint and dirt.'" Sherrill later reflected that "metaphorically my bureau scarf always had paint on it, so I was never the 'ideal' Westover girl." She admitted that she could never "muster up the spirit, enthusiasm and organizational skills" for most school activities, so she had no leadership position her senior year. Nevertheless, she said, "after my conversation with Miss D, I sort of knew who I was, and that I belonged. I won the fine arts prize and left Westover with a certain sense of accomplishment that owed a great deal to Miss Louise Dillingham."

Other moments of kindness nurtured the pupils in her charge. One of the girls was inspired by Miss D's faith in her, which was expressed during Faculty–Student Council meetings by "a quiet smile of encouragement." At the Lantern ceremony in 1958, the headmistress whispered to a struggling student with a learning disability words that changed her life: "Your light is burning brightly. Have confidence in it." One November the task fell to her to tell two sisters from Providence that their adored father had died of a heart attack. When the girls arrived in her sitting room, she very gently broke the news to them, then told them that she had made arrangements for them to go home that same day and stay as long as necessary. As the girls got up to leave, she suddenly drew to her large bosom the younger one, a little ninth grader with freckles who looked stricken, in a warm hug.

Another time, two ninth graders were seen holding hands, and a rumor arose that they were lesbians. When Miss Dillingham heard it, she summoned the other new girls to her sitting room. "Do any of you know what the word 'lesbian' means?" she asked. No one answered or got the answer right, so she gave an explanation. She went on to state that "two people who hold hands at the ages of twelve or thirteen could scarcely be labeled lesbian." Being away from home at such a young age among older girls whom they do not know is difficult, the headmistress continued, and their hand-holding should not be interpreted as anything other than seeking reassurance. And then she cautioned the girls to never jump to conclusions about others. "That took care of that, and never again did I hear anything about lesbians," remembered Eunice Groark. And after that, she thought of her headmistress as "a real straight shooter," and even "a giant among women."

In 1956, at the age of sixty, Louise Bulkley Dillingham was still a warrior on behalf of her young girls and her small school. During that era of Senator Joseph McCarthy's "red-baiting" hearings in Congress, agents from the Federal Bureau of Investigation arrived in Middlebury to look for subversive books in the school library, and she was able to turn them away with the force of her personality and her words. She was a powerful presence, especially in the eyes of an eight- or nine-year-old nephew. Young Terry Hallaran never forgot the evening his mother and father took him, along with his Uncle Ted and Aunt Hope Garfield, as well as his aunt's visiting sister, Aunt Louise, to a little French bistro in Cleveland. In the restaurant, Aunt Louise grandly—and rudely, everyone thought—waved away a steak that was not nearly rare enough for her to eat, forcing Terry's father to profusely apologize to the chef and owner of the restaurant the next day.

Miss Dillingham could also be strict and imperious with the students and staff. The evening before graduation one year, the seniors had an uproarious party. The next day, the class president and Miss Newton, who had been on duty, were told to report to the headmistress's sitting room. The senior sat on the floor in front of Miss D's chair and explained that she had made a bargain with her classmates: if they behaved well during spring term, they could have a party the night before graduation. The headmistress waved away the excuse, and she began explaining very forcefully and at great length why the senior's reasoning was all wrong. When Miss Newton tried to intervene by saying that the girl had good intentions, the headmistress glared at her and snapped, "Of course!" The teacher felt reprimanded, but she also came to realize that, in her way, Miss Dillingham was showing respect for students by holding them to high standards and telling them that it was important to have honor "in small things as well as in large."

Morning chapel line around 1960.
WESTOVER SCHOOL ARCHIVE.

This was also her attitude toward schoolwork. "Academically," said a member of the class of 1956, Westover "was a remarkable place." (To graduate, it took four years of English, three years each of math and a language, and at least one year of history and science.) In January of that year, evaluators gave Westover very good marks, especially for the "high caliber" of its mostly female faculty. It was evident to them that Louise Dillingham had accomplished a great deal with a small budget and loyal teachers. The educators expressed awe at the qualifications of Yale's Bruce Simonds, who was in charge of the piano department. Painting and drawing under the direction of Ethel Swantees was taught in unusual depth, they thought. They applauded the electives in creative writing and photography, but they wanted the school to offer more in areas like anthropology, religion, economics, as well as Asian and African history. They suggested a new space for physics and a new wing for the library. Reflecting attitudes about women's roles at the time, they also recommended vocational classes in home economics, typing, and driving. Miss Dillingham, however, told the trustees that she was adamantly opposed to devoting more time to nonacademic activities, since girls already cooked at Crossways and sewed for the Dorcas Society. Miss Newton later recognized that history had been taught "rigorously" through the years, "French had brilliant leadership, Spanish was weak, and Latin fared somewhat better." The way Mr. Schumacher taught art history was also "brilliant." Weaknesses in the mathematics and science departments were ignored, however. There were budgetary restraints, but the headmistress didn't think that students were interested in the subjects, and, even without them, seniors in the academic program were readily accepted by the Seven Sisters colleges, and those in the general course easily got into junior colleges.

Miss Dillingham proudly told a newspaper reporter during the 1950s that even though her students wanted more freedom than in the past, they were taking more responsibility; she also said that they were more mature, more studious, and more interested in careers than pupils in the past. The evaluators agreed, observing the "excellent atmosphere" at Westover, as well as self-discipline, enthusiasm, and interest in going to college. When the visitors interviewed the principal, she pointed out to them that "while training of mind and character require hard work, this work can be accomplished in an atmosphere which is both pleasant and healthy." As if talking about Charlotte Perkins Gilman's utopian *Herland*, she likened the female community of Westover to "a friendly household with high ideals." The evaluators had one last piece of advice for the headmistress: after they learned that almost all information about students was filed away in her prodigious memory, they suggested that it be made more available to teachers.

Years later, some students said they thought that ideas about women's emancipation and equality were implicit and obvious at Westover, and they did not need to be spelled out. One of Miss Dillingham's sayings was "walk with purpose, girls," and posture, or what she called "excellence of carriage," was graded every day. Others regretted that their intelligent and independent female teachers were unable to prepare them better for the slights they would experience beyond Westover's high walls. Teachers were more intent on developing young girls' values and minds, and "not so much the practicalities of how to be a woman intellectual in our culture," Miss Newton admitted. "We felt that we were giving them the intellects to be whatever they wanted to be." A member of the class of 1959, Betsy Shirley Michel, remembered that "we were told we had been sent to Westover to receive a fine education, but I'm not sure that anyone, teacher or student, had much sense of what we might actually *do* with our educations—beyond being the gracious wives of successful men."

It is evident that Miss Dillingham was not entirely oblivious about what lay ahead for those interested in the professions, since she began to set aside a few days before graduation every year for speakers to inform seniors about careers. But during vocational week in June of 1956, the talk was about the difficulty of combining marriage and work outside the home. A few years later, a visiting lawyer informed seniors headed for college that the field of law was not a good one for women. And in vocational week in 1961, speakers talked to the graduating class about the possibility of working in Africa. Most alumnae who returned for reunions a few years later were doing volunteer work, while a few had jobs as secretaries or teachers. One graduate was working for a Ph.D. in biology, and another was with the Peace Corps in Thailand. Clearly, most young women who wanted careers after leaving Middlebury were on their own.

8

A Great Lady:
Honors and Illness

WHEN LOUISE DILLINGHAM'S OIL PORTRAIT PAINTED BY THE mother and grandmother of pupils was unveiled in Red Hall in 1953, alumnae had spoken of the "great intelligence, warmth of heart, breath of mind and vision, and humility of spirit" of Miss D. "Long may she reign over our little kingdom." Four years later, the school celebrated her twenty-fifth anniversary as headmistress. She was given the Westover Award, which had been established by alumnae a few years earlier. The new president of the board of trustees, Elliott H. Lee, a retired banker from New York City and the husband and father of graduates, effusively praised her qualities of mind and heart as well. In response, Miss D said she was glad to have known Mary Hillard for more than a year before taking her place. She also said that she was grateful for what Westover had given her during the past quarter century, and for what she had been able to do for the school: turn it into a college preparatory school, foster democratic self-government, strengthen the honor system, and establish a policy of admitting pupils without regard to race or religion. That day in May she was given a number of gifts, including a color television set, a monogrammed Steuben glass bowl, and three hundred silver dollars for a painting vacation. She also received a tiny silver chair, which symbolized the gift that probably pleased her most—the establishment of a Louise B. Dillingham Chair (a fund of more than a hundred thousand dollars) to enable her to give a grant to a teacher every year and augment the salaries of the others.

Underneath her straitlaced demeanor, something about Louise Dillingham suggested a passionate nature; certainly she had great appetites for good food, cigarettes, caffeine, and cocktails. Her sitting room always reeked of stale tobacco smoke, and, beginning in the middle of the 1950s, students had noticed that their headmistress had a constant, even a "terrible" cough from chain smoking. People also knew that when she rode in an automobile with friends and relatives, as well as at other times, she would often suggest pouring drinks from a basket she always carried with her containing a bottle of liquor, an ice bucket, and little silver cups from South America. It was because of this ritual that she never learned to drive a car. "She didn't drive because she was a drinker," a niece explained, since she knew that she was not always sober.

Mental depression ran through the Dillingham family, and Louise and a number of her brothers and sisters had started to drink early and heavily as a way to deal with it. By the 1950s if not before, the eldest, Louise, had become an alcoholic. She held her liquor very well, and she was careful never to drink when in residence at Westover. In September of 1958 her health worsened. She was hospitalized for cirrhosis of the liver, and she was also forced to take a long leave of absence from her duties as headmistress. Her doctor, she explained in a letter to the worried alumnae, wanted her to take a rest "to dispel the miserable feeling which then plagued me." She went on: "Happily I can report to you that he was right, and that now, after a number of weeks without duties or responsibilities, I am indeed a different woman, endowed with new energy and interest in all that goes on." The first six weeks of her three-month absence were spent, along with her maid, at her sister Dorothy's home in New Hampshire, where her brother-in-law, Sherwood Smedley, taught chemistry at Exeter School. Miss Dillingham had once asked him to teach science at Westover, but he had not thought it a good idea to work for a relative. While in New Hampshire, she found it "exceedingly interesting" to observe a large boys' preparatory school, she told the alumnae. "I allow myself to hope, therefore, that my enforced absence from the school will prove to have been a really productive one, not only restorative but rejuvenating."

While she was away, Emma Hibshman, who had been an assistant principal since the early 1950s, was named acting headmistress, and she ran the school with the help of treasurer Marion Griswold and admissions director Rose Dyson. Miss Hibshman was an excellent administrator as well as a trusted confidante of Miss Dillingham's.

With her dignified, expressionless, and rather remote manner, she was the one put in charge of dealing with parents. "I'm sure they thought that they couldn't get too far," observed a former secretary at the school. "They had to state what was bothering them, and get it over with." That was the time when Miss Hibshman had to give up coaching the Dramatic Club, an activity she had greatly enjoyed for years, but she still managed to teach an occasional literature class.

In her autumn letter to the alumnae, Miss D had also written that she was looking "forward with great pleasure to January when I shall again be in the midst of Westover students, past, present, and future." It was evidently a heartfelt feeling, since in a letter

Studying in the Common Room under the portrait of Louise Dillingham. HUGH ROGERS.

written to the girls that fall published in *The Wick*, she expressed much more emotion than usual. "I have missed you very much in the last months," she wrote. "It will be a joy to be with you soon." She planned to return after Christmas, she went on, but Miss Hibshman would continue as acting head of school, while she herself got to know the new girls and make plans for the school's fiftieth anniversary the following year. At a picnic with art students at her home in Woodbury that spring, a senior remembered the way she had indeed joked happily with them as they sunbathed on her lawn. Another senior also recalled her smiling and laughing with delight that day as well as her "child-like pleasure in our company, which lit up her whole face and was totally innocent . . . and endearing, and transparent."

Despite her illness, Louise Dillingham was still an extremely forceful individual. She was pleased that her school was better than ever, academically speaking. After the Russians launched Sputnik in 1957, Americans were dismayed to find that, among the top ten percent of high school seniors, twice as many males as females went on to higher education. But at Westover it was rare that a graduate did not attend college, an achievement made easier as the veterans on the GI bill departed the campuses. Observers at the time noted her "keen, penetrating eyes and the concentrated power of her presence" as well as "an aura of exotic places about this New England head-

Helen LaMonte and her niece, Westover treasurer Marion Griswold, 1959. WESTOVER SCHOOL ARCHIVE.

mistress." On a hot August evening in the summer of 1959, a crowded meeting was held at Middlebury Town Hall about a planned superhighway that would cut through the heart of the historic village. Westover's headmistress was reported to have given such a "masterful" speech in opposition to the route that it influenced state highway officials to redirect it to the south and save the village—and her beautiful school.

At Westover's fiftieth anniversary in late October of 1959, cocktails were served in Red Hall on a stormy Friday evening, and then a dinner was held for more than four hundred people in a large green-and-white striped tent on the hockey field. As Dr. Wallace Sterling, president of Stanford University and the father of a student, spoke, the tent started to leak in the rain. In his remarks, Elliott Lee made the distinction that "Miss Hillard was the creator, and Miss Dillingham is the preserver" of the school. Betty Choate Spykman, a member of the class of 1914, wrote in a short and charming school history for the anniversary that "Miss Hillard made life romantic and exciting, and nowadays Miss Dillingham's loyalty and justice make it secure."

The next morning, a panel discussion about education with Judge Harold Medina, grandfather of a junior, along with fathers of other students, was moderated by Virgilia Peterson Paulding. A member of the class of 1921 and the first recipient of the Westover Award, she was an attractive mother and career woman who, among other activities, hosted a television show about books. During the night a violent windstorm had blown down the tent, so Miss Dillingham decreed that the chapel service planned for it be in the Middlebury Congregational church instead, but the storm's unrelenting torrential rains and winds made it difficult even to get across the village green. It was finally decided to gather everyone in Red Hall, where students sang as planned, and the Episcopal bishop of Connecticut and alumna husband Walter H. Gray presided. The improvisation worked wonderfully, people remembered. After all, the assembly hall and its balcony had regularly accommodated graduations of "more than five hundred people if not with ease but—warmly," as Jock Schumacher pointed out in his paean to the handsome room. On Sunday the sun came out at last, and the headmistress stood proudly at the entrance of the school in the afternoon and greeted hundreds of guests while the girls showed them around. "I think any school that can hold a major festival in the middle of a hurricane with the serenity and poise that was shown at Westover deserves to flourish for many half centuries to come," wrote the head of a New York City day school in a thank you note.

Absent that weekend but not forgotten was Miss Helen LaMonte, who had resigned from the board of trustees in 1948 and had been unable to return to receive the Westover Award in person in 1958. One of the many alumnae to visit her over the years, Betty Choate Spykman reported that "Miss Helen, at eighty-five, except for her helmet of white hair, is much the same as ever, a handsome small majesty who flings her cape across her shoulder while she strides about." In September of 1962, however, she returned to Middlebury to celebrate her ninetieth birthday. "What a birthday!" she wrote afterward. "If kindness would kill, I'd be dead after last week and all the golden words that were written and spoken to me." She had expected to feel old that day, she admitted, until Mary Willcox Wiley had arrived with her one-hundred-and-one-year-old father, a retired Cornell University professor. "After that a mere ninety seemed hardly worth notice and made me feel young again and gay," she wrote. She ended her letter, as usual, with wise words of advice: "Read your Bible, read your Shakespeare. Also read Salinger. Never stop growing, never stop learning, and never, never feel afraid." In the same spirit, she wrote to an alumna who lost a son the following year: "Here I am, the last of my generation, with all my friends and contemporaries gone, but can feel happiness, even gaiety of spirit, and the greatest interest and curiosity about all that is happening in the world at the beginning of the Great Atomic Age which is so full of promise, of possibilities for the human race." As usual, her inspiring words, penned in her meticulous, miniature handwriting, put everything in perspective.

A rumor had persisted throughout the years that Louise Dillingham had turned down an offer to be president of a college, maybe Bryn Mawr, to keep a promise to Mary Hillard to remain at Westover. Whether or not it was true, some friends and family members thought that during her long tenure as headmistress of a small girls' school she had made little intellectual effort and not fulfilled her earlier promise. At a time in America when there was little place for female intellectuals, she seems to have silenced herself in important ways. Although all the Dillinghams were bright, they were all in awe of Louise's braininess. Late one night at a family gathering after a great deal of drinking, her youngest brother, Sherburne, turned to her and remarked, "You should have been a man, Lulu." She was a person who "valued a trained mind and had one of the best ones herself that I have ever encountered," Helen LaMonte would say. "I always felt she should be a judge on the Supreme Court." For whatever reason or reasons, she indicated little interest in translating or writing or publishing in her fields of psychology and French or in the field of education. "And as she got older, she lived less a life of the mind," observed Adele Ervin, referring especially to the time after her leave of absence in 1958. "She knew she was ill and gave in to that."

The piles of books in Miss D's sitting room included prepublication copies of the latest Agatha Christie and other murder mysteries. At night when every window in the school was dark, there would be a light on in hers. While students had to turn out their lights at 9:30 P.M., she stayed up until three or four in the morning reading detective stories, as many as a novel a night. The only publication she ever listed on Bryn Mawr alumnae questionnaires was her dissertation (which had been published in 1927), but there was another piece of published work that she never mentioned. The truth is that in the 1940s she had won first prize in an amateur detective story contest, a discovery that was made "with total glee" by a pupil who had spotted the announcement in a mystery magazine bought in Grand Central Station to read on the train to Waterbury. "I cut out that page, tacked it on the bulletin board when I arrived at school—but *never* dared tell [Miss D] who had done this terrible deed," she remembered.

In 1960, President John F. Kennedy established the Commission on the Status of Women and appointed Eleanor Roosevelt to chair it, and in the following years federal legislation was passed to give women more equality in education and other areas of life. As the first stirrings of the women's liberation movement got underway, there was little evidence of restiveness in Red Hall. A thoughtful editorial by a student was published in *The Wick* in June of 1961 about the difficulty of finding time for both school traditions and academic work. At a Denver gathering of alumnae that autumn, the headmistress was asked by a newspaper reporter about J. D. Salinger's novel *The*

Catcher in the Rye, which had sounded an early note of a generation's rebellion and was popular on college campuses. She replied that she was aware that Salinger was supposed to be contemporary youth's F. Scott Fitzgerald, but she had not yet seen any interest in the writer at Westover. She was undoubtedly relieved. At graduation that year, she noted that she had gradually granted more privileges to seniors during their last semester, but she sternly warned them that "eternal vigilance is the price of liberty."

What was Louise Dillingham's attitude toward the women's movement from her vantage point at the helm of the virtually all-female world of Westover? She said very little about it, but those who knew her best had the impression that she believed that American women already had rights, but that they did not exercise them. Women could do much more with their lives, she thought, an indictment that, being aware of her own demons, perhaps included herself. While she may not have fulfilled her own potential, she did her best to help her pupils fulfill theirs. For many years she protected, advised, encouraged, and enabled hundreds of younger females. And she did set an example. "She was an original, intelligent feminist role model long before any of us consciously looked to feminist role models," observed a former student. Although Miss D was not feminine in a con-

ventional sense, she was very womanly in the best of ways. Once, after a girl got caught drinking beer in the senior garden two weeks before graduation, she was called into the headmistress's sitting room for a long talk that resulted in a revelation about the nature of womanliness. "It was always Miss D's honesty in dealing with people that impressed me most," the girl later observed. "Her sharp mind and humor could have intimidated us, but she was always gentle. Best, she never wavered from who she was. [She was] never full of feminine wiles, [but] always straight, always feminine."

Louise Dillingham also insisted on high moral standards, and she never had tolerance for deceit or cruelty. "There was a sense, even when I only knew

Louise Dillingham at Westover's fiftieth anniversary celebration. WESTOVER SCHOOL ARCHIVE.

the formidable Miss D, that one was absolutely safe with her. She was kind," said a graduate. For this reason, she tried to discourage the tendency of teenage girls to form cliques. In her early years as headmistress, when a pupil revealed the existence of a secret society called K. T. (for "keep trust" with the spirit of the school) started by her predecessor, she promptly eliminated it. Instead of social clubs, she encouraged groups to form around interests. She organized the Diction Club early on, and it was followed by debate, dramatic, art, language, and other groups, whose meetings after dinner were often followed by so-called "feasts" of sugar doughnuts or peanut butter and jelly sandwiches. For the sake of what she called an adolescent's "highest personal development," Miss D wanted each girl to discover her interests and abilities as a way to ignite her "creative imagination." One of her secretaries remembered that "the most exciting time was to see the light go on in a girl. The real problem girls for her did not know what they wanted to do, [who] had not had the clarification that takes place at this age." Not only would the clubs spark interests, the headmistress hoped, but they would also encourage girls to find new friends who shared them. So in 1960, when a junior and senior asked for permission to form an insider's group called "Pleides" to help boost morale, consisting of seven girls picked "for their sense of humor and liveliness," the headmistress turned them down, undoubtedly because the plan sounded exclusionary.

During her final years at Westover, Miss Dillingham was less attuned to what was going on around her. Her reliance on the belief that girls bring each other up went too far, and a number of them felt neglected and ignored. One young girl, who was unwillingly sent away from home halfway through the ninth grade when she was only thirteen, was "in my own little sad world," she remembered, as she struggled with a learning disability. She later called herself "insecure, a so-so student, a mediocre athlete, definitely a 'late bloomer.'" It was not until senior year that she felt better, believing that her difficult three and a half years at Westover would enable her "to fight with all my might whatever good fights might come my way." Despite Miss D's increasing detachment, she impressed another girl for "'nailing' my greatest character flaw at the Lantern ceremony," but her demeanor was "totally intimidating, unempathic, and therefore unhelpful." The graduate angrily added: "I blame the lack of warmth and caring on Miss D's austere manner. She was a despot, and we were the victims of her oppression. For those of us who needed more parenting, the school in the 1960s was a devastating place to be."

At other moments, however, Miss Dillingham was still involved and insightful. After the head of the singing group, the Undertones, returned from concerts, the headmistress used to ask her amused and penetrating questions about everything that had happened, an inquiry that taught the teenager to observe closely and remember well, which was excellent training for being editor of *The Wick*. Miss D also saw through a sophomore's persona of false cheerfulness after the death of relatives in a car accident. Although the student, Drayton Grant, was too afraid to speak to her, "she had me pegged," Drayton later said. In a letter to her parents, Miss D observed that she did not know if their daughter was happy or not, even though she always had a smile on her face.

As time went on and Miss Dillingham continued to drink heavily, she stayed for longer periods in Woodbury and was increasingly absent from Westover. In the past, she had eaten lunch and dinner in the school dining room, except on her day off and when she was away on fundraising trips, but now it was different. When she was in Middlebury, she often dozed off at lectures and concerts. Worst of all, her college counseling had become very poor. Even so, her detachment was more a cause of disappointment than anger to most of her pupils. One of them, who arrived the September when the headmistress was on her leave of absence in New Hampshire, always regretted that she and other members of her class had never known her better. "I have always been glad to have been exposed to a woman of such integrity," she later said. "I knew her well enough to now understand how much we missed."

Louise Dillingham, who was raised an Episcopalian, had explained early on that Westover was a Christian but not a denominational school, even though the Anglican Order of Service was used. Chapel services were still every morning and evening except on weekends. As always, morning chapel line was rehearsed the first day of the school year. Voice trials for four-part singing continued to be held during the first weeks of school, when everyone had to sing a hymn in front of the three Glee Club leaders and choral director Kenyon Congdon, and then after his death, his wife Carmen. The long Bible reading on Good Friday was still followed on Sunday by a sunrise Easter service at St. John's, when the minister would announce how much the Westover girls had earned for the visiting nurses by waiting on table, and Miss Dillingham would hand over a check. She had long sensed that her students liked music more than Bible readings during chapel services, and they also preferred thoughtful talks on "the *content* of one of the Gospels or a *factual* introductory study of comparative religions," she said.

When Miss Dillingham had presented a prize to senior class president Nancy May at graduation in 1935, the headmistress had uttered phrases from the Epistle to the Philippians that would eventually become her mantra. The words, used earlier by Mary Hillard when presenting another prize, praised "whatsoever things are true, whatsoever things are honest, whatsoever things are just, whatsoever things are lovely, whatsoever things are of good report." At graduation almost three decades later, Miss D spoke the beautiful old Biblical cadences again, and then she gave an intellectual explanation of them. It was typical of her talks, which often focused on a word or a phrase, sometimes an arcane word—a technique that was unsurprising for a talented linguist—and explored its meaning. Her formal remarks were almost always without stories, humor, or personal revelations; they were strong on ideas and ideals, instead. Written in pencil in her precise, neat handwriting on yellow legal pads, her drafts of speeches are full of erudite references to the Bible, Greek philosophers, and the French writers, like Montaigne, Pascal, and Flaubert, whom she knew so well. On that graduation day in 1961, she spoke the passage from Philippians again and began to elaborate on its meaning. Before she did, she paused for a moment and remembered that when doing graduate work in Paris, one of the most difficult challenges was the *"explication de texte,"* when scholars were expected to spend a year studying a short passage, but she promised to spend only a few minutes on it that day.

The following fall she left for another fundraising trip to try to raise money for scholarships and salaries. The prior year, appreciative alumnae had honored all twenty-eight loyal and underpaid teachers with the Westover Award, but honors and even the occasional grant were never enough. After elderly art teacher Ethel Swantees retired after two decades in 1962, Miss Dillingham hired a youthful prize-winning artist, Trudy Martin Barnes, who had been living with her husband and young son in a cold-water loft on the lower east side of New York and teaching at Manhattanville College. Even though the salary was small, she took the job because Westover was near an elementary school, and she was offered a farmhouse with enough space for a studio set in the rolling hills of Connecticut.

Young Mrs. Barnes thought that Westover had many petty rules, old rituals, and rigid regulations that were ossified in time. Several of the same teachers who had taught pupils' mothers now taught their daughters, and some of the teaching was less than inspired. Still, since the world outside Middlebury was rapidly changing, Miss Dillingham made a few modifications to the routine. From time to time, she allowed a small television to be brought into Red Hall for students to watch, like when astronaut John Glenn orbited the earth in 1962. The next year the birth control pill went on the market, and Betty Friedan published *The Feminine Mystique*, in which she called the prevailing cult of conventional femininity "the problem that has no name." It was also the year when Westover's debating team won against all-boys Westminster School, after arguing forcefully that a woman's place was not only in the home. Undoubtedly again in response to requests, the television was set up in Red Hall on a Sunday evening in February of 1964 so the girls could watch the Beatles on the Ed Sullivan Show. Miss D had her limits, however. She made the Undertones substitute the word "romeo" for "gigolo" in the Cole Porter song, "Anything Goes." And after she learned that girls had done the twist at a school dance, she labeled it "lewd" and banned all dances with boys' schools.

Meanwhile, fundraising was going slowly, so Miss Dillingham decided to enlarge the enrollment to increase income from tuition. In the 1960–61 year, the school had 176 students, all boarders, but many more had been turned away. For years it had been her desire to build a better gymnasium and stage, and then turn the small upstairs ones into more bedrooms. Not only would this plan meet needs identified in the most recent accreditation report, it would also enable her to admit more pupils. There was no talk of taking day students, since the headmistress believed that everyone "cherished" living under one roof. "'Family living' at Westover is indeed a unique aspect of the School," she told the

Trudy Martin Barnes (right) and pupil in the art studio, 1960s.
HUGH ROGERS.

trustees. A capital campaign for a new student activities building was kicked off, and enough money was raised to begin. Architectural plans were drawn up with a larger gymnasium and stage as well as a student lounge, a photography dark room, music and dance practice rooms, and a student publications office. In the original building, the architect found ways to expand the dining room, school room, and chapel, in the latter by removing the steep carved steps to the balcony. Groundbreaking for the half-million-dollar new building took place in November of 1961, and renovations on the main building began a year later.

The person put in charge of overseeing the construction was Roger Lort, the husband of one of Miss Dillingham's secretaries. He had been hired a few years earlier as the school's first business manager, so the board of trustees would be able to get more information about the state of the school's finances. A handsome Englishman with a degree from Oxford University, he was also asked to teach history and current events. Miss D enjoyed his erudite conversation, and she used to invite him to her house for drinks. He never forgot her amazing mind, and the way she seemed to remember everything she had ever read. He also never forgot her "phenomenal capacity for martinis," he said, and the way "she would be sharp and in control, and there was never a slurred word."

Still, Miss Dillingham's increasingly lengthy stays in Woodbury had become deeply troubling to the staff, teachers, and trustees. Ever since the headmistress's leave of absence in 1958, Adele Ervin's relationship with Miss D had been distant and difficult. It was "a professional estrangement" that made the alumnae secretary miserable and unable to work well, she explained in a letter to her dear friend Helen LaMonte. Every year, Adele said, she wrote and then tore up a letter of resignation. The administration, in her view, was settling "for what is less than is best in too many areas." Eventually Miss Dillingham became angry as Adele confronted her "over time with the effect of her absences (due to her drinking) and my encouragement of her thinking of retiring (I knew of the move to force that end)," Adele said. "My contract was not renewed." Distressed at the news, Helen LaMonte telephoned Elliott Lee and told him about the time that she and Mary Hillard had come to a parting of the ways. (Miss LaMonte had taken a sabbatical, not knowing if she would ever return, but after a year in Europe she did, and it was as if nothing had ever happened.) The older woman hoped that this would happen now, since she believed that Adele had done "more for Westover than anyone except Miss Hillard and L.B.D," she told her in a letter. Miss LaMonte went on to praise the old friend she affectionatley called "Miss Louisa B," and added: "With all her power and quick intellect, she is a selfless, genuinely humble-minded person." But Adele did leave Westover and move away from Middlebury to return to her parents' home in Manchester-by-the-Sea, Massachusetts.

Finally Elliott Lee, lacking the courage to confront Louise Dillingham himself, asked the president of the alumnae association, Shirley Melum Foote, to tell her former headmistress that the board of trustees wanted her to step down. When the student activites building was dedicated to Miss Dillingham in the fall of 1962, she announced that she would retire in June of 1965, unless someone was found to replace her sooner. She had not groomed anyone to take her place, so the board created a search committee. It initially asked Roger Lort and his wife, Lee, to take the position, but the couple declined the offer. Lee knew she was not an educator, and Roger wanted board members to help him find a job on Wall Street.

Miss Dillingham was saying little about what was happening, but everyone was aware that she was "being pushed out," in the words of Elizabeth Newton. It must have been an excruciating time for the headmistress, especially after all the honors that had been bestowed on her only a few years before. "The most casual photograph shows a face so tragic you can hardly bear what you see," observed Betty Choate Spykman at the time. Nonetheless, Miss D applied the code of honor to herself that she had so often preached to her pupils. Her words at graduation in 1963 were about freedom from fear as "an inner kind of liberation," and they suggest her struggle with her poor health, her pain over the loss of her position, and her apprehension about the future. "You yourselves gain freedom from fear when you think of the honest, the pure, the good, the true, the lovely," she told the graduates. "You know that these things are worth thinking of, worth living for. You act for them and you have not time for fear. Neither the bomb shelter nor the ivory tower is necessary or even helpful. Your freedom from fear is your own inner possession, a part of wisdom."

A year later, in the autumn of 1963, the appointment as headmaster of Robert H. Iglehart, a member of the faculty at Choate School, a boys' preparatory school in Wallingford, Connecticut, was announced. The timing forced Miss Dillingham to retire a year earlier than she had planned. Writing from her home in Owego, Miss LaMonte was appalled that Westover could find "no woman single or married who would consider being the Head." That winter Miss Dillingham put on a good face and said that she was glad to have met with the incoming headmaster often, and she expressed appreciation for his "younger, fresher outlook," as well as the hope that she would live to see the changes he planned to make at Westover. In reality, it was the time when Miss D's self-discipline about never drinking while in residence in her apartment at Westover broke down. Emma Hibshman was trying to run the school, but the president of the senior class felt resentful about all her responsibility for overseeing other students with little or no guidance from anyone. While the seniors dedicated the yearbook to their outgoing headmistress that year, few of them seemed to really mind that Louise Dillingham was about to retire.

In April of 1964, the alumnae association honored her at a large luncheon in the grand ballroom of the Plaza Hotel in New York City. More than four hundred and fifty graduates from every class and other guests gathered around tables decorated with yellow tablecloths and blue flowers. At the head table along with the outgoing headmistress, trustees, and representatives of the alumnae, faculty, and students was the keynote speaker, the president of Bryn Mawr, Katharine McBride, who decried "the waste of woman power in today's society." Indeed, after a decade of diminishing opportunities for women educators, Louise Dillingham would be the last woman to preside over Westover for more than three decades. In her remarks, she played with obscure words, as usual. She described the farewell luncheon as a "hypnapogogic" event, or a waking dream, like an experience she once had at Bryn Mawr long ago, when a psychology professor asked her to wake herself and write down her dreams. In her remarks, she described her memories as "happy ones, exciting ones, some dreary ones, some anxious, some tense, some just plain fun," and she graciously ended: "So it is no wonder that I am now in the happy state of euphoria . . . I am filled with gratitude for the past, pleasure in the present, anticipation of the future. I thank you all more than I can say."

That last spring the youthful new art teacher asked the retiring headmistress if they could trade paintings. Miss Dillingham chose to take only a very small drawing of a daffodil, and she gave away an oil painting of an orchid corsage. She allowed the young artist to go through the rest of her other paintings and select a few to hang around the school. Then the faculty gave Miss D a farewell party in the new LBD student activities building and presented her with a gold perpetual clock. They appreciated the fact that she had been very loyal to them, even overly faithful to a few elderly female faculty members, who lived at the school and had no place else to go.

Among the finest teachers was Elizabeth Kellogg, who had spent all her working years at Westover. When graduates during the Dillingham years looked back, many were glad that they had learned so young to develop what the English teacher called "mental awareness and self-discipline." She would describe what it was like to see this development happen over and over again. "It must be fun to watch a rare butterfly struggle out of its chrysalid, begin to vibrate and unfold its wings, crawl with all its strength along a leaf, and finally soar into the air," she said. "But it's more fun, from my point of view, to watch the slower metamorphosis of the bewildered Westover new girl into the well-developed Westover alumna, flying toward her goals. Even in the new girl chrysalid stage (and here I shall drop my weak analogy, for the new girl has considerably more spirit than the pupa, and the alumna is far from our idea of a 'butterfly!'), the student soon becomes aware of certain values. She learns to be 'honest with herself and others,' she sees the practicality of knowing how to study, and she begins to find her place in the school. From year to year her growth and development are noticeable. By the time she has become a senior, she knows why she is doing work that is sometimes absorbing, sometimes drudgery, and she takes her place in the life of the community to the best of her abilities." Still, added Miss Kellogg, she was sorry to see so many talented young writers in her classes become immersed in motherhood.

Still saying very little, Miss Dillingham indicated that she was pleased with Westover, but disappointed that she had been unable to raise much money for it. Around that time, the last living founder of the school loyally summed up the reign of Westover's second headmistress. "What was sound and good is still unchanged; what was outworn was discarded and fresh, vigorous elements [were] added," Helen LaMonte wrote to the alumnae. As the headmistress prepared for her departure in June, she told the trustees that she hoped that Westover would continue to be a reading and a writing school as well as a singing school. Then she sounded a warning note: it was important for the new administration to understand the importance of chapel,

Singing hymns outside the chapel door accompanied by *"the grasshopper."* WESTOVER SCHOOL ARCHIVE.

even though girls might not fully appreciate it until after they had graduated.

In May there was a final art club picnic in Miss D's garden. She appeared to enjoy it as much as everyone else. With her steel gray hair, dowager's hump, and "strong lines on either side of her mouth [that] made her appear stern," she had seemed unapproachable to a sophomore that year. But on that beautiful spring day it was "a completely different person who stood in her doorway to welcome us—softer, younger," recalled a senior, whose family had long been involved with the school. Another girl had a similar reaction: "I remember being rather frightened of her because her appearance was so severe. Big bosomed, double-chinned, skin-tight hair on the scalp, eyes that missed *nothing*. And then she smiled, and she became irresistible." Over the years, in fact, many pupils who had once feared their formidable headmistress would discover after they graduated that underneath the façade was "a beloved great woman." Anita Packard Montgomery, a member of the class of 1947 who had married a headmaster, used to see her at meetings of heads of schools. Her husband would get Miss D a martini, "and then we would sit down and have wonderful conversations and giggle and laugh."

At her last graduation after thirty-two years at Westover, Louise Dillingham wanted no one to mention her imminent departure. In her talk, she played with the five words in the class of 1964's motto: "According to thine own heart." In a departure from her usual emphasis on disciplining the emotions, she asked rhetorically: "What *are* you, this heart which is to guide you?" She then answered the question: "This thing which you are discovering is your *own* heart—your wholeness." It was as if she was speaking about herself, a person whose immense intellect now was balanced by a brimming heart. Then she backed off, returned to form, and advised her last class of young graduates "to earn the right to follow your heart by judging wisely."

That summer and autumn after her retirement, Miss Dillingham received visits in Woodbury from teachers and alumnae who gave what must have been distressing reports about the new regime at Westover. Some visits were lighthearted, however. One day in late November, three graduates drove up from New York City in an Alfa Romeo to take her to lunch. They were Clara Hoover, an actress in Greenwich Village, Priscilla Cunningham, who had married and just given birth to a son, both members of the class of 1954, and Susan Birge, who had graduated two years later. Miss D was "as energetic, witty, sympathetic, and generally wonderful as ever," reported Priscilla in a letter to a classmate. "Her penetrating intelligence, which one sensed in her eyes, was ever in her command, whether one was talking about life, books, or oneself. She wasn't only intellectual, she had great *joie de vivre*, too!" Priscilla went on to describe the way the older woman managed to get in and out of the small sports car—"a difficult feat for those more agile and less statuesque than herself"—with laughter and her dignity intact. And even when Clara backed into a parked car, Miss D maintained her good humor. It was only afterward, when Priscilla looked at the Polaroid photographs taken that day, that she saw "a far-a-way look" in Miss Dillingham's eyes that she had not noticed before. In fact, Louise Dillingham was seriously ill with only two more months to live. On January 14, 1965, the day she was supposed to undergo a tracheotomy for cancer of the esophagus, she died at the age of sixty-eight in Waterbury Hospital. The next morning, Emma Hibshman announced her death during the morning chapel service, only six months after the headmistress had left Westover. Her unexpected passing was "a great shock to me," Helen LaMonte, ninety-two, would write to a friend, adding that she had hoped that her much-younger friend would have had more time to paint and travel.

A few days later, a funeral service was held at the home of the deceased on Good Hill Road. Her old friend, the Rev. Charles Ives, the retired pastor of the Middlebury Congregational Church, stood in front of her large stone fireplace and recited the Biblical passages that she had repeatedly read to her pupils over the years. "It was a beautiful service," Priscilla Cunningham again reported to her classmates. The next afternoon during a memorial service at Westover, the new headmaster said that "in the delicate transition from a long, distinguished administration to a new and untried one, I experienced at first hand the greatness of Miss Dillingham." He added: "Her quiet support, infinite patience, and consummate discretion have been in large measure responsible for the graceful progression of a venerable institution into a new chapter of its history. I shall long remember her as a friend, as a wise counselor, as a great lady." The words "a great lady" were on everyone's lips. That day an editorial writer in *The Waterbury American* echoed them, saying that he could think of no better praise than calling Louise Bulkley Dillingham a great lady.

After the services were over, Louise's youngest sister, Hope Garfield, arrived from Cleveland. The two Dillingham brothers had already died, and her other sisters, Dorothy Smedley, by then of Wyoming, and Helena Davis of Montana, did not make the trip east. Louise had already given many of her rare and valuable books to Bryn Mawr and other educational institutions including Westover. Her will, which had been drawn up in 1952, left small gifts of money to a few close friends and her maid (for the education of her son). It bequeathed most of her silver, jewelry, antiques, and the remainder of her estate to her relatives. Her siblings had admired their eldest sister in earlier years, but by the 1950s her married sisters seemed to see her as an anomaly; certainly none of their daughters warmed to her or her school. The will also left her personal papers to her siblings, and, since few of them have ever been found, it's evident that Hope threw them away. Her sister Louise always had a strong sense of privacy, so maybe she thought that she would not have minded very much. It is difficult, however, for her former pupils not to mourn the loss of this legacy, a loss that insures that their erudite headmistress will always remain a little elusive.

9

Days of Desperation:
Rebellion and Falling Enrollment

TIME HAD STOOD STILL IN MANY WAYS AT WESTOVER UNTIL Louise Dillingham's departure. The school was virtually the way it had always been, with daily morning prayer and vespers services, an honor system more sensed than spelled out, and a variety of uniforms for classes, sports, dinner, and even for taking walks. After more than three decades of her reign, much of the faculty was elderly. Seniors had traditionally run the school, with the administration taking a hands-off approach, but this was especially true after Miss Dillingham became unwell. Even after her death, the new girl handbook still expressed her lofty thoughts: "Some of your reasons for coming to Westover may have been that you liked its atmosphere of ordered purpose, that you felt the enthusiasm of its community, and that you also felt there were contributions you could make to the School." As her dominating presence slowly dissipated, the world outside the Quad was continuing to change dramatically. The civil rights movement was well underway, ideas about equality for women were rapidly spreading, and college students were vigorously protesting the war in Vietnam.

In the board of trustee's urgency to replace the ailing headmistress, they had asked around for suggestions of names. The Rev. Seymour St. John, headmaster of Choate School, had recommended a French teacher on his staff, Robert Iglehart. The loquacious and ingratiating linguist made a very good initial impression on members of the search committee. Margaret Bush Clement, a member of the class of 1918, trusted the word of St. John, a Yale man, and the others ignored a number of warnings. They also overlooked the fact that the fifty-year-old Iglehart had neither a daughter nor any experience with girls' schools. What he did have was a wife, four sons (the three oldest were at boarding schools and the youngest was in grade school), two dogs, and an exchange student from Australia. Needless to say, the headmistress's small apartment became very overcrowded on school vacations, so plans were made to build a headmaster's house, to be named Lee House after board president Elliott Lee.

The board's confidence in quickly hiring Robert Holt Iglehart had a lot to do with his wife, the former Jane Whitcomb, a Vassar graduate whose mother had gone to St. Margaret's School and remained friendly with Helen LaMonte. When the Igleharts visited Miss LaMonte during the summer of 1964, the founder signaled her approval. "I felt that I know Jane because of her mother," she wrote to another former St. Margaret's pupil, "but I hadn't expected to see him and was as pleased as every one seems to be." A few months later, however, she acknowledged his wife's greater appeal. "Westover has been blessed by two great heads and a great loyal body of Alumnae and now a new third Head who rouses great enthusiasm and a wife who rouses even more and is a most charming hostess," she observed. In fact, the headmaster's wife was expected to be a de facto headmistress with a number of responsibilities. One of them was hosting Wednesday afternoon teas in Red Hall, which was more resplendent than ever that autumn with new crimson carpeting.

When the new headmaster's appointment had been announced the previous fall, he told editors of *The Wick* that he did not want to change anything at Westover, at least not right away. "However, once the girls stop yelling 'eek!' when I come up the stairs, and when the whole school has become adjusted to having a man around the house," a pupil wrote, "he does intend to effect some alterations." But right after school started in September, he imperiously eliminated morning chapel without consulting the students because it cut into class time. (When they vigorously complained, he quickly reinstated it.) The teenagers were happier about other changes, like being given permission to sign out and walk to a nearby store to buy candy and ice cream. "The school is happy and proud of the new responsibilities and freedom it possesses," one of them reported in *The Wick*.

Yet many of the young girls found the new headmaster severe and even scary. The tall, thin man was a "strange figure" who was "intimidating and almost menacing in his manner," recalled Jennifer Martin, who was a junior at the time. He summoned girls in their pajamas to his office at bedtime and then shut the door behind them. More than once he walked along bedroom corridors at night with his large bloodhound in tow, "to look in rooms and smile and leer," recalled Abigail Congdon. She likened him to Ichabod Crane, the scrawny, tyrannical, and poorly educated country schoolmaster in Washington Irving's *The Legend of Sleepy Hollow*. This new headmaster "was supposed to be freeing the kids from the bonds of the past, but he imposed his own bonds by terrorizing them on the corridors," Elizabeth Newton remembered.

Robert Iglehart soon infuriated parents, who heard from their daughters about his mercurial nature and "ghastly temper." If mothers or fathers complained, he became vindictive and punished their daughters by not giving them good college recommendations. It was also felt that he practiced favoritism by, for example, presenting long-stemmed roses during classes to seniors who got into certain colleges. He was clearly mistrustful of the pupils; there was at least one incident when he shouted angrily at a group of frightened girls, who were unaware that they had done anything wrong. One family withdrew their daughter in the middle of her junior year, regarding her young life "irreparably shattered by her experience with Iglehart."

He quickly angered the faculty as well by forcing the retirements of two beloved older teachers, Elizabeth Kellogg and Julie McLintock. "They were excellent and highly effective teachers. It showed absolutely no human compassion or what was good for the school," Elizabeth Newton recalled, who believed he resented their relatively high salaries. To replace them, he hired a married couple in their thirties with degrees from Yale undergraduate and graduate schools, Richard and Alexandra Rewis, who had a young son. He would teach English, and she would teach French. "I felt the world was crashing around me when Iglehart introduced his unwelcome (and really silly, many of them) changes," remembered Miss Newton, who bought a small house of her own in Middlebury at the time. Before long French teacher Howard Whittemore, a descendant of the family that

Students leaving the school around 1970.
WESTOVER SCHOOL ARCHIVE.

had helped establish Westover, left in disgust. As the headmaster's actions polarized and poisoned the atmosphere, morale fell to "an all-time low," Jock Schumacher later informed Elliott Lee. But luckily, the revered art history teacher, whom Inglehart had criticized for his "ways of informal teaching," stood his ground, and their disagreements "were later resolved into the normal, healthy agreement to disagree," the teacher later said.

A note of concern even crept into Helen LaMonte's letters despite her lifelong attempt to put the best face on everything, but she remained optimistic. "Several reunioners from Westover have written and all with enthusiasm about their Alma Mater," she wrote at the end of Inglehart's first year as headmaster. "The only unfavorable comment I had was that the Modern Bible is used in the Chapel instead of the beautiful old King James Version and I couldn't agree more. One thing I particularly like was to hear that Mr. Inglehart with the backing of the Trustees is not allowing smoking privileges to Seniors next year. The juniors were of course disappointed and so the Senior class talked it over and voluntarily gave it up for the last half of this year which I thought was A1 in spirit, don't you? I like both the Igleharts *very* much. Details are bound to change but I think they will keep the integrity of spirit and high standards."

In far off Owego, Miss LaMonte was apparently unaware that the headmaster had "taken away the honor system," in the words of Pamela Whittemore, Howard Whittemore's daughter. Early in the school year, Eleanor Acheson, editor-in-chief of *The Wick*, had written of her "profound respect" for the honor system because it assumed everyone's integrity, self-discipline, and sense of responsibility. "There will be reminders here and there, but never [will] the proverbial 'sword of Damocles' hang over my neck in the form of some teacher or prefect." Gradually, however, Inglehart began to substitute a different disciplinary system run by himself. "It has been harder on the senior officers in a way than on anyone else because they feel they're the last class to really know what can be done by the Honor System," history teacher Patience Norman observed to Elliott Lee during the following school year. It took a long time to build that "truly remarkable tradition," and now the headmaster's favoritism and "system of erratic privileges in the last two years has made it very difficult for students to know just what their privileges and responsibilities are." She went on: "I hope the student officers of this and next year's classes—the group I have felt most for in the current situation, since they have tried so hard to maintain what they sense is the most meaningful thing about the school at a time they are just realizing what it is—can be given a defined role and the help and support of every adult connected with the school, for they are the ones we really exist for."

Jock Schumacher agreed, also telling the board president that the temptation to make more rules should be resisted: "Genuine morality is very demanding. It is much easier, far less challenging, to submit to rules." He also stated in his letter that the headmaster did not understand young girls. "To discipline girls as if they were boys, to police them instead of helping them to make their errors steps of development is untenable," he said. "Their offenses shall not be taken lightly, for this would not help their self-respect. But any degree of overreacting and sermonizing to culprits is destructive not only to the individual student but to the atmosphere of the school as a whole." Furthermore, he wrote, instead of imitating a boys' school, Westover should remain true to itself. He was also worried that the increasing academic pressure was edging out electives in the humanities and, he thought, it was exhausting the girls. "It is appalling to see students enter the classroom in the morning in a state of stupor. Whatever the multiple causes of this perpetual fatigue, it is the most serious single symptom that much is very wrong."

Alumnae on the board, as well as those married to board members (whom the Igleharts derided as the "bedroom trustees"), became increasingly alarmed. After observing the disheartening changes at Westover, one of them remarked sadly to Miss Norman that "maybe it can still be a good school, but the tragedy is that people will never know what they missed." Many alumnae feared that Robert Iglehart didn't understand the nature of the school and was eradicating its very essence. Perhaps the most vehement opposition came from Adele Ervin, who now worked for the National Association of Independent Schools in Boston. "His unctuous manner momentarily disarms some people," she wrote to a trustee, but "his verbosity masks serious defects." To another trustee she wrote: "Make no mistake about it, the earnest mien and fulsome, plausible prose masks a frightening egoism and malevolence which has all but destroyed the school we love."

Finally, after a disastrous year and a half, the board bought Iglehart out of his three-year contract. In retrospect, it should not have been at all surprising to him. During his

Assistant headmistress and teacher Emma Hibshman.

WESTOVER SCHOOL ARCHIVE.

first months as headmaster, he had recognized that it would be "a delicate pass from Chapter II to Chapter III of a venerable and distinguished school story. I seriously doubt that any person (and surely any man!) could make of it less than a pretty rocky time." What Westover really wanted, Iglehart later told his wife, was "a curator, not a headmaster." In March of 1966, he called the faculty together in Room 21, Miss LaMonte's and then Mr. Schumacher's large wood-paneled art history classroom. As he announced his resignation, there was a palpable sense of relief in the room.

In her home in upstate New York, Helen LaMonte was surprised by his firing, despite the complaints she had heard from her many Westover visitors. "As you rightly know, it was a great blow to me when the news came for I had no hint that the situation was serious," she wrote to a friend in April. "Of course I knew that Howard had resigned, and that some did not like Mr. I. but it was true of both Miss Hillard and Miss Dillingham as I well know for people always came to me with their grievances against both those wonderful women." Elliott Lee had "tried valiantly to help and to restrain Mr. Iglehart but he wouldn't listen and was in too big a hurry to carry out his own ideas," she continued "V.[ery] hard on every one." She concluded the letter with her usual attempt to find a reason for hope by writing about spring: "It all passes so quickly and is such a Miracle, new every year."

Despite the hopes of alumnae who wanted the board to hire a woman, Mr. Lee went to see a dean he had heard about at Columbia University, John W. Alexander. He seemed an ideal candidate to be headmaster of a girls' boarding school. A sociologist and the father of three daughters, he was familiar with what he called "girls' development and girls' society" from spending summers with his daughters and nieces on his mother's farm. Born in Atlanta, he had attended a Quaker boarding school before going to Columbia and earning undergraduate and graduate degrees, where he later taught sociology before becoming an associate dean. He was the university administrator called upon whenever there was a student protest, and by the mid-1960s, as demonstrations against university policies and the war in Vietnam because more frequent and virulent, his position had become increasingly difficult. The board president's evident devotion to the small girls' school also aroused the educator's interest in moving from Manhattan with his new wife, Miriam, to the picturesque village of Middlebury.

The hiring of John Alexander, the year he turned fifty, was soon announced. In October of 1966, a Sunday afternoon reception for the couple with the faculty and staff at Lee House was followed by an evening meeting with the students in Red Hall. "We were more nervous about that than any appearance we had ever made," the future headmaster said the following spring after arriving to work with Emma Hibshman, who was again acting headmistress until June, but "that lovely crowd of girls in white dresses, seated on this red carpet, sprang to their feet. They cheered and they clapped, and I hadn't even opened my mouth. My only impulse was, 'Quit while you're ahead.' But knowing no fear, we went ahead."

John Alexander was kindly and much more approachable than his predecessor, but even so, some people were sorry when Emma Hibshman was replaced by another headmaster. Although she exuded formality, students and staff alike were fond of her. They also found her presence and her deep understanding of school traditions very reassuring at a time of turbulence. A staff member called Miss Hibshman's leadership "heroic" and realized that the assistant headmistress had always been in Louise Dillingham's large shadow. Especially after noticing a tremor in her hands, some pupils even felt protective of the older woman, who was by then sixty-four. *The Coagess* editors dedicated the 1967 yearbook to her for reviving what they called Westover's "fully renewed spirit." Under Miss Hillard and Miss Dillingham the school had "two great eras of leadership and inspiration," they wrote, and now Miss Hibshman was "responsible for the third." For his part, the headmaster-to-be graciously said that she "has done this year what she has always done, but has done more of it." He added: "She has shown us what the goal is to work for such a school as Westover, to give yourself to it, and to gain a life out of it."

When Miss Hibshman learned that she would receive the Westover Award that spring, she read over old alumnae reunion letters in preparation for her acceptance speech. She found it remarkable, she would say in her talk, that so many graduates had remained grateful for their excellent educations as well as for learning a good way of life. It must have been very gratifying for her to know this, since she had had so much to do with it during her nearly four decades at the school. At graduation a few weeks after getting the award, she spoke about the abstraction called happiness in a way that suggested she was speaking from her own experience. "It is not a *right* or a *gift* but something to be gained by your own efforts," she told the teenagers. She went on to say that she wished happiness for every member of the class of 1967, describing that state of mind as something attainable through a belief in oneself and the ability "to face life with inner strength and *with laughter in your eyes.*" A year later she retired after thirty-six years, along with admissions director Rose Dyson, and followed the next year by treasurer Marion Griswold. Within a few years, the old guard was gone.

Even before John Alexander was officially installed as headmaster, his troubles began. After reunion weekend in 1967, an alumna who had graduated a decade earlier wrote him to say that she was "shocked" to find pupils not kneeling in chapel and playing tennis in their white eyelet evening dresses. In response, he defended staying seated in chapel as an issue of religious freedom, but he admitted that both he and Miss Hibshman were disturbed by the growing trend of "slovenliness" among young people. He added that one of the student heads of school, the daughter of an alumna, had told him that Westover had "no right" to intervene in the private matter of personal neatness. It was important, he suggested to the alumnae at the time, that they focus more on the present than on the past.

At the same time, he recognized that Mary Hillard and the other founders had developed what he called "a very sensitive and delicate process" for encouraging individuality among young women, a quality he wholeheartedly endorsed. "Women weren't supposed to be as strong as the founders of the school wanted them to be," he later observed. The following fall, the Alexanders made the obligatory pilgrimage all the way to Owego to meet Helen LaMonte, right before her ninety-fifth birthday. "She has truly learned to live creatively and lovingly and to use her mind in the process. That is what I think Westover is about," Mr. Alexander said afterward. He added that he regretted that the elderly lady did not live nearer to Middlebury, so she could give him more advice. "I don't have any key ideas or comprehensive philosophy of education," he admitted at the time. "My views are somewhat pragmatic. I think our task here is to help an institution with a wonderful past, with great strength and promise, to become the best that it may be." In December he arranged to have Miss LaMonte listen by telephone to the singing during the Christmas candlelight service. For her part, she liked the Alexanders and said she felt "at rest about Westover once more."

Despite Miss LaMonte's peace of mind, the restlessness in universities was rapidly spreading to secondary schools like Westover. "We sensed the climate of rebellion and couldn't have put a name to it, but it made us brave," recalled Abigail Congdon, a senior in 1968. A few members of her class were ignoring rules while mocking school spirit and the principles of the honor system. Karin Lawrence, one of a group of so-called "subversives," was dismayed that so many of her classmates were oblivious to the nation's political and social upheavals. "I had boyfriends in Vietnam who were writing home horror stories," she later said, explaining that arriving as a junior had given her more exposure to events outside the walls of the school. She and her friends found a way to get up into the attic of the main building, where they smoked cigarettes and marijuana until the early hours of the morning. When she was too tired to get up and go to breakfast or chapel, she would sleep hidden under a pile of dirty laundry in her closet. "We simply were not going to bother with the rules we thought were ridiculous," she said. "It was passive resistance. We just said 'no, we're not going to do it.'" And she quickly realized that the seniors had no way to make them do anything and just hoped their attitude would not spread.

The latest headmaster was not the type of man to be dictatorial. As a sociologist, he was trained to expect and evaluate social change. As a Quaker, he believed in listening to all points of view and peacefully mediating conflicts. And as a liberal, he believed in the rights of individuals. He was the son of a minister who had led early integration efforts in the South, and he was also an ardent advocate of civil rights. He invited the African-American educator Kenneth B. Clark to speak about the need to solve racial problems in society. Like Louise Dillingham, he wanted the school to have more diversity, and, for the first time since the early 1950s, he enrolled pupils of color through a program called A Better Chance. When Martin Luther King, Jr., was assassinated in the spring of 1968, Mr. Alexander allowed students to honor the civil rights leader with a day of seminars on the history of civil rights, nonviolence, black power, and African-American culture. Afterward, a chapel service was led by a black minister, ending what was one of the first Martin Luther King days in the country.

An urgent matter awaited the new headmaster after his arrival in Middlebury:

maintaining Westover's accreditation. After gathering a great deal of data, the school passed an appraisal in October of 1968 but with a mixed report card. The visiting educators highly praised the "urbane and scholarly" Jock Schumacher as well as the young Robert Havery, an organist and choirmaster, fresh from a master's program at the Julliard School of Music. Before applying to Westover, he had looked into how many pianos various private schools owned and was impressed by Westover's half dozen Steinways, which signaled to him the school's serious interest in music. He was hired to lead the choral program and the excellent glee club, which had helped give Westover its reputation as a singing school, and to teach mandatory introduction to music and elective music theory classes. He quickly realized that many people associated with the school were still more oriented to the past than the present, let alone to the future. The youthful newcomer heard so much about a beloved Dr. Lewis that he assumed the former chaplain had recently passed away, so he was astonished to learn that the minister had died in 1940.

After Emma Hibshman retired, John Alexander named a contemporary, Elizabeth Newton, to be director of studies and assistant principal. He admired the English teacher's intelligence and toughness and later called their working relationship the best of his professional life. He also liked her ability. Her department appeared to the outside educators as "particularly impressive" because of its "liveliness, flexibility, rapport." Since the autumn of 1968, the English department had included James Weber, a long-haired, bearded Yale graduate in his late twenties with the Gaelic nickname "Shamus," which had been given to him by an Irish nanny. The evaluators also praised the school's three Advanced Placement courses but expressed concern about the absence of one in the history department, which they thought was in "dire need of reevaluation" under Patience Norman. In some areas, they went on, there was an overemphasis on true-and-false tests and overuse of textbooks instead of emphasis on topics and themes, they explained. Science was well taught but hampered by cramped classroom and laboratory space, they added. Alexandra Rewis was highly praised as a French teacher. Music and art were also well taught, and the art teacher "really taught her students how to see," remembered a student. But mathematics was poorly taught and was the worst department in the school, the evaluators flatly stated.

During their two-day visit, they acknowledged that the school had gone through "what may well have been the most difficult five years in its history." Despite having four different headmistresses and headmasters in five years, to say nothing of the high turnover among teachers, they said that "the morale of students and staff was remarkably high." A few months later, however, the headmaster felt the need to explain the honor system in chapel, since so many pupils did not seem to understand it. He said that after a senior reported a new girl as required for repeatedly breaking rules, the senior was ostracized by the younger students. The honor system was more about attitude than rules, Mr. Alexander tried to explain, and he admitted that "it doesn't always work well" because every pupil "has the power to weaken it or strength it." It was around that time when a visiting alumna found it "sad and shocking" to see the "the petulant demands and emotional self-indulgence" of the teenagers and the way the honor system had totally broken down.

By the spring of 1969, several younger girls refused to participate in germans and in West and Over team activities. They were impatient with traditions that seemed "more appropriate to a childhood they feel they have left behind," Mr. Alexander told the alumnae. At a school meeting in Red Hall that May, many girls demanded in the spirit of egalitarianism that they should have a more democratic student government. Also, despite a warning from the president of the senior class, the authority of older students was abolished. Instead, a plan was put in place for everyone to be responsible for herself and to only give reminders about rules to others. Meanwhile, more girls were dropping out every year, since many of them had more freedom at home. (One year four juniors withdrew: two for college and study abroad, and two for day schools, where one wanted to date and another wished to do social work). Many left gladly, but others were encouraged to leave because of their misbehavior.

In this atmosphere, education was becoming less and less important. During Victoria DiSesa's freshman year, when Miss Hibshman was acting head of school as well as the following year, there was still a sense of seriousness about learning, she remembered. But during her last two years until her graduation in 1970, this attitude eroded. The headmaster's excellent ideas for improving the curriculum were frustrated by both rebellious students and libertarian teachers. Although the young English teachers introduced their students to some excellent contemporary literature, several of them "often emphasized stylishly sensational reading and neglected disciplines of

Students walking across the Quad in winter. WESTOVER SCHOOL ARCHIVE.

thought and writing," Miss Newton later wrote in a report. The darkly handsome Carlyle "Crash" Clark had girls watching movies instead of writing papers, she pointed out. Another teacher, she said, referring to Richard Rewis without naming him, "substituted charisma, sensitivity exercises, and encouragement of obscenities in writing for any kind of even minimum standards of English teaching." Another teacher recalled that in their urging of self-expression at the expense of self-discipline, the Rewises were like "pied pipers." The couple was so popular, in fact, that the seniors dedicated their yearbook to them in 1970, just as Richard Rewis was running into difficulties with the administration.

Meanwhile, many men's colleges, followed by boys' prep schools, were going coeducational and attracting some of the most motivated female students to their well-endowed campuses. From time to time, Westover's trustees toyed with the idea of admitting boys, but the notion never got far because of the lack of money for a boys' dormitory. Mr. Alexander expanded an exchange program with nearby Taft and St. Margaret's schools to broaden the curriculum and create more contact with the opposite sex. It was an ideal arrangement, at least in theory. Pupils from all the schools took courses like calculus and physics at Taft, Russian history at St. Margaret's, and the Russian language at Westover. And during a week in May 1969, a dozen Taft and Westover seniors working on independent projects switched campuses, but more than twice as many Westover girls ended up taking classes in Watertown than Taft boys did in Middlebury.

Before long the Taft trustees proposed a merger—meaning that Westover give up its campus and move to Watertown. While Westover's board of trustees considered this offer, its headmaster worried that the boys' school was offering "such restrictive and submissive terms" that the arrangement would not be good for his school. "We do get the impression that many of [the boys' schools] simply wish to add girls to their roster[s] in order to keep the boys from getting restless and to keep the schools full," he added, suggesting that coeducation appealed more to adolescent than academic values. Mr. Alexander had other doubts about coeducation being right for Westover. He believed that away from what he termed "male domination," teenage girls develop more strength, self-confidence, and individuality. A poll published in *The Wick* around that time indicated that most teachers and pupils shared his sentiments about their female milieu, although girls liked the exchange program very much. But they said if boys were around all the time, they would be "too distracting" and "would never understand singing around trees" in the Quad. "We get the benefit of seeing boys especially on weekends but not the BURDEN of living with them," one stated. "There are seven miles between here and Taft and that's about perfect." When Westover did not readily agree to the proposal, Taft headmaster John Esty warned John Alexander that if the Westover trustees rejected Taft, he would find girls elsewhere.

It was unthinkable to the alumnae on Westover's board that their alma mater abandon its identity, to say nothing of its magnificent main building, designed so beautifully by a woman architect for girls. Meanwhile, the board was nervously aware that going it alone might fail. Nonetheless, in May of 1970 the members voted unanimously to refuse Taft's offer and remain in Middlebury. "Taft wanted to marry us, and we turned them down," recalled Virginia Stanton Duncan, noting that the boys' school wanted their girls, their loyal alumnae, and their large dowry in land. "In other words," she said, "Westover would be eradicated, and we would just become part of Taft. I would rather have seen Westover go down on its own with its flags flying than join Taft."

Board member Benjamin Belcher, who was president of his family's Benjamin Moore Paint Company, was aware that his three daughters had all "gained tremendously" from their years at Westover. Nevertheless, looking at the school's financial situation as a businessman, he was pessimistic. It was his opinion that the market for boarding schools was disappearing, since they were no longer a guaranteed path to Ivy League colleges. He also believed that girls' schools without links to boys' schools were in trouble, so he urged a relationship with Hotchkiss School. "If we can assume, for a moment, that Hotchkiss is available, what do the alumnae of Westover have to lose by a move of the school to Lakeville?" he asked. After admitting that its site on the Middlebury green was very attractive, he went on: "Certainly, a location on the Hotchkiss Hill overlooking the lake and the mountains would have to be even more dramatic and beautiful than Middlebury." He also thought that Hotchkiss headmaster A. William Olsen would have more respect for Westover's desire to keep its identity than his counterpart at Taft, and that the two schools could "work out a happy marriage." If not, Westover would have to raise millions of dollars to do something about what he called its "old and overcrowded" main building. "Even so," he said, "the gamble is great, since all the money and effort may well be in vain." Again, the board said no.

After the talk of an arrangement with a boys' school ended, John Alexander declared that Westover was now free to recommit itself "to educating girls in a distinctive way." Various ideas were floated about what this meant, including paying Taft to teach science to its girls and attracting more students by offering classes in unusual subjects like ecology, anthropology, archeology, and oceanography. There was also talk about interesting pupils and parents in Westover by using the latest teaching techniques and technologies, like audio cassettes for languages and computers for math. And suggestions were made about offering internships in the arts, ways to participate in politics, do social work in inner cities, and study in Europe in order to satisfy the urges of its teenagers to get out into the world.

Instead of becoming stricter or more permissive, John Alexander's instinct was to offer more choices, what he called "constructive freedom for intellectual, social, and cultural experience at school." He also wanted to give important information to the adolescents, so he organized lectures and discussions about dealing with authority, expressing sexuality, and taking illicit drugs. His most successful innovation was the establishment of an academic committee consisting of teachers and himself. It began to modernize the curriculum, like making basic design a requirement and offering anthropology and Russian or Asian history for European history. The committee also allowed students to take extra electives on a pass-or-fail basis. Furthermore, it created the independent studies program for seniors, where they could undertake art, music, writing, gardening, social work or other projects, in "an attempt to channel 'doing your own thing' and to open up academic possibilities," in the words of Elizabeth Newton.

However, nothing the headmaster did could calm down the growing discontent among students on the one hand and adults on the other. In desperation, he called together three hundred alumnae, trustees, teachers, pupils, and administrators to talk about the school's turmoil over a weekend in January of 1970. Even though Mr. Alexander, who was shorter than many of the teenage girls under his tutelage, became frustrated and angry when they ignored him or ridiculed his sincerity, he remained willing to be "a catalyst to find consensus to make sense of all this," he

Girls putting mail beside a place in the dining room.
B. E. HERZOG.

later said. That weekend, the participants discussed the crisis confronting traditional girls' boarding schools in an era of free speech and free love. Among the topics was whether chapel, classes, meals, sports, and study hall should be optional or compulsory. Pupils complained about living in the noisy and overcrowded building with more than two hundred boarders, and about the regimentation of the school day—everyone being in class, playing sports, or eating together at the same time—which resulted in little privacy and time to oneself.

It soon became evident that abolishing the old way of enforcing rules the previous spring had been a mistake. Mr. Alexander had wrongly assumed that students would be able to discipline themselves, Miss Newton later reflected. Instead, the adolescents cut classes, left early for weekends and returned late from them, and, in many other ways, did whatever they wished. Those who disliked Westover wanted to stay because of its permissiveness. Everything "unraveled with poor John," Miss Newton remembered. "Here was this gorgeous thing, and it was falling to pieces."

When the headmaster discovered that girls were signing out for church but going elsewhere on Sundays, his response was to offer alternatives to church services, like

John Alexander (left) and Joseph Molder around 1971.
WESTOVER SCHOOL ARCHIVE.

attending a religious lecture or Quaker silent meeting. Likewise, when students complained about going to chapel, its services were shortened to fifteen minutes and then decreased to three mornings a week. A student would speak one day (often airing a controversial issue), a faculty member the next, and on the following day a Catholic, Protestant, or Episcopalian clergyman would officiate. Even these changes were not enough. "The chapel experience can scarcely last another year or two," Mr. Alexander told the trustees in the spring of 1970, admitting that his offers of choices and compromises had failed. "Westover cannot survive for long as a conventional boarding school for girls in essentially its present form," he continued. "Today's girls simply will not accept it, whatever its past value has surely been and however firmly we try to hold the line."

A few months after the January conference, Victoria DiSesa, editor-in-chief of *The Wick*, felt disappointed and impatient because nothing had changed, as far as she could tell. So in the May 1970 issue, she attacked the way the school was being run. "There has been this past year at Westover a serious breakdown in the school's law and order," she wrote. "Girls have run away for a few days, boys are seen on upstairs corridors, and smoking and drinking at the school are apparent." She called John Alexander's administration inept and "confused," and she accused it of failing the school. "Students do not need to be talked to or pleaded with, but rather to be talked with and reasoned with," she added.

One afternoon when she was playing tennis, a very agitated headmaster walked over to her and anxiously said something about his wife being terribly distressed. One of the reasons he had been hired was because of his attractive wife, the former Miriam Heald of Nashua, New Hampshire. A 1950 graduate of Wellesley, she had worked with young girls before becoming an executive secretary at Columbia University. The couple had met there before setting out for what it anticipated would be a better life together in the country. At Westover, however, Mrs. Alexander felt personally slighted by various people and deeply upset by criticism of her husband. It was apparent that "her emotional fragility was a drain on his energy," in the words of a teacher at the time. And that May issue of *The Wick* had to be hastily confiscated.

The headmaster still had the sympathy and loyalty of some of the trustees. Benjamin Belcher did not blame him for the bewildering "revolt of our offspring." The former Nancy May, a trustee who had graduated in the 1930s as president of her class, found the teenagers at the time to be "an utterly alien species from my Westover contemporaries, who were shy, attuned meekly to the authoritarian tempo, bursting with ideals of honor and integrity, neurotic over tradition and spirit, lost in the world of that quadrangle." Dorrance Sexton, the husband of an alumna and the president of a large New York insurance company, had become president of the board of trustees after the resignation of fellow Princetonian Elliott Lee after the Iglehart debacle. He was an honorable man who was "worldly, savvy, and sharp," in the words of Adele Ervin. Mr. Sexton urged the beleaguered John Alexander to find an assistant headmaster to help him; accordingly, he soon hired a younger former colleague from Columbia, Joseph Molder, who moved with his wife, Beth, and three young children to Middlebury in the summer of 1970.

Meanwhile, the headmaster continued to be the messenger with the bad news. Entering girls, he told the trustees, now had more experience with illegal drugs than the present seniors had at their age. He had held long talks with every pupil who wished to return the following fall, during which he asked her to pledge not to use drugs at school. After the start of the 1970 fall term, he realized that students had paid no attention. He called a school meeting and warned the students that the police were enforcing drug laws and arresting drug dealers, including those with contacts at Westover. If someone was arrested, he warned them, it would be "a tragedy" for her and a serious blow to the school. Then he outlined ways that those with drug problems could quietly get help. "*If* the adults, by your default, must take on extensive police-like actions, a special quality of student-faculty relationship that has prevailed at Westover will be destroyed," he said.

That autumn some teenagers continued to demand more freedoms while others called for more order. After the anarchy of the previous year, Susan Clark, the new editor-in-chief of *The Wick*, noted in the October 1970 issue that there was a desire for the "return of authority." She wrote that "we've tried the personal liberty side, and it didn't work because liberty was carried to an extreme of self-interest." She urged both sides—the so-called hippies who wanted fewer rules and the preppies who wanted more—to defuse the "fever pitch" of "anger, unrest, and obstinacy." Another girl openly urged her classmates "to grab a pencil and paper instead of a joint" when bored. Meanwhile, a new director of residence, Helen Ferguson, the 1935 alumna who had grown up in Middlebury, was ineffective and forced to resign after admitting to a drinking problem. At the end of the year in the June *Wick*, teacher Polly Bartlett accused the seniors of being "irresponsible children" who "refused to grow up." To members of the class of 1971 who were complaining about "the general messiness and uneasiness at Westover," she pointed out that few of them had ever done anything about it. When they were sophomores, she reminded them, they had rejected the leadership of the seniors, and when they became seniors themselves, they had failed to take responsibility either for themselves or for the younger girls.

The rebellious class of 1971 protested against uniforms by wearing peasant skirts and workmen's shirts over them and blue jeans and hiking shoes underneath. They wrote on them in ink, ripped them, and left them unbuttoned. As juniors, half the class had refused to buy senior blazers because they regarded them as preppy and an emblem of the privileged senior status they disdained. Finally, the administration gave in, and the brass-buttoned and belted day uniform with its starched white color and black bow was waived on weekends, and then, after spring vacation in 1971, it was abolished altogether. Meanwhile, the required white cotton dinner dresses "were shrunk too small, dyed pink and covered with pen marks," recalled a student at the time.

Alumnae were appalled by the way the girls looked, and the headmaster did not know what to do about it. Around that time, Betsy Michel, who had been living in Paris, returned to Middlebury for a meeting of the alumnae association. Unaware of the extent of the student rebellion in America, she was "horrified" by what she saw as she walked through the Quad. She remembered Mr. Alexander saying something about "mature young women capable of making their own decisions," but she did not notice any maturity. "The spirit was wrong," she later recalled. Adele Ervin went even further, stating sadly in a letter to Helen LaMonte that the spirit of Westover has, "in essence, died."

Like other alumnae who had matriculated under the indomitable personalities of Mary Hillard and Louise Dillingham, they viewed the widespread breaking of rules as incomprehensible, so they tended to blame the headmaster. "There was very little discipline in the school because he was trying so hard to do what was right for everybody," another alumna, Virginia Stanton Duncan, later reflected. "Maybe if there had been a very strong disciplinarian as the head of the school, some of the things wouldn't have happened." Another distraught alumna thought that "ricocheting discipline leaves adolescents in a vacuum of pseudo independence which they simply cannot cope with"; she bitterly lamented that "in three years, a herd of confused teenagers can destroy over fifty years of quality heritage." Many parents were still sending their daughters to boarding school to learn to uphold the gracious and genteel traditions of the establishment. Mr. Alexander realized that they and the alumnae wanted him to somehow maintain "the old world" at Westover, and they acted as if he "had invented pot, and blue jeans, and sex." He still had an advocate in the ever-encouraging Miss LaMonte. "I think you are completely

WONDERFUL in the way you handle the young of this day without being a Dictator," she wrote to him.

That spring of 1971, the Westover Award was given to Rebecca Love Drew, a member of the class of 1934, who was a physician and pianist as well as the mother of three recent graduates. She hoped that returning to her old school would exorcise her girlish ghosts about being "Becky Love, the acned, gangling, noisy, uncoordinated gawk," and would fulfill a "fantasy about having Red Hall at her feet as a musician." If she been a boy and gone to Taft, she said in her acceptance speech, her achievements as an adult would have been taken for granted. "As a young, very militant goddaughter of mine remarked haughtily to me recently, when I was arguing with some of her radical (and even revolutionary) views on the liberation of our sex—'well, of course, you're a loophole woman.' I discovered that in her terminology this was scarcely better than being an Uncle Tom woman, and it meant that I had slipped through a loophole of an antifeminist society into a successful professional career, but this was clearly not enough."

This alumna, a woman of great dignity, went on to say in her talk that she had been delighted when idealistic social activists began applying to the University of Pittsburgh School of Medicine, where she taught, until she discovered that they lacked self-discipline. "If we assume that education should be an act of creating rather than mass-producing—that its aim is for each child to produce his own variously sized, asymmetric, intricate, gloriously resilient spider's web of intellect—then there are two" important requirements, she said. "One is intellectual discipline and the other is excitement. Both are necessary, neither is sufficient." She explained that "the notes *must* be right or one cannot express Beethoven, nor treat the patient. There should be no confusion among us that six times seven, or English grammar, or musical scales, or medical anatomy are 'fun.' But if the intellectual's spider web is to be strong and beautiful, it must have a well-constructed center. I assume that making such a center is very hard work for a spider; I am sure it is for a teacher, a musician, or a doctor."

"At Westover I learned to think," she continued in her talk. "'To Do' and 'To Be' follow, but only follow. 'To Think' without doing in our time is to me an immorality; to do without thinking is inexcusable in an educated person. 'To Be' is a mystery which I hope follows upon thinking and doing and upon their melding in one's soul. I cannot speak to that because I have not yet achieved it." Then she announced that she was going to play a Bach fugue, explaining that "in Bach one can see most intimately how these many voices can be disciplined into beauty without discarding passion." As she prepared to perform, she said: "It is a small musical offering to Westover and by its mood an impassioned prayer for her future."

The accomplished alumna's presence, as well as her careful words and her classical music, were reminders of what Westover used to be, a place of "discipline and responsibility, dignity and tradition," in the words of another alumna. "It wasn't only the chapel, which was a vital core of life," explained yet another. "It was also the sense of community, the sports, the nurturing of one's aesthetic appreciation in a love for poetry and art and nature . . . There were rules, which could rankle even then, but we wanted to be a forceful, giving, constructive part of a working whole." Although the culture of the country has changed, she went on, "I also like to think there is a place in the educational world where fourteen-year-old girls at school are given a sense of honor, of routine, of guidelines."

Then in June a poorly edited issue of *The Lantern* appeared with grammatical mistakes and the use of an obscenity. John Alexander had to decide whether to mail the literary magazine out and be criticized by alumnae, or not mail it out and be condemned by students. Finally, he sent it out with an explanatory letter. After getting the magazine in the mail, Miss LaMonte once again tried to console him. "When I reached the end and the word that so offended you, I passed over that quite calmly, too, thinking what a pity that in these times nothing is withheld." The elderly lady continued: "You live in an age that can't help but offend your fastidious mind, so try to take it as easily as you can and live on to see a happier day."

Her tolerant attitude was no longer widespread, and that spring the trustees suddenly stopped talking to the Alexanders. Applications had fallen off drastically, and so many ninth and tenth graders planned to leave for other schools that enrollment dropped by some sixty students. In a reversal of longstanding tradition, a few day students were admitted for the following fall. Since tuition was still the largest source of school income, a large deficit loomed. In June the trustees met to discuss the crisis, and the headmaster ended up submitting his resignation. In a letter to the faculty, he blamed his failure at Westover on the difficulty of dealing with teenagers in a troublesome time. It was a period, he later reflected, when he and his wife felt like they were in the middle of a battlefield, where alumnae, faculty, and students were all taking aim at each other. "It was," he said, "an impossible mission." In fact, very few heads of schools survived those turbulent years, except for those who were able to maintain the status quo for a little longer.

10

Regaining Balance:
Finding the Courage to Continue

AFTER THE DEPARTURE OF JOHN ALEXANDER DURING THE SUM-
mer of 1971, the board of trustees asked assistant headmaster Joseph Molder to be acting headmaster, while the selection committee looked for a permanent headmaster or
headmistress. Westover was "torn and anguished," in the view of Nancy May Rennell,
head of the committee. Recalling that trustees had turned down two women educators in favor of Iglehart and Alexander, she asked: "Why not concentrate on finding
a woman now?? There must be something to women's lib!" Rebecca Love Drew also
recommended that they find a female, since it might be difficult to find a good man.
"Westover has had its fingers burned twice now," she warned Dorrance Sexton, and it
had one last chance.

Probably the strongest words came from Adele Ervin. "For some sixty years
Westover was ably served by two women Heads—strong, courageous, first-class
individuals—who established a school of purpose and merit. In six years, two male
Heads—weak, ego-centered, second-class—have brought that same institution to the
brink of total collapse. And in this same period, the performance of the Board of
Trustees, the leadership of which also seems to be entirely male, leaves a good deal to
be desired," she wrote angrily to Sexton. Elysabeth Barbour Higgins, a trustee with a
daughter, Hilary, in the class of 1971, worried about the "Women's Lib overtones" of
her friend's letter. And Sexton, referring earnestly but ineptly to a feminist leader,
responded that parts of the letter "leave me with a feeling that Gertrude [*sic*] Steinem

would be proud of them." He also acknowledged that the next president of the board should be a woman. In her reply, Adele admitted that she was not much "in the velvet glove department," but said that "time is running out for Westover."

Meanwhile, Joseph Molder appeared eager to hear from alumnae, who were more and more pleased with him. Adele was glad to discover his sense of humor. Maria Randall Allen, who intended to show him Mary Hillard's essay in *The Education of a Modern Girl*, felt he had "an excellent grasp of things," and she was "ready to have another go at operation Have-Faith." After a long talk with the acting headmaster, Elysabeth Higgins felt sorry for him because he was inheriting a tight budget as well as teachers and students chosen by his predecessor along with the first group of day students while, she assumed, he had "next to no experience on any score," she wrote to Adele. She was glad he was against sensitivity sessions during classes and so many lectures about race relations and the Vietnam War and for more of them about the arts. He "is a good listener," she continued, and "he does not blow hard and pretend to know everything and to have all the answers."

In October, the faculty urged the selection committee to back him as headmaster. What Westover needs most, they stated, was stability. Joe Molder, they said, knows the school well and "the pitfalls of the past"; he also makes everyone feel "cooperative and optimistic." Pupils were polled, and every one of the ninety-eight teenagers who responded wanted Mr. Molder to be their headmaster. He was understanding, open, direct, and enthusiastic, they felt, and one young girl even noticed that he was well organized. "It's amazing how in just six short weeks, one man can lift the spirits and hopes of an entire school as much as Mr. Molder has," another told a reporter for *The Wick*. Years later a senior remembered that he "was like a shining white knight [who] came galloping into Sodom and Gomorra. In his kind and quiet way, he commanded everyone's attention. Thoughtfully, brilliantly, and persistently he won over the hearts of the students and faculty."

The selection committee's interview with the youthful acting head went very well. "What was impressive was how good Joe was," recalled Betsy Michel. "I think it surprised all of us, because he is a quiet, unassuming kind of guy, who chooses his words carefully." Committee members were also impressed by his strong support among pupils and teachers. The first ballot at the board meeting in January of 1972, the month the candidate turned forty, was unanimous in his favor. "Is everybody happy?" a girl asked rhetorically in the March issue of *The Wick.* "The students are, the alumnae are, the faculty are, the trustees are, I guess that means yes, everybody's happy."

Joseph Leighton Molder was born and raised in Worcester, Massachusetts, where his maternal great-grandfather had been mayor. His father, who came from a large family in Georgia, met his mother through her brother at Harvard. After the couple married, Molder's father went into her family's business, the Paul Revere Insurance Company. Young Joe, along with an older sister, had a privileged boyhood of private schools, winter trips to Florida, and summers on Cape Cod. After attending a coeducational elementary school, he was a day student at all-boys' Worcester Academy, graduating cum laude and as president of his class.

He remembers a happy childhood immersed in sports, especially the memory of "a wonderful little Scottish man called Mr. Wakefield" who taught soccer. "Most of all, he taught me that the 'call of the game' was stronger than the discomfort of playing on a cold, damp, dark wintry afternoon or the physical pain of pushing the body to its extremity of endurance." Molder learned to sail at an early age, and during the last year of World War II when he was thirteen, he gave sailing lessons to adults including college professors from Boston. During subsequent summers he taught at boys' camps and came to believe strongly in the importance of jobs for teenagers. At Oberlin College, where he graduated in 1953 with a major in sociology, he was captain of an undefeated soccer team and named an All American soccer player. After two years as a Marine Corps officer, he attended Columbia Business School, then worked at the university for twelve years in admissions, coached soccer, and advised students heading for graduate schools. In New York he became acutely aware of the growing generational unrest. During a protest at Columbia in the late 1960s, students took over his office, forcing him to sit on the steps outside.

During Molder's months as acting headmaster at Westover, the Equal Rights Amendment passed Congress and promised to give American women the same legal stature as men. Meanwhile, he had inherited a school where the honor system had completely collapsed, and the adolescents felt they could get away with anything. The practice of putting "Please Excuse" signs on bedroom doors for privacy was being abused. Study hall was no longer required. And because there were no more rules about lights-out at night, dormitory windows on the upper floors of the main building were ablaze until the early hours of the morning.

In the school year when Molder became headmaster, 1971–72, the student with the reputation for being most rebellious, Susan Ray, was president of the senior class. When she had been elected the previous spring, a horrified John Alexander had asked for another vote by only those who planned to return in the fall. Susan, herself, was shocked at being elected; although she liked to act like a hippie, she regarded herself as a loner. The headmaster set up weekly meetings with her, during which they developed rapport and mutual respect. She found him to be a reasonable and patient person with whom she could be honest, and who always listened to what she had to say. Unlike Mr. Alexander, he never got angry at her reports of misbehavior. Instead, "he became sad," she remembered, making her feel "badly" for him. She confessed that "I didn't want to disappoint him because he never disappointed me." She continued: "I considered myself a rebel, but this man made me feel that there was nothing to rebel against."

Despite their good relationship, Susan was unable to rein in others who were breaking rules. Around that time, a male teacher encountered a girl leaving the dining room with an enormous pile of sandwiches, which she admitted were for her boyfriend, who was spending the weekend in her room. Every week the new headmaster encountered another problem he had never dealt with before. He had watched his predecessor very carefully, he later said, so at least he knew what not to do. A senior that year later remarked on his "calmness," and the way he was "steady when fires were erupting and exploding all around him." She added that "he was quiet in manner but no pushover." And "he was comfortable matching wits with the occasional arrogance that young and cocky women can exude, and [he] did so with great humor and affection." He gradually quieted the school down by not overreacting or expelling students but by making it clear that a girl had to be invited back to Westover. "He took over in a very gentle way," remembered Elizabeth Newton.

Louise Dillingham's belief in older girls raising younger ones may have been more appropriate in the more peaceful past, but in the present when pupils refused to take responsibility and be leaders, this approach resulted in chaos. "My attitude was a hundred percent different," the new headmaster explained. Convinced that teenagers needed the guidance of grownups, he hired a number of young couples to live as residents in the dormitory in order to get the girls to understand and obey the rules. The sociologist-turned-headmaster later observed that it was "very helpful" having married men on corridors to help establish order. He also made sure that every pupil had an academic advisor. And he insisted on sit-down dinners over many objections, when an adult sat at every one of the new round tables in the dining room.

Early on, he realized that the young girls mistakenly regarded freedom and restraint to be opposites. Like Rebecca Love Drew, he knew that "individuality emerges not by flaunting one's liberties, but rather through purposeful self-restraint and training." Adults need to impose discipline until it is internalized by youths, he went on, the way a parent is supposed to say "no," when a daughter puts immediate desires before long-term aspirations. Aware that television made the younger generation aware of the many injustices in the world, he was sympathetic to their "feelings of despair, apathy, and even self-pity," which made it difficult for them to create "a purposeful community," he explained. To foster a sense of hope in young people, he added, it is "essential" for them to learn to take responsibility for their educations as well as for their futures.

Yet the young headmaster also liked to have a good time. When he had first arrived in Middlebury, he recruited eleven girls for a soccer team. "They were a giggly, self-conscious group at first," he recalled. "When two girls bumped into each other, or one slipped and fell to the ground, play would instantly stop, apologies would be profusely uttered, and only after equally profuse reassurances had been given would play resume." Soon they became better players and "began playing the game with abandon and skill," he said. Before long he was coaching three soccer teams and giving team members the impression of "a kind, accessible headmaster who really liked and cared about us." Another girl called him inspiring as "an amazingly talented and graceful" athlete who demonstrated "his patience and skill as a teacher on the playing field," and who taught "through example and gentle reminders." She added that they were more aware of his sense of humor on the soccer field than in, say, Red Hall. Also, the only time he raised his voice was while cheering them on. For someone so serious, another student said, he always had a smile on his face during their games. When watching the lanky headmaster run down the playing field, onlookers learned "about adroitness and the fast, unexpected—almost invisible—move that got the calculated result," Miss Newton noted.

The year before, a young, blonde Dutch physical education teacher had visited Westover, and Molder had recommended that she be hired to coach field hockey, volleyball, and softball. Anneke Rothman was living at the time in New York with her husband, American linguist Jules Rothman, whom she had met in Paris when studying at the Alliance Française. After retiring from teaching in Manhattan and witnessing a holdup near their apartment in Greenwich Village, he wanted to move to the country. As the Rothmans were settling into an apartment in Middlebury in the fall of 1971, Molder unexpectedly asked her to replace the long-time head of the athletic department, Gladys Haring. Mrs. Rothman was reluctant because of her shaky command of English but felt she had little choice. Her husband, a sportsman, helped her with unfamiliar sports terms that first year, and the headmaster was also "very supportive," she remembered.

Youthful Mrs. Rothman, with what an alumna called her "quick wit and booming voice," became a much needed voice of authority. She had been "a real devil" when younger, she admitted, so she knew all the tricks. "It's good to be firm with children," she observed, but "also to not see everything that you can see." Her first challenge was to make girls show up for sports; she sent warnings to those who did not and failed ten or fifteen of them the first term. "From then on there was no problem," she stated matter-of-factly. She was also the one who enforced the dress code. The headmaster was urging alumnae to tolerate what he termed the teenagers' "informal dress and manners," emphasizing that it was "attitude not etiquette" that mattered, but he had banned what he called "offensive, unclean, sloppy, or extreme" clothing. Anneke told the pupils that she, personally, didn't care what they wore, but they should care about the school's image. "And I would send them upstairs, and if they came downstairs with the holes [in their clothes] again, I would send them back upstairs. And I would send them back upstairs. I didn't give up. And I think I was fair about it," she remembered. "*Everyone* wearing holes had to go up."

She also insisted on teaching manners in the dining room, and in Red Hall, and everywhere else. "Discipline in athletics, abiding by the rules, [and] fair play were so instilled in me that I applied them in all branches of school life," she said. When she was in charge of the discipline committee, she never asked a girl to turn another in, unlike in the old days. Instead, she would investigate reports of rule infringements, and then either confront the student under suspicion or drop the matter. Sportsmanship was more important than winning, she told her players repeatedly. She might explain to a defeated team how they might have played better, but she never got angry with them for losing. Consequently, she was one of the few teachers at Westover who was very demanding while also being loved and respected.

Meanwhile, enrollment continued to drop alarmingly, especially among the boarders, as the larger classes graduated and smaller ones took their place. It would continue to decline to as few as 111 pupils, until in 1975 there were only twenty-two girls in the graduating class. "There was an elegiac air about the place," recalled the wife of a teacher. "At lunch there would be discussions about how it would make a nice country club or an old folk's home." While the trustees and administrators were understandably distressed, many of the remaining students liked the smaller classes, bedrooms of their own, and more places to be by themselves. During most of the 1970s, in fact, Westover would be about the size it was originally intended to be. Two instead of three beds were again in double rooms, and there were many more single rooms, making "life upstairs freer, less tense, and altogether nicer," a pupil wrote in *The Wick.*

A much smaller school caused a deepening financial crisis, of course. Three-quarters of the tuition income was gone, and the virtually nonexistent endowment was less than a million dollars. After graduation in 1972, a group of the most active trustees invited the headmaster to an informal meeting in the Common Room. Board president Dorrance Sexton was there, as well as his good friend Benjamin Belcher, and two other male board members. Alumnae Louise "Weedie" McKelvy Walker and Eunice Groark were there, along with another woman. Sexton began by speaking about the dire prospects of the school: it was a half million dollars in debt and nearing bankruptcy. He suggested taking a straw vote about whether or not Westover should stay open. As the trustees went around the room, three of the men voted "no" and two of the women voted "yes." When they got to Weedie Walker, who

The headmaster and students in line on the athletic field.

was president-elect of the board, she also voted yes. Sexton would be the last to cast a vote. Molder, who was listening intently, was certain that a successful businessman like Dorrance Sexton believed "in his heart of hearts" that the right decision was to close the school. Then Sexton spoke. If Weedie wanted to make a go of it, he said, he would vote with her. So in a tense, close, and courageous vote, they decided to recommend to the full board that Westover try to carry on a little while longer.

The following school year, 1972–1973, there was a recession, reducing the ability of parents to pay full or even any tuition at all. At the same time, an oil crisis drastically drove up the cost of heating the drafty old main building. Meanwhile, the school was continuing to try to compete with former boys' schools for female students. The effect was as if "someone had thrown a firebomb into the middle of Red Hall," recalled Eunice Groark. The way the trustees and administration were spending unrestricted endowment funds to keep going "almost bordered on the illegal," the attorney added. She was asked to look into how much more of the endowment could be spent before the school had to declare bankruptcy, and she even read the school charter to see where any remaining assets would go.

Westover was still surviving year-to-year, without anyone knowing whether each year would be its last. Richard Uhl, a recently retired Madison Avenue advertising man whom Molder had recruited to the board, traveled to Middlebury for a meeting on a bitterly cold, snowy day in the late autumn of 1976, where he found the trustees gathered around the fireplace in the headmistresses' former sitting room trying to stay warm. The treasurer's report was so dire that it was "another way of saying that the next year the school was out of business," he remembered. "It was a terrible shock." Weedie Walker had a vivid memory from that terrible time, too. "I shall never forget one cold night walking across the playing field in a crisp, crunchy snow to the main school building, which was ablaze with lights in every window, with a businessman friend and co-trustee, when he said: 'It is just like sitting helplessly watching the *Titanic* sink slowly in icy waters.'"

Molder, making use of his M.B.A. degree, rolled up his sleeves and got to work. He had "a tremendously good business head," acknowledged Adele Ervin later. "He kept the school going by cutting expenses in the right way. He was trying to buy time. We didn't see that right away." Early on, he promoted Jeannette Brown, a switchboard operator, to be head of housekeeping and then business manager, along with her hus-band (while enrolling their daughters, Patricia and Kathleen, in the classes of 1975 and 1977). "The rug in Red Hall was filthy," she remembered, adding that the school was being run with a large housekeeping staff that did very little. An energetic person from a large Connecticut family, she gave orders in a rapid-fire manner; she would also pitch in herself—raising window shades and sweeping the front walk—when there was no one else to do it. Before long, she cut her staff in half while having everything, from attic to basement, organized, cleaned, polished, and painted. She also managed to get a new kitchen staff to make better meals. Most important of all, she had insulation and storm windows installed and the heating system made more efficient. "She could turn straw into gold before your very eyes," marveled Eunice Groark. And, amazingly, as the operating costs of the school were reduced by a third, the handsome and historic building looked better than ever.

With his ability to spot talent, the headmaster promoted a secretary, Barbara Loveridge, to be director of admissions. Her job was to make prospective students and parents understand that Westover was academically strong, not just a place for girls unable to compete with boys, so she invited visitors to meet teachers and attend classes. She would ask students to show them around while worrying about what the girls would be wearing. Returning alumnae were frequently dismayed by all the changes. Parents were often at odds with their daughters about the merits of the school. Sometimes even board members could not persuade their daughters to apply to a girls' school; Eunice Groark would leave the board around the time her three daughters enrolled in coeducational preparatory schools. "It was a very difficult time. I could only say so much. The school had to speak for itself. It was not for everyone, but for some girls it was absolutely what they needed," Barbara Loveridge recalled. An outgoing and gregarious woman, she had "a wonderful motherly touch with everybody," Molder said. Even families who failed to apply praised her friendliness in their thank-you letters to him. She remembered that "I really did love that school, and I hope I conveyed that to people. I loved the warmth, the people, and almost every girl who was there."

Meanwhile, the headmaster wanted to make the teaching better than ever. He later reflected that he spent more time searching for excellent instructors excited by their fields than anything else. Gradually, he created a group of compatible young teachers who stayed for years, many for the remainder of their careers. They were offered housing in the lovely village and day care at Virginia House for their children, who grew up like brothers and sisters, seeing each other at dinner time and playing together afterward in Red Hall. He insisted that the board give teachers at least small raises every year for the sake of morale, implying that he would resign if they did not. Almost forty years later, Robert Havery, the choirmaster who had arrived in 1968, said it was still exciting working together with his accomplished colleagues. At the time the school had a reputation as a supportive environment strong in art and music, but people "were not recognizing the firepower of the academic program," Molder complained. Only five years after he became headmaster, outside educators would attribute most of Westover's appeal to "its very competent, imaginative, enthusiastic, and concerned teachers." Hiring gifted people was the part of his legacy of which Joseph Molder would be most proud.

Among the young teachers was young Ann Maiorino, the first person Molder hired after becoming headmaster. One of only three women in her class to graduate as a mathematics major from Fordham University in 1970, she then taught math at St. Agnes Cathedral High School in Rockville Center on Long Island. Petite and pretty with dark hair and hazel eyes, she had recently become engaged to a college classmate, Ben Pollina. When the couple decided to get married in the summer of 1972, she began looking for a temporary teaching job near New Haven, Connecticut, where her fiancé would be studying at Yale for a Ph.D. in mathematics. She had a grant to enroll in a master's program in mathematical scholarship for teachers at New York University, which was exposing her to some of the finest and most famous minds in her field. "It is here, in the inductive foundations of mathematics that one has the opportunity to be truly creative," she wrote a few years later. "Here a mathematician must engage every facet of his humanity, suspending disbelief and relying on his vision to propose a new coalescence of the elements of human experience." She still had a year to go when she asked her advisor for a leave of absence so she could move to Connecticut. He strongly advised against it, fearing that she would never finish, and he proposed a program where she had to attend classes in Manhattan only one night a week, so she was able to complete the degree the next year.

In the Yale placement office, she saw a small notice on the bulletin board about an opening at a school called Westover, which she knew nothing about. Since she lacked a teaching certificate, she needed a position at a parochial or private school. Driving to Middlebury for an interview, she was enthralled by the beauty of the countryside. Miss Newton greeted her warmly and escorted her to her sitting room, where they smoked cigarettes and talked about teaching and New York. When the young mathematician realized that Westover wanted someone to teach calculus, she was excited but also apprehensive. "I was dying to teach upper level mathematics," she recalled, but realized she had little teaching experience. When Joe Molder telephoned to offer her the job, she was so eager to say "yes" that she didn't let him finish his sentence. "It felt like a dream job," she remembered. The following year, the much older chairman of the mathematics department, Margaret Smertenko, retired, and Molder offered the twenty-five-year-old Ann Pollina the position. "That was a wonderful advancement for a young teacher," she later marveled.

The headmaster had developed a careful interviewing process involving students and teachers that allowed faculty members to veto prospective colleagues. The day of Ann's interview, pupils on the hiring committee took her to lunch. "She was very sweet, smart, and attractive," they thought, but perhaps a little too quiet, but Susan Wadsworth remembered saying that she thought the candidate had "hidden strength." The next year, Susan was in her calculus class, where Ann "spent half the year catching us up with what we should have learned the previous year, and then we moved into real calculus," she said. "Mrs. Pollina was always a most patient, kind, and enthusiastic teacher." Other students from the 1970s have similar memories. "Math was not my best subject, but I remember looking forward to her class and loved the way she explained things," said Debra Gartzman. Another girl did very well in calculus, thanks to her teacher, and eventually went to medical school and became a cardiologist. A thirteen-year-old, Ivette Caldera, who arrived from Nicaragua knowing little English, was always grateful that her "sweet young teacher" took the time to explain math very slowly to her "with tenderness and compassion," even saying the numbers in Spanish. To a teenager who had nightmares about math, "Ann was like a miracle," someone who, "in her loving, no-nonsense, humorous way," got her over her anxiety and doing advanced math.

Two years later, the Pollinas moved to an apartment in Virginia House nearer the teachers who had become their friends. "We came with like-minded people at the same

English teacher Bruce Coffin in class.
CHRISTOPHER LITTLE.

stage of life," Ann said. "We loved working together, we loved being together, and we wanted to make the school even better and stronger." One year, she and Shamus Weber of the English department put together an evening seminar for seniors and faculty, "Particles, Principles, Paradigms & Problems," about issues in literature, philosophy, math, and science. It was not necessarily the intent, but the intellectual excitement generated by such sessions began to rub off on students, especially the growing number of academically serious day and scholarship students. "It was a very heady time," Ann remembered. "We all had the sense that this was a wonderful place where we could make a difference." Once assuming that she would only stay until her husband got his degree, she gradually changed her mind, and Ben Pollina became a professor at the University of Hartford.

During those difficult years, the energetic Miss Newton was acting as the academic, faculty, and student deans. She had been at Westover since 1951, and her institutional memory was invaluable. It was she who wanted Shamus Weber, by then in his early thirties, to be chairman of the English department, and soon he was. The two strong-minded intellectuals from Chicago, both with degrees from Yale, used to argue about what to teach and how to grade, but with their shared streak of irreverence and deep love of literature, they respected each other and got along well. It was a "lively" English department, in the eyes of evaluators a few years later, with interesting electives and teachers determined to teach teenagers both to write well and to appreciate literature.

In May of 1972, the two had recommended that the headmaster hire a young teacher named Bruce Coffin. A native of Vermont, he had a master's degree in English literature from New York University and had taught in England and at a coed day school in New Jersey. He was used to being addressed formally, but during his first year at Westover, where some teachers were called by their first names, the senior class president called him "Bruce" for a few days, until he told her it didn't sound right. "Okay, Mr. Coffin," she said, and that was the end of that. Another student asked him to be her advisor despite all the red ink he used on student papers. "He was tough, he was serious, but all in all, I learned," she explained. His legendary corrections even continued after she graduated and went to college. "At one point, he sent me back a letter I had written to him, re-punctuated and corrected; with that infamous red ink, and a comment that he wasn't sure that Harvard was teaching me all that it could, and was I sure I wanted to major in English?"

In 1973, Joe Molder and Liz Newton, as her colleagues called her, attended a job fair at Wesleyan University in the hope of finding a Latin teacher. That day Alice Hallaran met them by mistake thinking they were looking for a science teacher. The headmaster was so impressed with the young teacher with degrees from Wheaton and Smith that he invited her and her husband, Michael or "Terry," to Middlebury for interviews. As the headmaster showed the Hallarans around, Terry, a doctor's son from Ohio, noticed the portrait of Louise Dillingham in the Common Room. He was stunned to realize that it was his aunt, who had "run some girls' school back East," he vaguely remembered. The Hallarans, both in their twenties, were looking for a place to live while Terry finished pre-med studies at Wesleyan, his alma mater. They agreed to be residents at Westover while Alice taught biology there. The next school year, 1974–75, Molder asked the Hallarans to chair the department. The young couple good-naturedly put together an excellent science program in a severely limited space, even building a greenhouse for it. Before long the curly-haired Terry, who also coached soccer and acted and sang male parts in student performances, was described in *The Wick* by the teenage girls as the "most attractive male on campus."

After Susan Ray, a girl named Ellen Harrington was president of the senior class. Early in the fall term, upperclassmen dropped water balloons from windows onto new girls, and Molder was trying to decide if it was a serious matter or a mischievous prank. He called Ellen into his office and asked her opinion. "Well, chief, I think I'd let that one go," she advised, and he did, and later believed that she had been absolutely right. She was able to defuse tension and trouble by encouraging other harmless practical jokes, like leading a cow into the schoolroom, all of which amused the headmaster. "Well, wouldn't you know they would come up with something like that," he would remark with a smile to the faculty, relieved that it was nothing more serious. Many teenagers appreciated getting his full attention, which is "a pretty unique gift to offer an adolescent," said a member of the class of 1974, as "he gave serious consideration (or at least the appearance of it) to the most outrageous proposals," thus dissuading them from "revolt and anti-administration feelings." When Susan Schorr was head of school the following year, 1973–74, she met with him often. With his "quiet, dignified manner," he also taught her how to be fair and how to be diplomatic, while keeping his opinions to himself and allowing her to try to solve problems her own way.

Margaret Thayer and her friends in the class of 1981 liked to stay up late studying in classrooms or singing and playing the guitar on the balcony of the chapel. They noticed that the headmaster kept a jar of candy on his desk in his office, which he usually left open at night. "Sometimes, during those late nights, looking for adventure or to satisfy a sweet craving, we would 'sneak' into Joe's office, 'steal' pieces of candy and leave feeling satisfied and victorious," she later confessed. She felt a little guilty at the time, but since he "never announced his discovery or displeasure of the crime, and continued to leave his office unlocked and the candy jar filled and on full display, we came to imagine that perhaps he either enjoyed the idea . . . or that he knew it was a minor infringement, a harmless crime, and that his moral focus was needed elsewhere." In any event, his leniency about taking candy "kindled our appreciation and respect for him, and we felt we had this secret bond."

Interestingly, it was younger teachers at the time who called for more order and older ones who resisted regimentation. Jock Schumacher had recently called for "universal human liberation" in a long article in *The Wick*, which was very sympathetic to the women's liberation movement. For a while there was tension between the newer teachers and Miss Newton, who did not like to think of herself as a disciplinarian outside the classroom, but eventually it dissipated. Once she invited several of her younger colleagues to her sitting room for a reading of Edward Albee's drama *Who's Afraid of Virginia Woolf.* As she and Terry Hallaran shouted the raw, argumentative dialogue of the lead roles, the students who overheard them—unaware that it was a play—were worried that the popular Terry was going to be fired.

The headmaster supported the desire of the younger members of the faculty for more regulations, but he knew he could not impose them. When he wanted to make another rule, his style was to ask a committee of students and teachers to study a situation and make a recommendation. Sometimes, as in soccer games, feint was involved.

When the matter arose about visits of boys to bedrooms, he told Anneke Rothman that it should, as usual, be decided by committee. "And it's not going to happen," he remarked, aware that the trustees were dead set against it. "What do you mean?" she asked. "We have to have meetings, and discussions, and make a compromise on boys being in the dorms upstairs? And then we make a decision, when we already know it's not going to happen? That's false democracy, Joe." And he replied, "Oh, do it anyway." And she did. "Even though at times you were not part of the decision making, you felt as if you were," she reflected later.

At times he was receptive to the girls' proposals, even teaching them how to present them effectively. "We were very creative, and in today's terminology, 'out of the box thinkers,'" remembered Mary Jane "M. J." Hemmings, who, as senior class president, persuaded him to let her class have the school's first prom and first senior trip. "Whenever we went to him with one of our 'out of the box suggestions,' he would bow his head, and shake it a little and give a slight sigh, and say, 'what have you young ladies been up to now?'" During lengthy meetings, he listened to suggestions, asking students to attempt to reach a consensus before putting a matter to a vote. If a vote was not what he had in mind, however, he would quietly say that the issue needed more thought. Then the girls went away until they came back with the right decision. In this way, rules were gradually tightened again about smoking, study hall and class attendance, independent study, and lights out at night.

Meanwhile, the young girls got to know the Molders as a family, and they realized that their headmaster was a respectful and affectionate husband and father. There was Mrs. Molder, or Beth, sons Steven and David, and daughter Marjorie, who were twelve, seven, and nine when their father became headmaster. When Marjorie entered Westover, Mr. Molder was "both a loving father and a very fair-minded headmaster," a roommate remembered. He expected his daughter to follow all the rules, even signing out when she walked across the playing field to go home to Lee House. The

A group of students and a teacher outside chapel, 1970s.
WESTOVER SCHOOL ARCHIVE.

Molders ate dinner in the school dining room almost every evening, and they welcomed girls into their home to cook. "It was as if we, the students, were an extension of their family," remembered an alumna. Another said he was like an ideal father: "We were entrusted into his care, and I felt that he never betrayed that trust." One time several students were invited to Lee House to help Mrs. Molder make the meringue and ice cream dessert called baked Alaska. "Of course it turned into a 'creative' exercise, with the result being the worst baked Alaska in history, but Mr. Molder just smiled and said, 'what have you young ladies been up to now?'" remembered M. J. Hemmings. Margaret Thayer idealized him as a parental figure, noting the contrast between herself, a teenager who was all "drama and craziness," and the "tall, quiet, shy, wise, family man." She notes that she was always "very aware of his presence—of this person I perceived as honorable, honest, noble, disciplined, humble, gentle, kind, loyal, good, wise and quietly inspired, by what I didn't know, but who I inherently trusted," she said. "Mr. Molder was a clear and present reminder of the possibilities and value of a steady and moral soul."

Beth Molder was born Elizabeth McElroy in Providence, the daughter of a Protestant minister. The couple met at Oberlin, but their romance blossomed when she moved to Worcester to work for the YWCA, and where he had a summer job with the Chamber of Commerce; they married in 1959. Beth and her younger sister grew up in Massachusetts, where her father had parishes, and later in Missouri. She admitted that she had arrived in Middlebury without enthusiasm but came to appreciate female institutions after seeing Westover's positive impact on so many young girls, including her own daughter. Beth had been an exchange student in Denmark, and at Westover she took a strong interest in the growing number of foreign students. She met with them individually, arranged international dances with other schools, and made the traditional meals of their native countries at Lee House. She was involved in other activities, as well. At first she volunteered her time and later received a small salary as Director of Community Relations. As hostess and partner of her more reserved husband, she was warm and outgoing. "She was extremely nice to everybody," said Jean Van Sinderen Henry, an alumna who lived in Middlebury and was married to longtime board treasurer Donald Henry. Beth Molder's kindness was evident one spring when she heard that a senior on a full scholarship could not afford to buy flowers to carry on graduation day like all her classmates. As the graduates were lining up and bouquets were being handed out, Mrs. Molder walked over to her and gave her some flowers.

Still, despite the couple's successes at the school, it continued to be difficult for the headmaster to navigate the gap between what the alumnae expected and how the students behaved. "The sudden shift in the culture was so great that you just couldn't bridge it," he explained. He also realized that the opinions of what he called "exceptionally active" alumnae tended to "overwhelmingly predominate over other viewpoints." Girls treasured relationships with friends and teachers, interesting classes and activities, and "a friendly and informal atmosphere," he pointed out. For their part, the faculty appreciated motivated pupils, interesting and able fellow teachers, independence in the classroom, participation in school policy, and fair compensation. And parents were concerned most of all about the school's ambience, the schedule, and the quality of teaching and advising. He could not recall a single time when a parent, unless she was an alumna, brought up the importance of chapel services. Yet, he said, he had rarely gone to a meeting of alumnae when the subject of chapel did not come up.

Besides chapel, he understood, alumnae also valued the old traditions, the honor system, and what he called the "decorum" of the girls. But it was useless, he still tried to tell them, to worry about the way teenagers dressed or wore their hair. "You could correct this, correct that, but it would always come out another way," he said about their rebelliousness, believing that it was wiser to use "persuasion and example rather than coercion." It was more important, he said again and again, to pay attention to what was happening in the classroom. In dealing with youth, "we work with a substance which parallels hard steel more than moist, fresh clay, and requires strong tools, patience and strength, in order to affect a gradual change," he believed. "The student is more like the force within the seed which propels the seedling when it germinates through the soil, and we are like the forces of the sun, rain and wind, which the young seedling or sapling must embrace, resist, adapt to, or [be shaped by]." Eventually, as alumnae saw their own children and grandchildren acting the same way as girls at Westover, they stopped blaming the headmaster for the way they behaved.

Joe Molder had always worked easily with the businessmen on the board, but they had come under increasing criticism from alumnae. In 1973, Weedie Walker, who had been involved with the school for a decade, became the first woman president of the board of trustees. She fiercely loved the small girls' school, where she said that her young mind and heart had been opened—"that sudden awareness, accompanied by a growing sense of judgment"—had happened at Westover. After graduating in 1932, she had a debut at the Plaza Hotel in New York City, and then she studied art history in Florence and traveled around the world. She married an executive at Bethlehem Steel Corporation, gave birth to three sons, and became actively involved in volunteer work in Pennsylvania. Now she walked through Red Hall "as if she owned the place," remembered a student at the time.

One of her first acts after becoming board president was to write her old teacher, Helen LaMonte, undoubtedly for courage in dealing with the challenges ahead. Miss LaMonte, by then a hundred and one years old, had recently refused her small pension from Westover—because "I feel that I have overextended my three-score years and ten so outrageously," she explained—and was instead sending small checks to Middlebury in response to the school's fundraising appeals. She replied to Weedie with words of encouragement from her bed, reminding her former pupil of her strength. "You will give many hours of your time and wisdom but grow in the giving," she wrote. She ended her letter by declaring her "absolute confidence in your always being the little Dresden doll who can put on the tires." When Weedie Walker spoke at graduation a few months later, in May of 1974, she read at length from her teacher's long letter, including the wise words: "Expect change always; without it there is nothing. It is all part of growth."

The letter, Mrs. Walker told the graduating class, reminded her of the way Westover had always emphasized spirituality and the arts, especially when she had graduated during the last year of Miss Hillard's reign. Then the board president, who was around sixty years old, gave the graduates a bit of traditional womanly advice in that era of the women's liberation movement. "I just can't tell you how really great a feeling it is to *enjoy* being a woman, to be proud of it, and feel an inner strength, which women must have in order to be able to give strength to others," she said, adding that she knew this despite never going to college or holding a paying job. "You may not want to choose the life I've led, but I will give you one hint I have found very helpful—learn to think as much as possible like a man, but act and enjoy being as feminine as possible while you are doing it." Then she added: "It's pretty effective."

Only a few months later, Dorrance Sexton warned her that Westover was still not attracting enough pupils to cover its operating expenses. It would be better to "close this year than to attempt to stagger through until our assets are exhausted," he wrote. Ominously, fundraising had fallen way below the level of the year before, and he most likely did not want to continue raising and giving money to what he regarded as a lost cause. "My reasons are numerous," he continued, "but not least of them are a feeling of moral obligation to take care of some of the older faculty, and that a school of Westover's standing should bow out gracefully." Around that time Weedie had lunch with him and Benjamin Belcher in Lakeville, and she was informed again that there was no way to keep the school going. As she drove back to Middlebury, she despaired of even finding a buyer for the beautiful old school building. Another time, when she and her husband were on a hunting weekend with the Sextons in the Poconos, Dorrance told her again that there was no hope. At this point she became angry and defiant. "I knew I had been elected at a time when closing down the school was possible, but after that night I felt a real personal responsibility to *make* it work. I became 'a woman in a hurry'—stubborn, stubborn, stubborn."

Meanwhile, "Joe wouldn't talk," remembered Adele Ervin, who had joined the board. He also seemed stubborn, and he would not listen to anyone. "He had a vision, but it was not articulated." In fact, he wanted Westover to stay a small, independent, primarily residential girls' school that offered an excellent education. Molder, who had done advanced work in math and was teaching the few physics students, had a mind like a mathematician's that "angled and meandered about a problem," another administrator said. While working long hours and resisting taking a raise, he would observe, he would ponder, and then there would be, in effect, a mathematical breakthrough and a solution to a problem. "He was silent, but he ran deep," noticed Eunice Groark, like so many others. But Weedie Walker thought that the quiet, young headmaster needed to be pushed and prodded, and she called him almost every day for lengthy conversations.

The two struggled for control of the agenda and, since the stakes were so high, there was enormous tension at board meetings. One of the areas of deep disagreement was scholarships. Molder wanted to give them generously, while Weedie Walker and other trustees resisted doing so in the face of huge deficits. He argued that "if you have an empty bed, and you give a twenty thousand dollar scholarship, it's not costing you

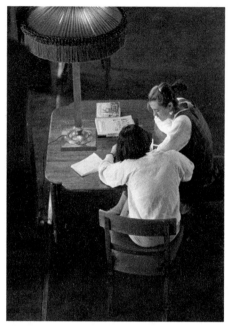

Studying in Red Hall under a lamp with a Victorian lampshade. SVEN MARTSON.

anything," especially if a family pays a portion of the tuition. "Rightly or wrongly, I stood alone in my belief that by far the best, quickest, and in the long run least expensive results would come from investing in financial aid," he said. An anonymous donor who pledged one hundred thousand dollars for scholarships during that time turned out to be the headmaster himself, drawing on family funds.

He also conceived of a scholarship for daughters of teachers, perhaps after meeting young Holly Kennedy. At the age of thirteen, she had arrived all by herself for an interview, getting to Middlebury from Pennsylvania by train and taxi with a suitcase in one hand and a bag of books and a teddy bear in another. When the admissions director looked around for her parents, the girl explained that her father was dead and her mother, a teacher, was at work. Holly was given a full scholarship at Westover before going on to Harvard. "We used the endowment to purchase good students," recalled Eunice Groark. As Molder tried to enroll a wider diversity of students of ability, regardless of their religious or racial backgrounds, there were a few African-Americans in almost every class, including M. J. Hemmings, who won an award for her independence and courage before being elected president of the senior class. She later credited Shamus Weber for helping her in English and Ann Pollina for getting her to enjoy and excel in mathematics before entering the University of Pennsylvania as a math major. After initially resisting going to a nearly all-white school, she said that Westover "saved me from a different kind of life. I blossomed there. It allowed me to be everything that I could be."

Meanwhile, some trustees worried that Joe Molder was not an extroverted "Mr. Chips kind of headmaster," in the words of Richard Uhl, and because of his Yankee reserve, he was unable to effectively promote Westover. Others, like Adele Ervin, feared that he was not committed enough to the idea of a girls' school. She urged him to visit alumnae around the country, the way she and Miss Dillingham had done in the

1950s. Instead, what he wanted to do was "to build the school from the inside out," he said, by attracting the right teachers and pupils, and allowing the school's reputation to spread by itself. "In terms of personality, I'm an inside person, not an outside person," he said. A trustee argued for hiring an assistant headmaster "to be a bit of a pied-piper" for the school. "Somehow or other," he wrote to the board, "Westover must regain its confidence and pride." Early on, the Molders had visited Helen LaMonte, where they were charmed by the way she had made her way over to a bookcase and chosen children's books exactly the right ages for their youngsters. "No one with such a good face as Joe's could be anything but good," she had written to Weedie Walker afterward. But, still, an unnamed member of the board noted in a confidential memorandum at the time that "like it or not, goodness does not sell itself."

So the headmaster hired a young man named Jerry Van Voorhis to be assistant principal and "a kind of Mr. Outside" to travel throughout the country to recruit students. Soon he had another challenge after Westover was asked to be featured in a documentary about independent schools for CBS's "Who's Who" television program. The school was asked to "'bare its soul,' directly to the American public," according to Van Voorhis; the trustees agreed to do it because it was an extraordinary, if risky, opportunity for publicity. Some people thought the girls' school was selected because Theodate Pope Riddle's neoclassical design was so photogenic. Others credited Adele Ervin, who had suggested her alma mater when CBS contacted the National Association of Independent Schools, where she worked. Yet others wondered if the choice had anything to do with the fact that Babe Paley, a member of the class of 1934, was the wife of the CBS board chairman William Paley.

In any event, in the fall of 1976 the network spent a week shooting hours of film featuring senior Mary Duncan, who had previously attended a public school. Miss Newton, who loved directing student plays, was in her element, suggesting scenes and camera angles, all the while making sure that the school schedule was not disrupted. A few months later, the seventeen-minute segment was aired to an audience of thirty million viewers. There was footage of students sitting in Red Hall, singing in chapel, and meeting in the Common Room, where they talked before the camera about making close friends, becoming more independent, and concentrating on their schoolwork at the small country school. "I felt they did an amazing job of capturing Westover in a very positive and warm sense," observed Weedie Walker, reflecting the prevailing view. The publicity boosted everyone's pride in Westover, and, said Van Voorhis, "it got the school back into the game."

The next month Molder's son Steven flew the headmaster and Jerry Van Voorhis to upstate New York to show the film to a frail Helen LaMonte, who was unable to get the program on her television. She must have been startled to see Westover girls without their distinctive uniforms, and she didn't say very much. It may have made her remember the elation with which the school had originally opened. Or maybe it reminded her of the distressing difficulties during the past few years. Whatever the case, the centenarian caught a glimpse of a racially diverse group of attractive and thoughtful teenagers of the same age as those she had taught so well so many years ago. Afterward, she graciously wrote the headmaster that her nursing home "is a good place for me to be in my second century but my heart is always at the School where I worked and lived for so long and to see it once more and the lively faces of the girls now there gave me happiness beyond all telling."

The same month the CBS film was shown, in January of 1977, the trustees held their winter meeting. Present was Manhattan lawyer Hubert "T" Mandeville, who had just rejoined the board. He had first joined in 1968, when his daughter Meredith was a student. A graduate of Yale's engineering and law schools, he was a patent attorney with a number of business investments. He was appalled that the school's budget remained in the red and that the last of the endowment was being spent. He was also tired of hearing about the board's inability to raise money, inhibited about fundraising because of its fears that the school might go under. The next day, a Sunday, he telephoned Weedie Walker and offered to give Westover half a million dollars if it could raise a million dollars within three months. The board became galvanized, accepted the challenge, and named Van Voorhis chairman of the fund drive. Mrs. Walker, who had repeatedly remarked that Westover would close over her dead body, began traveling to even the smallest gathering of alumnae to ask for money. Mandeville "held her feet to the fire and at the same time was her most important cheerleader," recalled Betsy Michel. He extended the deadline and, finally, by the spring and the summer of 1978, the challenge grant was more than matched.

In May of 1978, as Weedie Walker stepped down after five years as president of the board, she received the Westover Award. In her acceptance speech, she pointed out the many ways the school was finally succeeding. Everyone thought that the class of 1978 was wonderful. Students' test scores and college acceptances were improving and most students were studying hard once again. The school was reaching full enrollment, the endowment was growing, and the budget was expected to be balanced soon. "I have been bold enough to leave a dream for Westover," she had written to incoming board president, Patricia Castles Acheson, a few months before. "I have wanted the kind of spirit we found in our Westover heritage available for girls in the future . . . And I just happened to be in a position to do something about it. I have held tenaciously to that goal—some say stubbornly. It *is* in sight."

The headmaster was also praised that spring for his part in saving the school. "As it turned out, Joe was the perfect choice" for his position, observed Betsy Michel. "He had the determination and he had the depth." The educators on the 1978 accreditation committee were very impressed by his open and competent managerial style. He had taken over the school at "a time of disaster" and "steered it through its darkest hours and into a new day," they wrote in their report. "Without him, we doubt if Westover School would exist today." Now the school for girls was ready to move from "a time of survival to one of confidence," and they suggested that it begin planning for the future.

11

Classroom Innovations:
Learning from Girls

FOR AS LONG AS ANYONE COULD REMEMBER, WESTOVER'S SCIENCE department in the old Methodist church's stables had been too small. When physics was first offered in the 1930s, Louise Dillingham had made room for it in the basement of the main building. Three decades later, the biology and chemistry classrooms were still crowded and noisy, and the space for physics was "almost desperately inadequate," noted the 1968 accreditation committee. Ten years after that, the chemistry lab continued to be so cramped that science teacher Terry Hallaran worried about flammable fumes sparking an explosion. Nonetheless, Terry and his wife, Alice, "cheerfully arrange and rearrange the different classes and inspire students with their own interest and expertise," the educators observed, while enthusiastically adding interesting electives and an Advanced Placement class. Meanwhile, the number of students taking science had increased dramatically, making the overcrowding worse than ever. While the school had been struggling to survive, it had been impossible to do much about the situation, let alone match impressive science facilities at former boys' schools, which were now attracting girls interested in science.

Now that the headmaster and the board of trustees were optimistically looking toward the future, they began talking about what to do. Joe Molder pointed out to the board that the school's excellence was due to its fine faculty, not its facilities. But, he went on, classrooms must be up-to-date if they were going to convince potential pupils and their parents of the advantages of going to a small and pretty school, let alone to maintain its accreditation. Westover, which had a fine collection of art history books but relatively few volumes in the sciences, had also outgrown its lovely Mary R. Hillard Memorial Library. Novels were shelved in the Common Room, while reference books were placed here and there. The original school building and its idyllic surroundings are so attractive, Molder told the trustees, that Westover had been able to rest on this strength for too long.

At first there was talk among board members about again putting science classrooms and laboratories in the basement of the main building, or in the infirmary, or in Virginia House. Around that time, businessman C. Lawson Reed, Jr., a graduate of Hotchkiss and Yale, joined the board. (His wife, the former Dorothy Whittaker, was a member of the class of 1941 along with Emily Detwiler Uhl, whose husband was already a trustee; also, the Reed daughters, Janet and Dorothy, had graduated from Westover in 1964 and 1968.) Patricia Acheson, the new board president, soon became an enthusiastic admirer of the new trustee, saying that he had "a mind like a steel trap" as well as intriguing and progressive ideas about education, which were widening everyone's perspective.

The trustees were still searching for "a unique mission" for Westover, something that would call attention to the school. It had been founded early in the century when private boys' schools excluded girls, in an era when men and women were expected to live very different kinds of lives. Now as gender roles were becoming more alike, there was an urgent need to find a compelling reason for educating girls together. Only a few years earlier, Matina Horner of Harvard had published her research about the "fear of success" among college women, but its implications were not yet widespread. Lawson Reed urged the board to do something bigger and better than what it had in mind: to build an entirely new structure devoted to science, which would also hold all the school's books. Not only would a state-of-the-art science building be a dramatic break from the past, but it would also show the school's seriousness about educating girls for the modern world. The decision to go ahead with

Science teacher Terry Hallaran.

this plan, when Westover was just emerging from near bankruptcy, was "a pretty gutsy move," admitted trustee Betsy Michel later, but "we never lost our momentum—we couldn't afford to."

This new building became Mrs. Acheson's cause. Annual fund and capital gifts were increasing—Molder called the generosity of the alumnae "perhaps the greatest strength of the school"—and by September of 1981 more than $1.5 million had been raised, but double the amount was needed to break ground. "If we make our goal and make the building a reality, there is no question in my mind that Westover will once again lead the pack," the board president wrote to her predecessor, Weedie Walker. "We have lost students, as you well know, because of our antiquated science lab. People don't take in A.P. scores as they do physics facilities. It is my dream to see this building."

A member of Westover's class of 1942, Pat, as everyone called Mrs. Acheson, had undoubtedly pleased Louise Dillingham by graduating cum laude from Bryn Mawr, her headmistress's alma mater. She went on to teach at the National Cathedral School for Girls in Washington, D.C., and elsewhere, as well as to write several history textbooks. Her boarding school classmates recalled her as brilliant but intense and outspoken, and

A class meeting in the newest library. SVEN MARTSON.

some of them had wondered whether she would be the right person to head the board. The headmaster had also worried, so several trustees had taken her aside and told her to run the board, but let Joe Molder run the school. And she did. "Nothing at Westover surprised me more than to see the success of our partnership," Molder later said. In fact, Pat Acheson became an effective and inspiring leader who was determined to make Westover, once again, what she regarded as the best school in the world. There was never any doubt that her young daughter, Eleanor, would go there, too. "I knew I was going to Westover before I even knew it was a school," she would later say.

On the recommendation of noted architect Edward Barnes, the board's building committee hired young architects Charles Gwathmey and Robert Siegel of Gwathmey Siegel & Associates. "After a few false starts," Pat Acheson reported, they "really got the spirit of the place," and in a few months came up with what she called "the perfect plan." What everyone loved about the architectural drawing was the way it meticulously repeated motifs from Theodate Pope Riddle's masterpiece like the look of the slate roof and the creamy stucco walls. A long covered arcade, joining the old building to the new one, had the same arches and herringbone brick walkway as the original cloister. (Some people were disappointed that the plan eliminated the large, bright corner schoolroom, and for years afterward boarders would have to do their homework in the lower level of the LBD student activities building.) In an ingenious touch, steps leading down from the arcade to the playing field would serve as a grandstand. And a tower at the far end, echoing the existing big belfry on the original building, would become an observatory, making it possible to offer astronomy as an elective.

With three spacious and sunny science classrooms with handsome black stone surfaces, each with teaching and laboratory areas, there was at last enough room to offer all the academic requirements as well as many electives like botany, geology, meteorology, earth science, marine biology, and ornithology. Deeply involved with the design, Lawson Reed, who had founded the scientific Xomox Corporation in Cincinnati, had insisted that the building be equipped with enough cables for the eventual installation of advanced computer technology. Besides the large space for science, which even included a small greenhouse, the new library had shelves for twice as many books as the old one. On Westover's seventieth-fifth anniversary in the spring of 1984, the $4 million Adams Library and Whittaker Science building was dedicated. The following February, the building graced the cover of *Architectural Record* magazine and went on to win seven prizes, including the American Institute of Architects' most prestigious design award.

Even so, the original square-sided structure remained the heart of the school. Around 1970, when the school's teenagers were rebelling against its traditions, they surprised the administration by resisting suggestions about updating the Victorian décor in Red Hall. It was there, only a few years later, when an elderly Archibald MacLeish gave his last talk in Red Hall, which looked the same as when he had first seen it when visiting his aunt, Mary Hillard. His final visit in 1979 was also the fiftieth reunion for his wife, Ada, whom he had met in the school dining room long ago. His memories were very alive to him that May day. The prize-winning poet evoked his Aunt Mary—the "tall figure, the dark eyes, the thrilling voice." He observed with a touch of wonder that his indomitable aunt had been dead for almost fifty years, and now, at the age of eighty-seven, he had lived longer than she. It was only after his aunt had died, he reflected, that he understood why she had so angrily opposed his giving up the law and moving to Paris to become a poet. Practicing law, she had believed in the early 1920s, was "an instrument of human service," while writing poetry was merely "self-indulgence or self-aggrandizement." She had been wrong, he said, but as a daughter of a New England minister, she only had faith in certain forms of what he called "human helpfulness." In any event, the poet concluded, Mary Robbins Hillard's strong and benevolent spirit "has filled the lives which began to find themselves in this building—those lives and the lives they brought into being." He added: "It is here now. It is in this room."

Meanwhile, tantalizing new theories about educating girls were emerging from the turmoil of the 1970s. Harvard psychologist Carol Gilligan's first book, *In a Different Voice*, initially published in 1982, would eventually be called the little book that started a revolution. Noticing the way females were routinely left out of studies of psychological development, she had undertaken her own studies of them. The young psychologist ended up rejecting the way morality was regarded by males: ranking "blind justice," or abstract principles of right and wrong above concern for the welfare of others. In her book, she described another kind of morality that was more common among girls, "a sense of integrity [that] appears to be entwined with an ethic of care." As she argued that girls reason—and learn—differently than boys, she became known as the founder of "difference feminism." In her research, she also noted that the voices of schoolgirls tend to become hesitant at puberty, a time when many of them lose self-confidence and start to fear that their former expressiveness will lead to punishment or isolation. And if girls cannot give voice to their genuine thoughts and feelings, they suffer psychological damage, she said.

Reading Gilligan and books by others, Ann Pollina became excited about applying their insights to better ways of teaching mathematics to girls. Joe Molder, with his own interest in the field, encouraged her. "Joe was one of those people whose door was always open, and you could always walk in and talk to him about *anything.* He *loved* new ideas," she remembered. "I could always sit down with him and talk mathematics. He was always the intelligent audience." When she had arrived at Westover in 1972, few students were taking math after their sophomore years. This concerned her because without it as many as half the college majors were closed to them, including the rapidly developing and highly remunerative field of computer science. One of the first curriculum changes she made was to redesign a third year of math and call it Intermediate Algebra instead of Algebra Two, so that girls who were apprehensive about numbers would not be afraid to take it.

Elizabeth Newton had quickly become an admirer of the innovative young teacher, calling her "brilliant" for the way she was getting girls enthusiastic about math. The older teacher also found the younger one "charmingly vivacious" as well as "highly cultivated" because of her love of reading, especially the novels of Jane Austen, which the mathematician liked to read over and over again. "Real life," Ann liked to say, is less about "dramatic events" and more about "small moments," as well as matters the English novelist wrote about—"loving and losing, and family and friendship, and honesty and honor in the daily lives of all of us." Speaking rapidly and precisely in a soft voice (oddly enough, not unlike Louise Dillingham's way of speaking), she liked to tell the teenagers to spend an hour reading Jane Austen for every hour watching television.

For a Jane Austen fan, the goings-on at a school for girls must be endlessly interesting and appealing. Even during the early 1970s when teenagers were testing the rules, they adored their math teacher, who was not much older than they. Since she was from New York City, nothing they did shocked her, she said, and she did not regard them as disrespectful as much as "not always doing the right thing." When she had to discipline a girl, she spoke to her like a daughter, talking calmly and clearly while being "subtle, strong, and very rational," remembered a student about one of those sessions. The girls also noticed that Ann enjoyed teaching those who struggled with numbers as much as those who found them easier. "Not only did she take the time to help me understand, she never made me feel I was incompetent for not understanding," said Deidre Sullivan, who arrived in Middlebury the same year as her teacher. Deidre also admired the way she taught: "Ann took the time to insure we were developing logical, critical thinking skills—certainly more of a life skill than memorizing algebraic formulas." When Deidre's class of 1976 dedicated their yearbook to the twenty-seven-year-old teacher with long, loose black hair, they thanked her for her kindness and understanding and especially for her friendship.

In her administrative role, the stern and stylish Liz Newton was still running day-to-day activities with a firm and occasionally unforgiving hand. Since arriving at Westover in the early 1950s as a young scholar in awe of Miss Dillingham, she had demanded intellectuality in her classroom and theatricality on stage. Always a brainy and impassioned presence, she now seemed weary of teaching and acted as if her patience had finally run out. As she prepared to retire to her little house in Middlebury in the spring of 1985, she said she still loved "the Westover style," meaning the beauty of the school, inside and out. She liked watching waves of young girls pass through the grades—"eternally young and fresh, eternally standing on the brink of womanhood with all that means of strength and weaknesses, unexpected stability, unexpected capriciousness, and always departing after a giant step toward being a completed person," she remarked when receiving the Westover Award. After she retired, the last of the old guard was gone. A number of other staffers were named to replace her including Ann Pollina, who took Miss Newton's title as director of studies. "There was no doubt in anyone's mind that [Ann] was the best person for the position," said the new president of the board of trustees, diminutive Polly Townsend Hamill, who had attended Westover on a scholarship and then graduated first in her class of 1959.

In retirement Miss Newton lent her expertise to a review of the curriculum, chairing a committee of teachers. "It was time to stand back and look at the edifice as a whole," she explained. "Was it out of proportion—even ramshackle? Were there too many tempting courses for the brilliant—or merely ambitious—students? As a result, were they overworking, or spreading themselves too thin?" The resulting report went on: "Despite years of experimentation—or was it tinkering?—with schedule, was student time being used to the best advantage?" After a number of meetings, it was decided to make more use of techniques like role playing and study partners. Team teaching was also encouraged, and calculus and history classes got together to study subjects like the effect of Newton's laws of motion on the Enlightenment. Outside evaluators continued to praise the teachers, observing that "the competence and dedication of the Westover faculty provides the school with its greatest strength."

One of the reasons the curriculum review had been undertaken was that teaching had become more challenging as American culture changed. Years earlier James Coleman, a well-known University of Chicago sociologist and the author of *The Adolescent Society*, had warned about the negative impact of adolescent values on academic performance, but now the mass media had amplified its impact. Incoming pupils had less general knowledge than earlier generations, since they had read fewer books and attended less demanding schools. At the same time, loosening family ties left many teenagers on their own. Some, like the young Laura Nash, a four-year day student with divorced parents, found Westover "a magical, regal place of serenity" that felt like her real home. She found the routines and rhythms of school life so emotionally grounding that she was able to focus on studying. But many others were unwilling or unable to study very hard or obey the rules. Early in the decade a dean of students, Blair Jenkins, was brought in to establish order, and before long she was glad to say that she was spending more time advising than disciplining girls.

It had been suggested in the late 1960s that girls be grouped by ability, especially in languages and mathematics. But most teachers at Westover were opposed to rigid tracking in such a small school "because of the lockstep effect, the pejorative social consequences, and, for the less talented, the lack of stimulation from brighter minds," the curriculum committee explained. Instead, they wanted the strongest and weakest students to sit and learn side-by-side. Since the school was now on a trimester system, it was possible to offer a large number of courses of varying paces and areas of interest including Advanced Placement classes in every department. In the language department, for example, a demanding ancient Greek elective was available, as well as a simplified form of written Latin. Courses in the arts taught discipline to less studious girls while offering enrichment and excellent preparation to others. This system allowed a pupil doing poorly in one area to excel in another. One of them was a failing freshman in Shamus Weber's English class, who took a digital photography class with Michael Gallagher and went on to win national photography awards. In the math department, the attempt to avoid "the iron mold of tracking," as the committee put it, was most successful of all in devising classes at many levels. It soon became difficult to restrain the teenagers from taking too many electives. Graduation requirements were raised, but even average students began to graduate with more credits than necessary for a diploma.

Early in Joe Molder's tenure, the English department was given "great freedom" to develop a wide range of classes. In order to teach writing well, Shamus Weber proposed separating the teaching of writing from the teaching of literature. What evolved was a demanding writing skills requirement along with a number of literary electives from Shakespeare to James Joyce. Even though he was department chairman, Shamus chose to teach what he called "formal writing" to freshmen, believing it was important for "the crankiest and most experienced teacher to teach the youngest students." Almost every year, pupils' poetry and prose, which was also published in the prize-winning *Lantern*, won national and state awards; girls also won top scores in Advanced Placement tests. "Given his head, he had the force, resourcefulness, and popularity to implement goals of precision and discipline in imaginative contemporary ways," Miss Newton and his colleagues observed.

Over the years, many members of Shamus Weber's young audiences in the spacious, lofty old church building, now called Hillard House, were inspired by his ideas and knowledge, his love of poetry and prose, as well as titillated and amused by his irreverent remarks. It was he who encouraged Mary Gelezunas, a day student from Middlebury on a four-year scholarship, to take his elective on James Joyce's *Ulysses*. After studying *The Odyssey* as a freshman, she found Joyce's novel "made sense as I traveled with Leopold Bloom through 1904 Dublin as a twentieth-century Odysseus." She caught fire intellectually, and at lunch she and her friends used to sit at a table they called a "salon" to talk excitedly about what they were learning. "The atmosphere was of pure intellect; discussions flowed freely as we breathed the heady air of ideas and images, of history, of literary possibility, of reading and writing poetry. The days were so fully packed that I always think of Blake's 'eternity in an hour' when remembering the times of infinite potential, of trading words, of intensely writing papers," she recalled. Without "canned worksheets or standardized tests, I felt like a student in the classical sense." It was a time of "intellectual ecstasy," she continued, when she and a younger girl, Divya Singh, began an underground newspaper called "The Beat," which discussed those ideas along with complaints about other students' apathy. As a senior, she became editor of *The Lantern*, and it won a prize that year. She went on to Wesleyan University, which she thought no more difficult than Westover, while its larger literature lectures were less thrilling than what she had experienced at a younger age in Hillard House.

Even though adolescents in the 1980s seemed more sophisticated than in the past, the staff thought they actually needed more "personal support than in earlier and more naïve times"—eight hours a week, and if there were family or other problems, as many as twenty hours a week. John Alexander had introduced academic advisors, and since teachers had few duties outside the classroom, they were able to talk to students in the afternoons. After evening study sessions, boarders could go to the residents' small apartments for snacks, television, and talk, and corridor birthday parties and other gatherings were held. A peer support group starting in 1982, led by social worker Eileen Tateo, taught the teenagers how to listen and speak to resolve conflicts and personal problems. The Health Center also offered counseling. It was decided that every sophomore must take a class about sexuality, which emphasized matters like self-esteem and maintaining good physical and psychological health.

English teacher James "Shamus" Weber in the old library under the portrait of Mary Hillard.
SVEN MARTSON.

Many graduates have expressed gratitude for all this attention. "When I first arrived at Westover in the fall of 1980, I felt scared and alone," admitted Frederica Barney Yates, but soon she became aware of the "all around genuine caring," and she warmed to the sincerity, sensitivity, sensible advice, and "relaxed, easy manner" of the adults. Ann Vileisis, another four-year day student from Middlebury, remembers that she could always find someone to take her philosophical questions seriously, especially Alice Hallaran, whom she admired for her egalitarian marriage and balanced way of life. "I appreciated her warmth and her ability to talk about anything," Ann said. As well as giving generously of their time, teachers and staffers were admirable examples of "openness, tolerance of differences, willingness to compromise, patience," according to the latest accreditation committee.

So much concern and involvement with students "might be verging on spoon-feeding," worried a few grownups, and at least one of them wondered if the school was becoming a hothouse for wilting plants. Around that time, Valerie Lee, a professor of education at the University of Michigan, was asking if some girls' schools were practicing a subtle form of sexism or sex role socialization (what she called "engenderment") by protecting and nurturing their young pupils too much. In her research, she found that academically strong schools like Westover usually managed to find a good balance between "individualist and relationist" tendencies, meaning the mental and emotional aspects of life, although not without difficulty. "What does that mean—nurture too much?" Ann Pollina later asked in exasperation, observing that girls often need more encouragement than boys because of their lower expectations for themselves. In the decades to come, most of the younger alumnae continued to say that they appreciated all the reassurance they had received at Westover, although one said that she wished she had been made to stand on her own two feet a little better.

Alice Hallaran also thought that many of the young girls needed to become more determined and independent. She, along with Blair Jenkins and science teacher Chris Norment, proposed a challenging outdoor program that pupils quickly nicknamed "survival." With roots in an earlier Outing Club, it was also an alternative for those who disliked team sports. Afternoon and weekend hiking and camping trips were made to woods, lakes, rivers, mountains, and an island off the coast of Maine. Alice, once an Outward Bound instructor, persuaded the teenage girls to backpack, rock climb, whitewater canoe, and build shelters in every kind of weather while learning to appreciate the world of nature. In the spring, members of the program camped alone on the island for several days and nights with few provisions except for matches to start campfires and tools to catch or find food. Ann Vileisis admitted that she had never been physically active before participating in the program, and she has remained very grateful for it. "We started to take responsibilities for our bodies," she remembered, and found it "exhilarating, life-affirming, and wonderful."

Ever since becoming headmaster, Joe Molder had wanted to enroll as many motivated students as possible to inspire the faculty and other pupils. It had occurred to him that gifted teenage musicians from overseas at the Julliard School of Music in New York needed to study other subjects besides music, so he made inquiries. Soon the young Korean pianists Soomi Lee and her cousin Mihae Lee were members of the classes of 1975 and 1976, respectively, studying in Middlebury during the week and in Manhattan on Saturday mornings. The cousins later said they were glad that Westover had given them rounded educations—even though they struggled to play sports and, because of language difficulties, to master the material in English classes—before becoming concert pianists. The idea worked so well that Robert Havery would eventually teach an Advanced Placement music theory class to young musicians. A formal arrangement between Westover and the Manhattan School of Music in New York was established by the end of the 1980s.

"All the vital signs are positive and strong" at Westover, an evaluation committee wrote in 1988, except for declining applications and admissions because of a downturn in demographics, a depressed economy, and the ongoing unpopularity of girls' schools. It remained difficult to explain the reasons for educating girls apart from boys. So many schools had gone coeducational in the late 1960s and early 1970s that fewer prospective parents had gone to single-sex schools, and many of those who had gone remembered them as old-fashioned. Mothers who had loved Westover could not get their daughters to even visit or apply. Often it was grandmothers who suggested their alma mater to their granddaughters. The idea of going to a school without boys seemed so strange to fourteen-year-olds that, if they decided to go, their friends were shocked. Enrollment also dropped because the headmaster repeatedly refused to lower admission requirements, even threatening to resign over the issue in earlier years. As a result, enrollment had fallen to around 160 students.

To enroll enough qualified students, Molder realized he had to attract boarders from around the world. Princess Zein Al Hussein, one of twelve children of King Hussein of Jordan and his English former wife, was among them. During her two contented years in Middlebury, Zein had round-the-clock security. When the diminutive King Hussein arrived for her graduation in 1986, there seemed to be more bodyguards than guests in Middlebury that day. During the visit he offered to finance a student exchange program, and soon afterward one was arranged between Westover and the Ahliyyah School for Girls in Amman.

With girls coming from such diverse worlds as the royal palace in Amman and islands off the coast of Maine, more rules had to be written down. The school had to carefully spell out differences between collaboration and cheating, sharing and stealing ideas, scholarship and plagiarism. In the past, the pupils "all came from the same family," an older alumna told a teacher, at a time when there was an unspoken understanding about how to behave. Without rules and regulations spelled out, it would be difficult for a girl from the Bronx, who liked to rap at night, to get along with a roommate from Seoul, who wanted absolute silence after eight in the evening. Tensions remained between so-called preppies and hippies as well as those from wealthy and modest backgrounds. One scholarship student never forgot that a classmate's father sent a helicopter for her at a nearby airfield. The Glee Club still sang Renaissance motets but now also performed songs by women composers and South African and Israeli music. Before long there would be a gospel choir. When the singers began to give concerts in cathedrals abroad, and language students traveled to France and Spain on spring vacations, it helped equalize experiences among those from different backgrounds. And since uniforms—white linen sailor outfits with navy piping—were only worn occasionally, there eventually had to be categories of appropriate dressing explained—class dress, formal dress, and informal dress—governing specific articles of clothing and footwear.

As experiencing diversity became more of an integral part of an exemplary American education, Miss Hillard's notion about "the right kind of girl" had completely changed at Westover. In the 1980s the African-American Latino Student Association (or WALSA) was organized, and there would also be a Jewish Student Association, an Asian Culture Club, and a multicultural festival celebrating diversity. Adults are always trying—in chapel, classrooms, and in private conversations—to get girls to respect oth-

Chaplain and English teacher Thomas Hungerford.
© GABRIEL AMADEUS COONEY.

ers' differences. Ann Pollina says that at Westover distinctions are more obvious but also more genuinely respected. "There are all kinds of ways kids fail each other and trip over themselves," she has said, "but it's easier to handle the problems in a small school that respects individuality."

In the spring of 1981, the headmaster had hired Thomas Hungerford, a thirty-one-year-old Californian with a master's degree in theology from Yale, to be chaplain (as well as to teach English, and with his wife, Mathilde, to be residents). Joe Molder had finally decided not to abandon the controversial one-morning-a-week chapel service, since he had come to believe that the overriding purpose of the school was to pass on ethical values. The young chaplain quickly discovered the alumnae's strong feelings about St. Margaret's Chapel. The first question every older alumna asked him was why services were only once a week. When most of them were pupils, they had spent hundreds of hours in the lovely little chapel at morning services and evening prayers. Many had felt happiest during those hours, especially during the Dillingham decades when so many teachers and staff members were detached or indifferent toward the emotional wellbeing of the girls.

Years earlier, when Molder was still acting headmaster, an alumna on the board had written him a long, emotional letter about chapel, at a time when both pupils and teachers were protesting against mandatory attendance in the name of religious freedom. The singing was uninspired and speakers even criticized the chapel program itself. "I appreciate [that] this matter is fraught with difficulty: between placating the students and a secular faculty on the one hand, and satisfying the profound concern of many Alumnae and parents on the other," Elysabeth Higgins began. She explained that "there was something in the Chapel's sphere—something esthetic, if not religious. Many heard their first great music there; it grew familiar and became a cherished experience. Others discovered that language could be handsome, powerful, mysterious . . . Some learned, per force, to reflect—as distinctive from, to think. Others enjoyed the sense of unity—of a whole place, together without the distraction of personalities; even an historical sense, too, of being in touch with what went before and was still to come. So—some looked, and some listened, and some rested; but all felt, and were served. And most, whether consciously or unconsciously, put back into the daily life of the School what they had received. It is for this reason—and not because one generation was pious and the next is not—that so many Alumnae believe that when Chapel is discarded or misused, it is the School which has been profaned."

As the school became more diverse, the controversy over chapel took another turn. Hungerford, an Episcopalian, realized that if everyone had to attend, services could no longer remain exclusively Christian. "If the chapel space does not belong to all, it belongs to no one," he stated. He was aware that long ago it had been dedicated, not consecrated, and that now it must become more ecumenical to embrace girls who were Jewish, Jehovah's Witness, Muslim, Buddhist, Shinto, Hindu, or had no religion at all. He and a student chapel committee asked them to lead services and explain their religious traditions. There were various special meals, like an Islamic Eid al-Fir meal to mark the end of Ramadan. Services were also held to commemorate the Holocaust, to celebrate Earth Day, to mark Martin Luther King Jr. Day, and to reflect on other events throughout the year. Inevitably, the presence of the Christian cross on the altar was questioned, and by 1988 it was occasionally removed for non-Christian services; eventually it was absent except at Christmastime, Easter, and on alumnae weekend, much to the dismay of many older graduates.

Still, the ambience and the architecture of the little Tudor chapel with a cross on its roof remained those of a Christian space. It was possible for students of other faiths to be exempted from chapel, especially the Christmas candlelight service. Once, a few Christian girls argued that if Jewish pupils were exempt from the service, then they did not have to participate in the Passover Seder meal. Feelings became so intense that the Jewish girls asked the chaplain to cancel the celebration that year instead of holding it in what he called "a spirit of rivalry." He later pointed out that the religious minority understood the spirit of the chapel better than the majority. Afterward, there was a school meeting in Red Hall, when the Jewish students sat on the stairs and talked about how painful it felt to be a religious outsider at Westover, especially at Christmastime. The wound healed, and a decade later the head of the chapel committee was Jewish.

As the years went by, Hungerford realized that the weekly chapel service—along with the traditional processional and recessional chapel lines—was an important ritual that connected every class to each that came before. It was also a quiet time for the teenagers to reflect about issues of identity and self-worth, honesty and lying, vanity and beauty, education and ignorance. Another excellent reason for the morning gathering, he would say, was to heal and strengthen the community of girls. "When there are problems in the school, you feel them in the chapel," he explained, adding that the occasion acted as a mirror and as a lightening rod for the mood of the school, "and that is the way it should be." As a result, any difficulty can be better addressed and made better during services.

Educators and others are reluctant to speculate about whether nature or nurture is responsible for differences between the genders, because no one really knows for sure. Poet Adrienne Rich came down on the side of nurture after teaching writing in New York City in the late 1960s to disadvantaged minority students who wanted to go to college. In a speech to women educators, she said that before the students could express themselves, she had to create "the conditions for learning" by addressing "racism, oppression, and the politics of literature and language." Then, when she taught at a women's college a few years later, she was surprised to find the same sense of lack of entitlement. The young women had to be encouraged to take themselves seriously, validate one another, and believe in the importance of their history as women. "I would suggest that not biology, but ignorance of our selves, has been the key to our powerlessness," she said in her speech. She also urged the teachers to "listen to the small, soft voices, often courageously trying to speak up, voices of women taught early that tones of confidence, challenge, anger, or assertiveness are strident and unfeminine."

Yet during the heyday of the women's liberation movement in the 1970s, gender differences were played down. Ann Pollina had been a teacher for two years after college in a large coeducational high school, where she had taught everyone the same way. "If you had said to me at the time that girls learn mathematics differently from boys, I would have been furious," she said. But after teaching girls apart from boys at Westover, and then giving birth to two daughters, she began to change her mind. She recalls playing with her older daughter, Emily, and trying to get the three-year-old interested in building a city with blocks. Instead, the child took a yellow toy truck and began knocking over the blocks. When Ann asked her what she was doing, she said she was vacuuming. At first the young mother was horrified and wondered what was wrong with her daughter, but gradually she realized that her assumption was wrong, that constructing a city or creating a civilization was not necessarily better than taking care of the ones already in existence. She would also understand something else: "If I populated the land with little people and suggested that those people needed homes, my daughters instantly became architects and civil engineers."

Mathematics is "a very masculine field," Ann Pollina has explained. "There is a certain kind of analytical learner, many of whom are boys, for whom just posing a question, if it's an interesting question, is enough. But it's not enough for other people. Not enough for many boys and not enough, I think, for a majority of girls." Interestingly, she describes her own learning style as atypical of her gender, since from an early age she has enjoyed solving mathematical problems simply for their own sakes.

Mathematics teacher Ann Pollina with a few students.
SVEN MARTSON.

In any event, when male academic institutions opened to women in the 1970s, they expected females to adjust to them. And when the girls did not learn math and science as easily as the boys, teachers tried to make girls more aggressive, analytical, and competitive in the classroom. In this way, in Pollina's opinion, they sent the wrong message: that what is female is inferior. "To teach girls well in mathematics, begin from the premise that there is nothing about them that is wrong or in need of remediation," she would write, and she urged other educators to discover girls' special strengths and to utilize them.

Taking advantage of girls' sociability and helpfulness, she had them arrange chairs in circles or semicircles to encourage conversation and to work together in pairs or groups. In classes, she would explain a mathematical concept, and then ask them to try to work it out on the blackboard together. "If girls like to collaborate rather than compete, [then] design bigger and better problems that need the work of many minds," she has written. She also created a friendly atmosphere, where teenagers felt comfortable asking questions, taking risks, and learning from their mistakes. She would walk around and help, then offer afternoon tutoring, evening study sessions, and math anxiety clinics. "What was extraordinary is that Ann provided us a clear and ready path to learning complex ideas," remembered Ann Vileisis. "We weren't fearful or reserved about math—we just tackled it with confidence and enjoyed it." As their teacher enabled them to learn calculus and other complicated mathematical concepts, they became proud of what they could do.

Ann Pollina's own calculus professor during her freshman year of college had a way of teaching that was both caring and extremely effective, and it profoundly affected her. "The good teacher is the one who dares exposing not only mind but heart and soul," she would write. "The essence of good teaching is the willingness to sustain a terrifying proximity to ideas much larger than yourself and to the minds and hearts of those you seek to teach." One day she walked into a class, dropped a textbook on the floor, asked the girls what she had done, then drew them into a fascinating discussion about the nature of reality. "After that geometry class, I understood that math was a language that we use to find the truth of things," a student said. To increase the comfort level, she liked to bring coffee and doughnuts to class and invite pupils to her home for Indian food. Another of her students, who went on to major in engineering, recalled that "she would help you when you needed help, or you could just sit quietly in her home and do your homework." The girl, Allie Conway, elaborated: "You had no excuse not to do your work because she made herself so available that it was almost embarrassing when you did poorly. She really cared about making sure we knew our math, and we loved her for that."

Most of the girls in Pollina's classes over the years were more interested in solving practical than abstract problems, especially ones that contributed to the good of the world. "If I want to teach exponential functions in my calculus class, we talk about world population growth," she said, or land use problems, demographics, or the environment. She has described female adolescents as "altruistic knowers" as well as "connected learners." She has also found ways to harness their abilities "to synthesize, make connections, and use their practical intelligence," as she put it in an educational journal. Girls, she noted another time, "will do the same things, they will achieve the same ends in math and science, but they won't do it the same way" as boys. In this way, she was well aware of going against the grain in the field of education: "What I propose is change that is radical, as all attempts to change the prevailing paradigm are radical."

When she had started teaching at Westover in the early 1970s, only two or three seniors in a class of fifty were taking calculus, but within a decade most were attempting it—including those more interested in the arts, even though calculus was not required to graduate. At an open house for prospective pupils more than a decade later, a father who was skeptical about girls' schools was only half listening to the math teacher speak. "Suddenly I sat up, and my hand shot up in the air," he recalled. "Please could you repeat that?" he asked. "Certainly," Ann said. "Seventy-five percent of our senior class is taking AP calculus." Christian Daviron and his daughter, Juliette, had visited a number of top coeducational prep schools, and he knew that none of them could say the same. His daughter entered Westover, and, although she had always thought she was bad at math, she ended up taking and passing calculus, too. "We don't think that any other school in the country could have given her the confidence to achieve what she achieved," he says. "For Ann Pollina, 'cannot' is a word that does not belong in the English vocabulary."

Observing Pollina's success with her students, Joe Molder decided to compare Westover to coeducational schools in an attempt to show the advantage of teaching girls together. Comparing nine seniors of exceptional ability in Westover's class of 1986 to girls of similar aptitudes at Exeter, Andover, Choate Rosemary Hall, Groton, and Taft, he discovered that his seniors "outperformed them by a considerable margin" on Advanced Placement tests. Girls of lesser ability also did better than comparable girls at the other schools in biology, English and French literature, American history, and other subjects. Furthermore, all the girls at Westover were taking more Advanced Placement classes and doing better in them than their counterparts. But in mathematics their achievement "may be unique among schools," the headmaster wrote in a brochure. "You do what works," said his youthful director of studies, matter-of-factly, "and what worked was dramatically different."

12

Backlash:
Defining the Difference

AS HALF THE GIRLS' SCHOOLS IN AMERICA DISAPPEARED, ONLY A few voices were raised in opposition, like the eloquent one of Adrienne Rich, who had attended a female high school before going to Radcliffe College. Teaching teenage girls together was especially important, she believed, because those are the years when "polarization between feminine attractiveness and independent intelligence" is widest, or, in other words, when attention given to appearance often undermines the ability to think. She was well aware of the many ways that the world sabotages schoolgirls—from making sexist assumptions to ignoring sexual harassment. "If there is any misleading concept, it is that of 'coeducation': that because women and men are sitting in the same classrooms, hearing the same lectures, reading the same books, performing the same laboratory experiments, they are receiving an equal education," she had declared in her 1978 speech. "They are not."

In the late 1980s, the remaining girls' schools started to take a stand. British-born scholar Rachel Belash, head of Miss Porter's School, and a counterpart, Arlene Gibson of Kent Place School in New Jersey, organized a meeting of all-girl schools in October of 1987, and then, at Joseph Molder's invitation, they gathered in Middlebury the following spring. Before long they organized the National Coalition of Girls' Schools with a membership of fifty-six schools. "Ours is a coeducational world—no doubt about it— and single-sex education needs its defenders, promoters, believers, and proselytizers," Belash wrote in *The New York Times Magazine*. "Yes, some people think girls' schools are anachronisms, but they succeed, better than most people realize, and remain necessary in a world where men and women still do not work equally together as professionals." The next year, on the heels of the publication of Carol Gilligan's second book, *Making Connections*, same-sex Emma Willard School took out in *The New York Times* and *The Wall Street Journal* feisty advertisements that promoted educating girls apart from boys and denigrated "St. Grottlesex," a nickname for a group of formerly male prep schools in New England.

Next, the coalition commissioned a study of attitudes toward schools for girls. It revealed that parents assumed that math and science were better taught in coeducational than in girls' schools. This astonished and dismayed Ann Pollina, who realized that few people were aware of what was happening at Westover. She also blamed this impression on bias, saying that "women are still fighting our battles for gender equity on a primal level." She realized that girl-only schools had been struggling so hard for survival that they had neglected to oppose this widespread attitude. "We are, however, beginning to do so at Westover," she declared in 1991. She also adamantly rejected the stereotype of the schools as refuges from unfair classrooms. "This must not be the message of single-sex education," she added in an article. It was evident that she understood that the relatively few girls' schools must enlarge their mission as well as their message. "We are a natural laboratory for the investigation of how girls learn best," she continued, adding that what teachers of girls have learned over the years should be used to improve the nation's classrooms for girls and boys alike.

In June of 1991 she, along with math teacher Louise Gould of Ethel Walker School, co-hosted a symposium, under the aegis of the new coalition, about teaching math, science, and technology to girls. Gathering at Wellesley College, eighty-seven educators met at a time when women's progress in computer science and similar fields had stalled. Over the next few days, as the educators shared ideas and information, they talked about teaching girls technological abstractions through stories, substituting sports or rocket metaphors for those that pupils invented, finding ways for them to see them- selves as experts, and many other matters. Judith Jacobs, a mathematics professor from California, spoke about her success with using journals: "I find that when my students write about how they feel as they are learning mathematics, as well as how they are doing in mathematics, they have amazing growth." Claudia Henrion, a mathematics professor at Middlebury College in Vermont, mentioned the importance of telling young women about the female mathematicians in history, the womanly tradition of stitching quilts in geometric patterns, and the mathematical symmetry everywhere in nature—in leaves, spiderwebs, honeycombs, shells, ice crystals, fruit, and even in their own bodies. Many of these techniques were already being used in math classes at Westover, and soon others would be added as Pollina brought quilts into classrooms as well as Byzantine, Navajo, and pre-Columbian decorative patterns to demonstrate various mathematical principles.

All this was soon validated in an important way. An influential group, the American Association of University Women, began releasing reports verifying what teachers of girls already knew. Its *Shortchanging Girls, Shortchanging America* revealed the reasons why many adolescent girls had less confidence in themselves and poorer grades than boys after twelve years of schooling. These startling findings were widely reported by the national media, and many parents started taking another look at schools for girls. The AAUW's following reports suggested solutions that sounded exactly like descriptions of the best girls' schools. Educators were urged "to celebrate girls' strong identity, respect girls as central players, connect girls to caring adults, ensure girls' participation and success, and empower girls to realize their dreams." Certainly all this sounded like the nature of a female community like Westover. "We didn't even talk about it because it was just there," Molder observed.

Since Ann Pollina was getting what he called "remarkable results" in math, he wanted to achieve them in science as well. Soon a program called Women in Science and Engineering, or W.I.S.E., got going, along with a scholarship fund for girls of color. Arnold Cogswell, who was on the boards of both Westover and Rensselaer Polytechnic Institute, arranged for participants to go on to the university. In the early 1970s, boarders had been abandoning Middlebury on weekends, while Molder had wanted Westover to become more of a residential school again. Since most of the faculty refused to teach on Saturday mornings, classes were offered like typing and driver's education followed by sports in the afternoons. Later, arts courses that needed longer classes began to meet on Saturdays, and then the W.I.S.E. students did as well.

Pollina, who had by then been named dean of faculty, also became director of this co-curricular program, which introduced pupils to physical, structural, and electrical engineering as well as to computer programming. Students started out by taking apart a lawnmower, and then they moved on to building robots and writing computer code.

Ann encouraged the young girls to use computers in their own ways, "as a tool, not a toy," she explained, or, in other words, for cooperating and communicating with others instead of playing violent war games. To give the girls a sense of mastery, she allowed them to monitor the school's computer labs and to work on its Web site. In years to come, the sophomores in the W.I.S.E. program would often be the largest group of girls from any Connecticut school taking the Advanced Placement computer science exam. In 1998, sophomore Sarah Schipul, a day student from Watertown, Connecticut, was the only female in the state to get the top score in the challenging exam. The Westover program has attracted several sets of siblings, including the Sieller sisters, also from Watertown; the Emeagwali sisters, originally from Nigeria; and the Pollina sisters. Many of its graduates are pursuing studies or working in the fields of computer science, industrial design, environmental studies, and nuclear, biomedical, electrical, chemical, and civil engineering.

All this was exceptional, especially for a small girls' school, outside evaluators would say at the end of the 1990s. "In English classes students learn principles of etymology so that they may derive the meanings of words on their own; geometry students learn practical surveying; in history, through role playing, simulations, and debate, students learn to express contrasting arguments; languages are taught in the native language; science courses stress real life applications of abstract principles," they said. They were also impressed by the way several departments taught intellectually interesting classes together, like the history and literature of New York City, and a class called "Peoples, Plagues, and Poxes," offered by the science and history departments. And in the art studio, girls worked from skeletons and live models under the eye of an exhibiting artist.

In the spring of 1994, this art teacher, Trudy Martin, invited Judy Chicago, a controversial feminist artist, to Middlebury for a day. A few parents called the headmaster to complain, but Molder stood his ground and invited them to attend. Before the visiting artist's arrival, the Common Room was turned into a gallery with a selection of work from "The Birth Project," her collaborative work of childbirth images sewn by needlewomen in California. Some students read the artist's memoir, *Through the Flower*, while others worked on their own collective needlework projects. When Arts Day arrived, there were lectures, videos, and discussions about women and creativity through the ages, including one about childbirth, moderated by Alice Hallaran and other mothers on the staff, called "Does It Hurt?"

Judy Chicago must have immediately recognized the visual affirmation of the design and decoration around the school, like the round rosettes in the school emblem and the blood-red fabrics of Red Hall, many of them symbols of femininity and fecundity. There that afternoon the artist told the teenagers that they were lucky to be attending a girls' school: "Women have worked really hard to make schools for women, because spaces where women can be by themselves give us a chance to get strong. And we need that. It takes a lot of strength to stand up for yourself in the world, and to keep on doing it," she said with honesty and humor, drawing on her own difficulties in the art world. "I hope you will remember that it is most important to try to hear your own voice, and to have the courage to stand up for it, even if everybody tells you your voice is not worthwhile." She also talked to her adolescent audience about a widely misunderstood word, telling them that those who want equal rights for females should not be reluctant to call themselves feminists. At the end of a slide talk about her work that evening, she was given a standing ovation.

As people became more interested in female education again, more than thirty new girls' schools opened during the decade. They included the Young Women's Leadership School, a public school in East Harlem. With the backing of private philanthropists and the New York City school chancellor, it was launched in 1996 with a class of seventh graders in a neighborhood office building. When parents heard about the new school, they rapidly enrolled their daughters and filled a long waiting list. Despite its popularity, the girl-only school ignited a fierce debate. Separating the genders suggested to some feminists that girls could not compete with boys, and the New York office of the National Organization for Women opposed the school. The American Civil Liberties Union pointed out that the Supreme Court's historic *Brown v. Board of Education* decision had emphatically rejected the concept of separate but equal in 1954. Both NOW and the ACLU immediately

Learning together. SVEN MARTSON.

Seniors in a procession during graduation. SVEN MARTSON.

filed complaints with the U.S. government, charging that the school for girls was biased against boys.

A generation earlier, the Supreme Court had been concerned about Negroes getting inferior educations, but now the issue was teenage girls getting superior ones. While the courts had virtually ended the debate about separate but equal in regard to race, the discussion was evidently not yet ended about gender. Supporters of girls' schools argued that when separation of the sexes is voluntary, it should be treated differently under the law. They also pointed out that the comparison between race and gender is inexact, since males and females live together in families. Law professor Denise Morgan, an African-American graduate of the all-girls Chapin School as well as Yale University, declared at a symposium in 1997 that girls' schools are not a retreat from gender equality but another way to achieve it through a kind of affirmative action. Girls, especially those of color, frequently found a sense of safety and freedom in female environments, educators stated. Professor Valerie Lee had endorsed parochial girls' schools in the 1980s (for improving academic attitudes, achievement, and aspirations), but she was unable to prove the benefits of their private secular counterparts, except for their impact on those from disadvantaged backgrounds. Indeed, the Young Women's Leadership School had better attendance and other results than other city schools, as it sent virtually every graduate to college.

In the mostly white milieu of Middlebury, girls of color have experienced "culture shock" over the years despite Westover's welcoming attitude, says Izukanne Emeagwali, but she and many others have also thrived there. A classmate, Nailah Staples, the daughter of a dance teacher in Boston, attended because it was the first school where "the smile was not false," she told a teacher at her all-girl middle school, Mother Caroline Academy. Other African-Americans in their class of 2001 included twins Dana and Dena Simmons, who lived in the Bronx. Dena especially excelled, and while at Middlebury College afterward, she won a Fulbright scholarship to study public health in her native Dominican Republic and then won Westover's Distinguished Young Alumna Award.

The school had at last achieved what Louise Dillingham had tried and failed to do in the 1950s: enroll a group of minority students in every class.

In the age-old debate about distinctions between men and women, English feminist Mary Wollstonecraft declared three hundred years ago that it was not nature but nurture—girls lacking the educations of their brothers—that was responsible for women's supposed mental inferiority. Again, in the late twentieth century, feminists still worried with good reason that any imagined or actual differences between the genders would be held against women. Now some educators were challenging that position, arguing that pretending sameness in every way meant ignoring inherent female strengths. The attention that Carol Gilligan and other feminist scholars paid to "difference" was intended to examine, not necessarily exalt, any female virtues and to challenge the prevailing male standard. Humanism should be a goal for everyone, they thought. They also meant to use gender as a metaphor for relational and rational ways of being, not to generalize about all males being one way and all females another.

Meanwhile, Ann Pollina persisted in her belief that girls develop and learn in their own unique ways. "The part that saddens me is the notion that equal in the American lexicon must mean the same," she said. "Maybe I'm spoiled by my training in mathematics. Even in this very exact subject, we allow there to be a difference between equal and identical. Some equations are identical, the same regardless of the values or the variables involved. Others are equal only if the variables have a specific value. It is all a question of value." It is easier to treat everyone as the same in the classroom than to acknowledge different kinds of intelligence and learning styles, she added. Another time she conceded that "we face a remarkable challenge—trying to achieve equity for our girls while allowing for difference." She also regretted the divisions among feminists because it slowed female progress. "Regardless of the kind of feminism that you espouse, and what you believe, the empowerment of women is the goal," she stated. She found the controversy over the Young Women's Leadership School "both disheartening and understandable," since it reminded her that people were unaware that girls' schools could be progressive and empowering. In fact, female educational institutions are validating when they are academically demanding and vigorously create "a culture that liberates women's strengths."

In such a culture, girls tend to be very open and honest with each other. When they are "learning, thinking about things, and becoming more confident about who they are—it's fantastic," said Alice Hallaran. A member of the class of 1956 remembered feeling overshadowed by men and silenced in their presence until she went to Westover and then to a women's college. "Once you've gotten the freedom to speak your mind, it's difficult to give that up," she said, adding that she never did give it up. Even at Harvard in the 1980s, young women were still acting intimidated in classes with young men; they talked more easily in classes that were mostly female or led by a women professor. At Westover in 1997, girls from a number of classes emphatically told a questioner that they could be themselves and outspoken while at school. They did not have to worry about the way they looked, either. Kate Walker, a ninth grader, had always wanted to go to the school so many of her "strong" female relatives had attended. Perhaps in a test of its tolerance, she decided her first year to cut off her long brown hair, which fell almost to her waist, and to shave her head. Administrators were nonchalant about her bald head, and her young classmates thought it was "cool," but, unsurprisingly, boys at a dance treated her like "a dragon lady."

Meanwhile, loud female voices resonated in the school's hallways, and students told those who asked that living in a community of girls was "exciting and expansive." Michelle Brooks, who had been teased at her prior public school for acting like a hippie, was encouraged to express herself in her own way. She overcame her shyness to play the role of Juliet in a performance of *Romeo and Juliet*, which was directed by professional actors from Shakespeare & Company, a repertory theater in residence at the school. She was like "a little flower that suddenly blossomed," marveled her mother, alumna Monique Corbat Brooks. The library began putting out a reading list of books titled *Of, By, and About Women*. Science classes were sure to mention figures like Madam Curie, who studied with other women before winning a Nobel Prize in physics. Electives over the years have covered the works of such women writers as Virginia Woolf and Alice Walker, "women warriors" in history, and female contributions and viewpoints in the arts. As a result, many girls become proud of themselves. "You put women in a situation where they are first-class citizens, where their opinions are *the* opinions, where their values are *the* values that are trusted and respected, and that's what they learn to believe about themselves," says Ann Pollina.

In this atmosphere, Westover's male teachers have learned to be more considerate and courteous. When Bruce Coffin first arrived in Middlebury after teaching boys and girls together, he harshly criticized a pupil's paper in an afternoon conference. The next day, everyone in the class acted angry at him and refused to answer questions. He realized that she had complained to her classmates, and that they had taken her side—unlike boys, he observed, who would be gleeful about such an incident. Likewise, Terry Hallaran, who had attended Wesleyan when it was a men's college and students shrugged off professors' critiques, was taught to be more tactful. Elizabeth Newton had to take him aside and tell him that he had unwittingly terrified a girl in one of his classes. Astonished, he wondered what he had said or done, and he gradually concluded that adolescent girls are "a different species" than boys. When one of his students gives what he calls a "remarkably wrong answer," he is now more diplomatic about it.

Robert Havery, who has traveled with the Glee Club to concerts around the country and in some of the greatest European cathedrals, has repeatedly heard remarks about the poise and self-assurance of his young singers. These qualities emanate, he has explained, from the freedom they feel to express themselves at school and, in fact, the expectation that they must in class. "I think we are very often impressed by our students, by their intelligence and their creativity," he said, "and they get that kind of feedback from teachers." This is important since educational researchers have evidence that the respect and praise of male teachers has a particularly positive effect on young girls. The headmaster has also expressed pride in the aplomb of his graduates. "Our girls go off to coed colleges, and they come back and invariably say that they are the only girls who speak up in class," he said, adding that they often have the confidence to go on to graduate school, too. And later in life the alumnae are more likely to put their intelligence and abilities to work. An alumna now in her fifties, who says the school gave her a college-level education, marvels that "my friends from my Westover days are brilliant women who still enjoy being brilliant women."

By the early 1990s, Joseph Molder had been at Westover for twenty years, and, since scholarships had always been his close to his heart, the trustees

Choral director Robert Havery directing the Glee Club.
SVEN MARTSON.

deeply pleased him by crea ing a scholarship in his and his wife's names. On his sixtieth birthday the same year, staffers dressed as if for games of soccer or tennis and playfully tossed balls at him during a morning party in Red Hall. He was beginning to think about retiring and finding someone to take his place, so he hired an attractive young woman to be assistant principal and dean of students. Over the years, he had created an administration noted for its openness and collegiality, but suddenly everything changed. Many thought that the newcomer's style was divisive, and long-time faculty members found themselves taking sides, resulting in unrest and unhappiness. "Westover suddenly became political, which it never was before," recalled Ann Pollina. "That was probably the hardest time for me because this is not, by its nature, a political place." A senior that year felt that the new dean was "fake friendly, fake smiling," and she was struck by the contrast between her and the forthright Anneke Rothman, whom she regarded as "tough" but "sincere and trustworthy." After a traumatic year, when a number of teachers and staff members left or were fired and students were put on probation or expelled, the new administrator herself departed.

Anita Packard Montgomery, a tall, attractive alumna from the class of 1947 and of Vassar, had become president of the board of trustees as her husband, Tad, a head-master, retired. While she was president of the Alumnae Association in the 1970s, two of her five children were at Westover, when "it was about as bad a scene as I could ever have imagined," she admitted. When she had attended a generation earlier, it had never occurred to her to disobey or even displease her headmistress, the indomitable Louise Dillingham. When the trustees met in the Common Room where Miss Dillingham's oil portrait hung, Anita would imagine that the searching eyes in the painting were staring straight into hers, and she would find herself saying silently to the picture as a meeting adjourned, "Okay, okay, I did the best I could."

Under her leadership, the board kicked off the most ambitious fundraising effort ever undertaken by a girls' school, the Second Century Campaign, intended to double the endowment. The qualities she needed in abundance were listed under her senior picture in *The Coagess*: "Forth she went, independent and undaunted." Fundraising was greatly helped by all the new publicity about the benefits of girls' schools as well as small schools. It was also aided by the arrival of Sharon Holladay in the development office, which "suddenly became a very efficient machine," Anita remembered. The demographic draught had ended and applications were up, so it was a time of growing optimism. By the mid-1990s, incoming students had the highest test scores of any class since 1970, the year before the enrollment had taken a dramatic plunge. Meanwhile, the admissions office was able to offer financial aid to more than half the applicants, a larger percentage than at comparable schools.

Anita Montgomery had "a real faith" in Joe Molder, she said, even though she knew he would never be the kind of headmaster who was comfortable making small talk at cocktail parties, and the Montgomerys and the Molders became close friends. One day he telephoned her to talk about whether Westover should join a gay alliance being organized by other independent schools. She remarked that he was very lucky that she was board president, and when he asked why, she told him that she had insight into the matter because one of her daughters was a lesbian. After much discussion between them and at the school, it was decided to neither encourage nor isolate any gay students. Instead of joining the alliance—mindful of a potential image problem for a same-sex school—Westover started a Gay–Straight Alliance. In this way, all the adolescents could together discuss issues of sexuality, like the normality of younger girls idealizing older ones. Developing a crush on someone does not mean a girl is bisexual or gay, they learned, but if a girl declares herself to be gay, she is expected to follow the policy prohibiting sexual contact at school. It has turned out that many more heterosexual than homosexual students have been suspended for breaking this rule.

After the debacle with the young administrator, the headmaster had hired Janis Gilley, a straightforward teacher with four children and five step-children, to be dean of students. One of the issues he wanted her to deal with was the hazing that had taken hold after Miss Dillingham's retirement. Upperclassmen, for instance, were frightening new girls with the possibility of being "a leftover" instead of being chosen a West or an Over. A new tradition called "dirge" had also started, when seniors blackened their faces, dressed in black, and marched onto the corridor of the youngest girls while singing and banging hockey sticks. Incoming girls were also blindfolded, sworn to silence, and led or dragged to the pond and threatened with being thrown in. Molder knew from long and hard experience that it would be impossible to ban these practices outright. Older students felt strongly that they had a right to treat younger ones the way they had been treated. So Jan Gilley formed a traditions committee, and every year a few modifications were made until, by the end of the 1990s, the more cruel customs were changed or ended. More pleasant traditions were put in their place, like walking new girls on a path illuminated by lanterns to the pond to be welcomed by seniors, who sing to them and set out onto the water little yellow boats with lit candles as a greeting. In this way, school traditions—including the germans, the lantern ceremony, the graduation circle, and all the others—continued to arouse the warm and fond feelings that Mary Hillard had intended so long ago.

In the 1990s Theodate Pope Riddle's architectural masterpiece was also added, along with the area around the Middlebury green, to the National Register of Historic Places. During the decade, the school grounds became more attractive under the headmaster's interested and caring eye. Landscape architect and historian Diane McGuire, who had restored the Beatrix Farrand gardens at Dumbarton Oaks in Washington, D.C., was hired. It was she who discovered Farrand's 1912 drawing of Westover's foundation plantings among the earlier landscape designer's papers at the University of California at Berkeley. Even though the accompanying plant list was missing, McGuire was able to make educated guesses about the original plantings, like the barberry hedges alongside the front walkway. She also designed large lanterns to top the pillars on either side of the entrance and benches carved with the motif of the Tudor rose. Old herringbone brick walkways were relaid, and a granite cobblestone curb was built. The landscape architect also added rose arbors to the senior garden, and had playing fields regraded, and the pond dredged. Before she was finished, she had traditional sugar maples, lilacs, tulip trees, and crabapples planted around the grounds.

The beauty of Westover's grounds and structures symbolized the state of the school as Molder moved closer to retirement, when he and Beth planned to move to their home in Middlebury overlooking Lake Quassapaug. After almost a quarter century, the quiet New Englander was said to be the longest serving headmaster of any girls' school in the country. Some thought his greatest achievement was keeping the school a place for girls, while others were sure it was simply its survival. The year of his retirement, 1997, also marked the successful conclusion of the fundraising campaign, which enlarged the school endowment to more than $21 million. "Even for a close observer, it isn't easy to know how all this has been accomplished or by just what qualities," Miss Newton mused about the headmaster's style. "Vision, of course. Constant scrutiny of contemporary theory and practice. Evolution of firm goals, patiently accomplished. In meetings, the low-key leadership, silent for long minutes till at last the best thought and judgment prevail. Under attack, the smiling good humor that is completely natural. Making small changes over *here* that later result in enormous progress over *there*."

A few years earlier, he had uttered words at graduation that a senior never forgot. "He told us not to have a superficial life," recalled Victoria Campbell more than two decades later. "It is simple advice, yet deeply meaningful and more complex and harder to live by than it appears. I knew what he meant as we sat there, clutching our white dresses, eager to embark on our journeys, eager for the summer to come and life to begin. He meant to live a life where what we do means something to ourselves, our thinking and independent selves. By not living a superficial life it means to stay clear of the easy road, that patience is hard won and painful, yet ultimately rewarding because our own integrity remains intact."

Victoria and her friends used to talk late into the nights in the dormitory, "dreaming of our adventurous lives," she remembered. A decade after graduation, she realized that "it is so easy to lose ourselves, our wonderful, spirited, ebullient, hopeful, contemplative, imperfect Westover selves." She went on: "It is easy to relinquish those days and become something else, someone society deems normal and conventional, someone who keeps everything in line and goes through the motions, buys nice things, and has a nice, pretty veneer of life. And yet this is precisely what Mr. Molder warned us against by telling us not to live a superficial life." She admitted that Los Angeles, where she worked as a writer and actress, is "one of the most notoriously superficial places on the planet." But, she said, "I try to live those words every day by not coasting through life, by living for my own truth no matter how unpopular or alone I feel, by not feeding into the material frenzy and 'perfect life' syndrome which plagues us in a silent, insidious way." She said she still intended to live "a real, breathing, messy, chaotic, colorful life and not a superficial one. I promise you Mr. Molder!"

On a rainy Saturday in May of 1997, more than eight hundred people who knew the Molders gathered under tents on a playing field for a day of sporting events, student performances, and other activities in the couple's honor. During the speeches and giving of gifts, the retiring headmaster sat smiling and taking it all in, even when his two sons rode in on a pair of fancy new bicycles for them. The mood was festive despite the weather, and even though everyone sang "Auld Lang Syne" at the end, "it was not a sad day but a celebration of his years there," remembered Rosa Gatling Williams, who was celebrating her twentieth reunion. In his remarks, Molder mentioned that Rosa's young daughter had just given him a card made from coloring paper, thanking him for her wonderful mother. "Now, in my twenty-six years of headmastering, a goodly number of parents have credited us with improving their daughters, but this was the first time that a daughter had credited us with improving her mom! In the child's mind, a school full of love is a school that makes great moms." Rosa, one of seven siblings from a Waterbury family, recalled him fondly from the time he was trying to enroll more African-American students. She never forgot the kindly way he showed her and her parents around, and his evident desire to have her attend. That day she fell in love with Westover, and even though friends at home wondered if it was a reform school, she stayed for four years.

The notorious class of 1972, returning for its twenty-fifth reunion that day, made the Molders honorary members of their class. "Apparently our class had quite a reputation, and yet I never felt that he prejudged us," explained Joan Gerster. A classmate, Edith Noble Bacon, realized that he had "single-handedly brought Westover back from a very dark place and moved it front and center." She added: "I feel very fortunate to have known him. He is one in a million; a truly amazing, marvelous man." By then, they regretted having made fun of his difficulty in remembering their names and pronouncing them properly. Like others, they recognized that during the years of rebellion and resentment about rules and regulations, his steady hand had enabled Westover to adapt to another generation and then go on with its spirit intact. "I think what Joe managed to do, miraculously and well, was to keep enough of that core of beauty that's at the center of the school and change it, direct it to a new center," observed Ann Pollina. He had "weathered that tumultuous time with incredible grace," she said, because instead of making tactical moves, he always did "what he thought was right."

For a long time, he had thought that Ann would be the ideal person to take his place. It was clear that the ebullient and extroverted dean

Joseph and Beth Molder. SVEN MARTSON.

was a natural leader. President of both her high school and college student councils, she also took the lead at Westover. "At first there was respect for her intelligence and her expertise in presenting her ideas," remembered Trudy Martin, but before long she "was acting as an authority in faculty meetings, regardless of who was supposed to be in charge of them." Earlier, she had been uninterested in the promotion because her daughters were young, and she was deeply involved in innovating new ways to teach math to girls. Now she was asked again. The board wanted the school to be better known outside the educational establishment, so she agreed to let her name be put forth. She knew that being headmistress would make it easier to promote the work at Westover she cared so passionately about. She also hoped that the position would also enable her to be a "gadfly" who kept people talking about girls' schools.

Anita Montgomery informed the headhunter that the school had a strong inside candidate with enormous support. As he looked into it, he thought he had found something negative when a pupil told him that she did not want Mrs. Pollina to be promoted, until he learned the reason why—she didn't want to lose her math teacher. In a decision that seemed inevitable, the board voted unanimously to make Ann Stephanie Pollina, at the age of forty-eight, the sixth head of Westover School. The news was received "with great joy" by students and staff, the board president reported, because the teacher's "wisdom, sense of humor and warmth have made her a valued, trusted and beloved member of the Westover community." That month Anita jotted a note to a board member that "the reception of the news by the faculty and students would have made you cry, and Ann's response was just perfect. I think we are truly blessed and also think that we deserve this kind of a break." The following spring, as Anita celebrated her fiftieth reunion, she stepped down as president of the board and received the Westover Award.

The background of Westover's new leader was seen as quintessentially American, but in a different way from those of her predecessors. Born in New York City in 1948, she spent her early years living in a brownstone in an Italian neighborhood that became known as East Harlem, among a large extended family of immigrant grandparents and many aunts, uncles, and cousins. Her father, Frank Maiorino, the eldest of nine children and the patriarch of the family, ran a printing business in lower Manhattan. There, in middle age, he had met his wife, Stefanya or Stephanie Wyskiel, who worked in the office as a secretary. She had moved to Manhattan during the Depression to find work and send money home to her Polish immigrant family in the mill town of Manchester, New Hampshire.

When Ann was around ten and her brother twelve, the family moved to Bayside, a neighborhood on the far edge of the borough of Queens, where the children continued to go to Catholic schools. Ann, who always adored school, went on to a co-institutional high school in Queens, Bishop Reilly High School, where girls and boys had separate classes but joint activities, "which in some ways is the best of all worlds," she has said. When she turned sixteen, she worked on Saturdays and in summers in the credit office of Lord & Taylor on Fifth Avenue. It was the 1960s. She was on the Fordham debating team, and she used to argue with her father about feminism and the Vietnam War. (Her mother, on the other hand, was "a model of decorum," in her daughter's words, who banned arguments from the dinner table.) Although father and daughter vigorously disagreed, he was never angry with her personally. His attitude toward her—as well as her years in all-girl classes—made her unafraid to be outspoken.

At her October 1997 installation in St. Margaret's Chapel, alumnae and others drew their little rush-and-wood chairs closely around their new head of school (the word "headmistress" was banned as old-fashioned). In her remarks that day, she touched on the topic of misconceptions about schools for girls. She vehemently disagreed with the notion that they were only for shy girls, especially since the latest research showed that few girls flourished in classrooms with boys. Instead, she emphatically stated that any kind of girl can benefit tremendously from the culture in a female community. That autumn day, she turned to the assembled pupils and told them that "you are here not to hide from the real world—you are here to learn to build a better world." And, she added, "because of you, and your potential to change the world, I am proud to be head of this school." She had already graciously acknowledged that she was taking over a school in very good shape: the next year it would win virtually unanimous approval from evaluators, especially for the "depth and richness" of its academics, the excellent relationships among everyone, and its focus on its mission. She indicated that under her leadership there would be changes in style but none in purpose, explaining that "Westover has great momentum as it approaches its one hundredth birthday."

13

The Ethic of Care:
Defending Girls' Schools

UNFORTUNATELY, A FEW MONTHS AFTER ANN POLLINA'S INSTAL-
lation, the important American Association of University Women suddenly backed off
from advocating girl-only classrooms, saying in the spring of 1998 that attention should
be given instead to improving education for the vast majority of girls in the nation's
coeducational schools. It was also concerned about the legal and political consequences
of endorsing the separation of the sexes in public schools. Its report, which published
conflicting or neutral—not negative—data about girls' schools, "is at worst uncertain"
about their advantages, a *Wall Street Journal* editorial stated, and it concluded that it was
"a case history of how politics trumps policy nowadays in this country." Most contributors to *Separated by Sex: A Critical Look at Single Sex Education for Girls* acknowledged that
the research showed that girls learn better apart from boys, but, they asked, was this
because of the absence of boys, or better schools, or more supportive parents, or some
other reason? Whatever the case, Westover's new principal fired off a letter of protest
to *The New York Times*, which went unpublished.

The backlash against girls' schools grew, and the next month *The Atlantic Monthly*
published a harsh attack by the writer Wendy Kaminer, a member of the Smith College class of 1971. When she had attended the Massachusetts women's college more
than twenty-five years earlier, she had experienced more sexism in its genteel female
atmosphere than among other Jewish students at her public high school on Long Island,
she wrote. "Since their inception in the nineteenth century, all-girls schools have fos-

tered femininity along with feminism. They are models of equivocation, reinforcing regressive notions of sex difference at the same time that they educate women and help to facilitate their entry into the professions," she declared.

Ann Pollina responded again, asking rhetorically in a published letter to the *Atlantic*'s editor what was the matter with femininity coexisting alongside feminism. What is really wrong, she wrote, is that all too often girls feel they must choose between the two. "What Kaminer sees as equivocation in single sex-schools, I see as balance," she said, adding that "I do not think we will ever be successful in our quest for equity by androgyny." In her letter, she also mentioned that she urged the future scientists and engineers in her classes to retain their caring natures. "We have all come to understand that not only can they do mathematics in spite of their traditionally feminine concerns, but that they will do better mathematics because of them." She believed they would do this by bringing their altruism and other approaches to the profession. While girls need math, she emphasized another time, "in my heart I firmly believe that math needs girls." This idea has to do with her conviction that integrating relational and rational styles heightens creativity and leads to intellectual breakthroughs. "We get further, we do more, we're wider open, we learn differently, we learn different things about the universe, and we pose different questions," she has explained. Scientists like Barbara McClintock, who won the Nobel Prize in cytogenetics, as well as the primatologists Jane Goodall and Dian Fossey, have advanced the research in their fields by being attentive to relationships, she has pointed out.

In these letters and elsewhere, Pollina has promoted an ethic of care, which includes an ardent defense of women's traditional work. It is a viewpoint that is unusual for an innovative educator who believes in the empowerment of girls. Women should not have to apologize for staying home and caring for children or elders, she says, or for taking time to cook and do other housework. She has taken exception to the slogan of a supposedly pro-girl advertisement—"If you want her to succeed, give her a chemistry set instead of a doll"—because she believes girls should be given both. "This is a *very, very* hard message to get across," she has admitted. Still, she is sure that affirming the gentler virtues long associated with womanhood actually validates schoolgirls, since these values are inherent, or at least deeply ingrained, in girls. "We accept traditionally male work as the important work, we teach our daughters to aspire to it exclusively, then we wonder what happens to their self-esteem," she also wrote in her letter to *The Atlantic Monthly.* She has also challenged the educational establishment for neglecting to encourage caring attitudes and activities in young men. Aware that educators, especially in former boys' schools, were saying that they were now giving equal attention to girls, she has pointed out that she had heard nothing about praising male students for babysitting or giving time to community service. This is very important to do, she has said, since the ability to nurture and be sensitive toward others enables everyone to get along at home and at work.

Ann Pollina's installation as head of school, October 16, 1997.
TOM KABELKA, COURTESY *REPUBLICAN-AMERICAN.*

For years, Westover's leader has realized that girls' schools should be valued as laboratories for how most females—and many males—learn best. This is a pragmatic approach since the schools educate relatively few pupils, and it enlarges their purpose. Still, the ongoing debate about their merits is missing an opportunity to discuss the nature of an excellent education, Ann has pointed out. "Why is not the educational community beating down the doors at all-girls' schools in search of this information?" she has asked. "If we truly valued things female, we would be more willing to learn from the experience of girls' schools, trusting that education that is good for girls is simply good education." It is "almost sexist," she ventured another time, to ignore what they have to tell us. She and other educators have long known that something intangible—a kind of energy and excitement—can happen in a classroom without males. From 1978 until her retirement, feminist philosopher and theologian Mary Daly insisted on teaching only female classes at coeducational Boston College because of what she called this "gynergy."

In the midst of the backlash, Ann Pollina invited Maggie Ford, president of the educational research arm of the American Association of University Women, to a debate in Middlebury. After her guest spoke in Red Hall, Ann took her turn. Although she acknowledged that a school for girls is likely to be criticized for clinging to "a traditional philosophy," she declared that the honoring of humane values is "a revolutionary philosophy" in contemporary America. She touched on many topics that evening, insisting that what teachers of girls have always known is very relevant today. "If these were men's institutions, we would be complementing them on their educational foresight and naming the techniques after them. Every educator knows about the Socratic method and the Harkness table, the brilliant pedagogical techniques that work very well, particularly in the all-male environments in which they were formed," she said. "If Socrates was a woman, and if she was teaching all girls, I am afraid the research would have said, 'Isn't it lucky that she stumbled upon this trick of asking open-ended questions?'" She went on: "We should have a Wellesley organizational culture, like a Socratic method, or a Westover circle like a Harkness table."

Around that time she began to refer to Westover girls as "*all* my children," perhaps because she is the school's only headmistress to be a mother. "This job is every mother's dream," she likes to say, since she is entitled to boast about her many accomplished daughters, who win state and national prizes every year. No doubt as insightful as her predecessors into her pupils' personalities, she has the advantage of firsthand experience. When she became head of the school, her real daughters were thirteen and eleven years old; the older, Emily, was already at Westover and her younger sister,

Elizabeth, attended the Middlebury elementary school. Their mother wanted to continue teaching an advanced calculus class since, she often says, there's "a part of my soul that lives in the classroom." When Emily was ready to enter the calculus class, her mother worried about being able to fairly evaluate her own child, and whether or not she should teach the class at all. The two had "a long, hard conversation," the principal recalled, when her daughter reminded her about their promise not to do anything differently after her promotion. The day when the mother walked into the calculus class for the first time, Ann was surprised to see her daughter's face merge with the faces of the others. "It was a moment of revelation," she said, when she realized that she had been a teacher longer than a mother. When Emily

Two students studying together.
© GABRIEL AMADEUS COONEY.

raised her hand to answer a question and began, "Mrs. Pollina . . . ," everyone laughed, and then when another pupil raised her hand and started, "Mom . . . ," they burst into laughter again, dissipating the tension.

Emily, a member of the class of 2000, wanted to be treated like the other girls, but she also needed to talk to her mother about school. "She developed this little routine, where she would say, 'Permission to talk to you as a mom?'" Ann recalled. Then she would listen to her daughter and do only what a mother would do in the situation, taking no action as head of the school. Once, when she learned about some misbehavior and asked Emily if she knew about it, the teenager said she would be the last to know. Ann interpreted this silence as the way the other pupils protected her daughter from divided loyalties, and she praised it as a "remarkable" form of kindness. Elizabeth, who graduated with high honors in 2003, followed her older sister's lead. As a mother of two different kinds of daughters who both thrived at Westover, Ann has said that motherhood has deepened her understanding of the school.

In the past, inspiring role models of women who did it all have been few and far between, but now Ann Pollina—wife, mother, and professional—is regarded as an admirable example of a modern woman. Warmhearted and given to affectionate embraces, her authority rests on the teenagers' respect for her authenticity and intelligence. "No matter what was going on at Westover, Mrs. Pollina made her flawless efforts to appear happy and put-together, except in circumstances when an appearance of that sort would be detrimental," remembered Alyssa Siefert. "For example, there was a period during winter term in which there were a number of emotional disciplinary committee meetings (in which such cataclysmic events as seniors getting expelled occurred), and I clearly remember the concern and the compassion on Mrs. Pollina's face as she orchestrated an all-school meeting one night. After the meeting, several students came up and hugged her, and as always she gracefully fielded their questions and eased their worries." Alyssa, who was head of the Athletic Association, liked to joke and laugh with her during their weekly meetings together. "I think that if I had to describe Mrs. Pollina in a single word, I would choose 'graceful,' for she is an exemplary and brilliant woman who handles every situation she finds herself in with grace," the graduate continued. "I could not ask for a better head of school to lead the unique and nurturing environment that she has fostered at Westover."

As always, the ambience of the school is subtly but profoundly influenced by its historic architecture, which sets the tone of the living and learning going on inside. The century-old drawings of the original quadrangular building hang in Red Hall and along its balcony, giving generations of girls a chance to see the initial plan for a smaller boarding school. "Architecturally this place births community," Ann Pollina has observed, referring to the communal spaces and circular routes of the square-shaped building. "The way the school is designed forces, requires, and celebrates interactions among students," she says. "It's very hard to be cliquish." Like previous principals, she is a fierce defender of its architectural integrity. When it was suggested by outsiders that the Theodate Pope Riddle structure be enlarged to make more spacious apartments for residents and more gathering places for students upstairs, she firmly rejected the idea. Adding on to the old façade is "not an option," she stated, and neither is the other option of eliminating ten or eleven student bedrooms to make more interior space in what is already a small school.

When it was necessary to expand in the past, Mary Hillard, Louise Dillingham, and Joseph Molder had dreamed about adding outlying buildings until they eventually became realities. Even though Miss Dillingham was in declining health in the early 1960s, she brought into being the student activities center with its gymnasium and stage, called "one of the finest buildings of its kind in the country" at the time. Three decades later, however, as athletic and performing arts programs expanded and competition for pupils increased, the LBD building had become outgrown. Since Middlebury was no longer isolated in the countryside, sports teams were competing with many other schools, and Wests and Overs became more spirit teams than anything else. To avoid late evening athletic practices and drama rehearsals, each activity needed its own space. So to design an overall master plan the board of trustees hired architect Graham Gund, who, like other architects before him, regarded the original building as an architectural masterpiece that must remain dominant in any new design.

Around that time, Mary Fuller Russell, a member of the class of 1930, unexpectedly left to her alma mater in her will $6.1 million, the largest gift in the school's history. After graduating, she had briefly taught sports at Westover, so it was decided to start the expansion with a new athletics building and name it after her. In October of 2000, a Dixieland band led a festive procession of students and staff carrying colorful balloons to a groundbreaking ceremony. "We learn things with our bodies as well as our minds," Ann Pollina explained at the dedication the next year. The very large and light-filled Fuller Athletic Center, with squash, basketball, and volleyball courts as well as a fitness room and a rock climbing wall, sits appropriately at a lower elevation than the main building and, placed at a slight angle behind Virginia House, creates another courtyard that gives the campus the comfortable feeling of a small village.

The transformation of the LBD building into a state-of-the-art performing arts center followed. In the spring of 2004, six alumnae—former Julliard and Manhattan School of Music students—gave a fundraising concert as the work neared completion. The renovated theater with four hundred fixed and moveable seats was built with a catwalk around its interior, echoing the encircling balcony in Red Hall, and with a modern lighting and sound system workable by students, making it an ideal teaching space. Playwright A. R. Gurney met with acting students when it was finished and reminisced about his late mother, Marion Spaulding Goodyear, a member of Westover's class of 1926. He told them that she had often spoken about how the school in Miss Hillard's day had stimulated her love of learning. (Nevertheless, female characters in several of his plays, which gently satirize the ways of old-fashioned WASPs, are identified as Westover graduates.) Finally, a Joachim Schumacher art gallery was constructed in the entryway, a fiftieth anniversary gift from the class of 1954, who had known the enthusiastic and often enthralling art history teacher in his prime.

Afterward, it was time to focus on enlarging the endowment, decided the board of trustees, by then headed by Louisa Jones Palmer, who graduated with the class of 1954 and from Radcliffe before becoming a foreign tax expert at Ernst & Young in New York. A much larger endowment was necessary to safeguard the school throughout its next hundred years, the board said, because almost half the teachers in the country—including the loyal group that Molder hired in the 1970s and 1980s—would be retiring soon. With far fewer following in their footsteps, Westover will have to compete for the best of them. Throughout the years, its principals have understood that finding gifted and genial teachers is their most important challenge. "True education is a face-to-face, mind-to-mind process," Ann Pollina has said. "You get good people in a school, you have them interacting with young minds, and you can create a *great* educational structure."

Graduates gathered around the Senior Tree in the Quad. SVEN MARTSON.

When Harvard president Lawrence Summers suggested in the winter of 2005 that women lack innate ability in math and science, his words hit Westover like a bombshell. Ann observed that "it was a wake-up call, and it knocked girls out of their complacency," especially for the admired W.I.S.E. students. Outraged and defiant, they immediately rejected his remarks but, nonetheless, organized a panel discussion about them over pizza in Red Hall. During an interview at a Waterbury radio station, Lindsay Chromik admitted it was "scary" that such an influential person would say such a thing, Alyssa Siefert said she was "shocked" that he had said it at a conference promoting diversity in math and science, and Annie Zheng conceded the importance of learning that "there are still people in the world like that." Another teenager withdrew her application from Harvard and went on to study engineering at Columbia instead.

During the brouhaha, the media began speculating again about why the numbers of women with doctoral degrees in engineering and computer science were so small. "Every gain women have made in the past two hundred years has been in the face of experts insisting they couldn't do it and didn't really want to," noted Radcliffe alumna Katha Pollitt in *The Nation*. She went on to say that if career paths were designed with women in mind, they would allow time off to raise children without penalty and peak later. "By treating this work culture as fixed, and women as the problem, Summers lets academia off the hook." Westover's principal reiterated her belief that the sciences would be "richer, broader, better" with more women scientists. Still, she was worried. All too often she saw W.I.S.E. graduates go off enthusiastically to engineering schools and later change course because the attitudes and teaching techniques in the mostly male colleges made the work unrewarding and "joyless." A year and a half after Summers misspoke, a blue ribbon panel of women educators under the aegis of the National Academy of Sciences bluntly blamed the situation on bias. Although the damage was done, Summers was soon replaced by a historian as well as a graduate of a girls' school and a woman's college, Drew Gilpin Faust, who was named the first female president of Harvard University.

In the aftermath, the old debate about differences between men and women took another turn. Research in its early stages on the living human brain by new imaging technology was suggesting that male and female brains differ structurally at birth, develop at dissimilar paces, and work in distinct ways. While uncertainty continues among women about whether or not to emphasize these distinctions, it is becoming increasingly apparent that the genders take their own mental routes to the same place. Whatever the case, evidence indicates that females use neural connections on both sides of the brain more often than males, especially in the active and intense emotional part. Studying the mentality of girls has, in fact, led to widespread concepts in society like "emotional intelligence," the "relational self," and "the feeling brain," Carol Gilligan has observed. Perhaps because of the reflective mental activity of schoolgirls, their teachers have long liked to give them a few moments to think before answering questions, a pause that is difficult to protect in a classroom with more competitive boys.

Educators should devise tests that use girls' "abilities to synthesize, make connections, and use their practical intelligence," Ann Pollina has written. If scientists eventually find absolute proof for what she has long believed—that many girls think differently than most boys—this will be yet another reason for teaching girls together, at least for a few transformative teenage years.

Over the past century, among the many changes at Westover is the pace of school life. "The work is very challenging, and the girls are pushed, they push themselves, and they prod each other as they go out of their way to bring everyone along," Pollina says. It is unlike the tempo in Mary Hillard's day, when not everyone left school with a diploma and went on to college, as she envisioned married women living one kind of life, and professional women like herself living another. In those days, no one expected middle- and upper-class women to do it all. Even during the Dillingham decades, when almost every graduate headed to college, there was a general course of study for others. Since those days, the country, or at least its meritocracy, has become intensely competitive. "The real culprit, if there is one, is our culture," explains the third female head. The effects are felt everywhere, including the "enormous pressure" to excel at Westover, in the words of a recent graduate, but the stress goes along with a sense of pride that so many students win top scores on nationwide examinations.

Nonetheless, this pressure worries teachers, who look back nostalgically to earlier decades, even to the early 1970s when it was difficult to get girls to study at all. "We've lost some things as well as gained some things along the way," Shamus Weber says, noting that fewer pupils take the time to write what he calls "great" papers. In the view of Alice Hallaran, we are "too driven, too serious, too self-critical, too intense, too productive, just plain too busy to enjoy what we are doing," as she implicitly raised the question of the purpose of a good education. "We want to do it all and do it *all well*. Is this possible? Perhaps the answer to that question is not as important as asking, 'Are we fulfilled?' Are we doing an injustice, a disservice to our students, particularly as women, in making them think this is the road to success? Should we be encouraging, even demanding, that they make some tough choices, as their future lives will require?" she asked. "I wonder what Mary Hillard and Theodate Pope Riddle would say were they here today? Would they applaud and cheer us on? Or would they say 'stop thinking, stop doing, and let yourself BE!'"

These are not easy questions to answer. Intensity is also "part and parcel of what is wonderful at Westover," Ann Pollina has pointed out, because it is a way for teenagers to discover and develop their interests and abilities. After going to all-girls classes herself, she felt she could be anything, she remembers, and she wants her many daughters to feel that way, too. "If I have one hope for each of you," she tells them, "it is that you will take away from this place one passion: one thought that has captured you, one activity that excites you, the seeds of a dream. If you are truly fortunate, as I have been, your passion will be your work." She understands that they will have to make difficult choices: "It may be that they don't do all of those things at once, or at college, or beyond, but they can, and they know they can." But her graduates do not have to do it all just because they can, she also tells them: "You don't have to marry. You don't have to have kids. You don't have to have a career. You don't have to do all those things to be a successful woman."

It is also true that too much emotional intensity can easily arise in a female environment, especially under the stress of getting into college. While pressure exists to go to prestigious Ivy League universities, the college advisor also suggests smaller colleges where graduates might be happier. When girls ask their principal whether one elective or another would look better on college applications, she says her answer is always the same: "Who cares? What will look good to a college is the course of your heart. So my answer to you is, 'Which one do you want to take?'" To put the anxieties of the adolescents in perspective, she makes a point of reading interesting obituaries of women to them in chapel, noting what is finally meaningful in life. Chapel services are more valuable than ever as peaceful times to do nothing but listen and let one's mind wander. "Like play, which has no explicit end outside of itself, daydreaming can be a very good thing," the chaplain says. Other ways to work off tension are playing sports, participating in the performing arts, and parties like Saturday night "rockouts" in Red Hall. Also, there is still the thrill of the unexpected Mrs. Riddle's Holiday, or Head's Day as it is now called, the surprise holiday when classes are canceled.

Going to a school like Westover is a temporary withdrawal into another world, where girls are valued for both their brains and their hearts. Teachers sometimes worry—with reason—about what will happen after graduation when most of them go on to coeducational colleges. Before then they e-mail and instant message with boys, and seniors can invite them to visit their dormitory rooms. Even so, a majority of young alumnae in a poll who believed they were better prepared than their peers for college—in writing, public speaking, participation in class discussions, and interactions with professors—also realized that they were less prepared for relationships with men outside the classroom, at least initially. Ann Vileisis wished she had known more about women's history before going to Yale and been better prepared for the kind of sexism she encountered there. During her freshman and sophomore years at Westover, she and her friends had wanted boyfriends, but gradually she realized that "it wasn't the time in our lives for it, and after we let go of it, we were happier." It was a time for learning and a time for other kinds of enjoyment. As always, it was a time for friendship. When Erin Zwack was a senior in 2004, she mused in a chapel talk about her unlikely rapport with classmate Allison Grande, calling herself a "slightly insane, loud person," and her friend "kind, sane, and quiet." She theorized that each of them—and perhaps all good friends—recognized "something" similar in each other, while finding in their differences a way to expand their own experience. Another alumna now in her fifties has remarked that at Westover she "never learned to flirt, but I got a great education."

Westover, of course, has never pretended to be a utopia like the one in Charlotte Perkins Gilman's novel *Herland.* As always, boarders complain about claustrophobia, confinement, and being in a nunnery, especially during the winter months. Secretive groups play pranks like putting goldfish in toilets, shaving a dean's cat, and once even spray painting male genitalia on the grass of a playing field right before graduation. Sometimes it is difficult for adolescents to learn to be honorable human beings. And rules, of course, continue to be broken. After some sophomores brought liquor to a school dance, one of them became so intoxicated that an ambulance had to take her to a hospital. Ann Pollina reacted with toughness along with compassion, calling the incident "very naive experimentation" by "deeply good kids" and suspending ten students—those who drank and those who knew about the drinking. During her decade as Westover's leader, she has continued to win praise from pupils and parents alike. Her "serenity under pressure, her ability to listen, her passion for fairness, and her leadership qualities are remarkable, and we and our daughter count ourselves very fortunate to have met her," a father has observed.

What has stayed the same over the past hundred years is the attention given to moral education. Mary Hillard often sounded more like a minister's daughter than an educator in her desire to inculcate values. When attempting to integrate the school in the 1950s, Louise Dillingham insisted that Westover must be "a *good* school" in an ethical way. Like Miss Hillard, she had students memorize the lovely St. Paul's Letter to the Corinthians. Joseph Molder carried on the emphasis on ethics by hiring a chaplain and continuing compulsory chapel attendance when it was rare at other schools. He kept up the traditions, too. "When I think of the Molders, I am reminded of I Corinthians, Chapter 13, which was often read in the chapel," said a member of the class of 1980. "'Charity suffereth long, and is kind; charity envieth not; charity vaunteth not itself, is not puffed up,'" she remembered, quoting the old Biblical words. "'Doth not behave itself unseemly, seeketh not her own, is not easily provoked, thinketh no evil.'" The present principal tells incoming students that "you will be asked to grow both in learning and in goodness," and she often talks about the importance of honesty, loyalty, courage, kindness, and generosity. The Distinguished Young Alumna Award, which was initiated on her watch, goes to "an inspired intellectual, artist, athlete, philosopher, or entrepreneur," who also has "integrity, responsibility, and commitment to community." Under the aegis of the charitable Dorcas Society, juniors now learn about philanthropy by raising, investing, and donating money. And it is mandatory for every pupil to give a number of hours a year to community service: tutoring, visiting convalescent homes, or serving at the Waterbury Soup Kitchen.

Mass media messages about teenage "mean girls" and "queen bees" annoy Ann Pollina because she doesn't believe their behavior is inevitable. When a girl is unkind, disrespectful, or acts in an exclusive way, she is likely to be confronted by a grownup who asks her to empathize with the person whose feelings she hurt. "You can't be cool and mean at Westover," the principal says. "If you create a culture where that's not okay, they adjust," she says, snapping her fingers, "just like that." Westover, she also says, is a place of "incredible challenge without competitiveness." She has gone as far as to say that there is something "absolutely glorious about the society of women." Outsiders have noticed the school's openness and warmth, which teachers talk about proudly. "The school is very down-to-earth, very friendly, and the kids are very happy," says Alice Hallaran. Her husband, Terry, sees "a generosity of spirit" in the way pupils not only accept but try to get to know those from different backgrounds. Shamus Weber observes that they are tolerant of "quirky" classmates, the types of teenagers who might be ostracized at other schools. When Rachel Bashevkin taught public speaking, her students disliked judging each other's talks by holding up numbers because it seemed too harsh, so they decided to rate them differently. "There's a way that girls critique each other that's compassionate, and [when I learned this] that's when I started falling in love with this place," she explained.

A cohesive community can, of course, create a culture-within-a-culture that helps instill enlightened values. It is not that impressionable young girls need protection from the world as much as they can use insulation for a while from increasingly powerful and undermining messages in the mass media about how they should think, do, and be, and especially how they should look. A member of the class of 1969, Elizabeth Stern, a social worker who has raised a daughter, bemoans "the dumbing down" of girls around the age of thirteen. Like many graduates, she would go to Westover again in a heartbeat, even though she was rebellious while there. She wishes that her daughter had gone there, too. In the counterculture of a school for girls, a young female has "a different kind of authority" and "a freedom to experiment," observed her classmate, Jeannette Byers. And this is a source of a girl's contentment as well as her growing confidence.

In the twenty-first century, Westover remains an intact and intimate community of two hundred or so girls, but now it exists within an electronically wired global village. Even though it had Middlebury's first telephone, this new development could splinter the school's cohesiveness. Long ago, Mary Hillard censored comics and crime stories in the daily newspapers, and now her most recent successor is grappling with the much greater challenge of the dangers and distractions of technology. When the Internet became widespread, it was deliberately decided not to wire bedrooms so the girls would be more likely to talk face-to-face rather than send each other e-mail messages. (Everyone was provided with telephone voice mail, and boarders have message blackboards on bedroom doors.) Now wireless access to the Internet exists throughout the school, and students and teachers can surf the Web everywhere, even in gathering places like Red Hall. It has been necessary to make rules about online reliability and safety, like demonstrating the risks of recklessly using social Web sites. Some Web sites are blocked, and rules limit access to others and the use of cell phones to specific times and places, so they do not interfere with studying and making friends at school. There is the additional concern that words about the importance of a close community do not resonate as loudly with potential pupils as restrictions against electronic communications. Westover is gradually finding ways to adjust to this new world, in its determination to remain a vibrant community within a virtual world.

Proponents of girls' schools often point to the testimony of graduates, who give their schools top grades for education and for encouragement. Certainly Ann Vileisis found it "exhilarating" to be part of a community centered on learning, and there her love of learning grew. Like so many others, she said

Red Hall with balloons on an alumnae weekend.
SVEN MARTSON.

she was able to be herself—an intellectual girl—and by the end of her freshman year she was "completely in love" with Westover. Going there, she says, "has given me a tremendous core strength and deep confidence and sense of capability." Almost all the forty-eight young alumnae who responded to a recent poll said they had liked being part of a small, supportive society. Some had decided to enroll because of the school's beauty, its small classes, or its ambience. One was impressed on her initial visit by the "intensity and sense of passion" of the pupils, while others liked their friendliness and apparent happiness. There is an "incredible sense of community and love that exists at the school," said another respondent. They would tell prospective pupils that their former school is a place to discover genuine interests, develop individuality, and make lifelong friends. "Westover let me be myself," said one of the alumnae, echoing the familiar refrain, so she graduated "truly knowing and appreciating" herself. Another said she had gained "strength of mind, body, and spirit." Going there is "an amazing experience" that you do not fully understand until it is over, another of the young alumnae said, "but it will never leave you and always help you."

At times it sounds a little like the imagined female paradise of *Herland*, envisioned by Mrs. Gilman so long ago, a place where well-mentored and high-spirited girls are eager learners, who share what they know and express themselves freely. The fictional Herlanders also live in harmony with nature, and now at Westover there is an ongoing effort to be ecologically prudent and protect the environment. Today the school is a collaborative, nonhierarchical community, where much ongoing conversation takes place about whether this decision or that will conform to what is called "the Westover way." Female scholars have observed that the conversational voice, unlike the colder appraising eye, is often used metaphorically by women when describing themselves. "Unlike the eye, the ear operates by registering nearby subtle change. Unlike the eye, the ear requires closeness between subject and object. Unlike seeing, speaking and listening suggest dialogue and interaction," according to the authors of *Women's Ways of Knowing.*

Another young alumna dreams about "the possibility of an open-minded and accepting community," and, as a result of going to Westover, is "more optimistic about changing the world." This is exactly what Ann Pollina wants to hear. Like Mary Hillard, who was intent on sending her young ladies "out into Vanity Fair *fortified*," as she put it, Pollina is passionate about her purpose. "We need to send out a phalanx of girls who are going to do what the *world* needs, which is to embody those qualities of care and nurture and community that our culture is *desperate* for right now. The culture *needs* our girls," she says. She wants them to make the world a place that recognizes and rewards themselves and others for their abilities and their altruism. "Infusing society with strong, well-trained young women who have learned in an atmosphere that celebrates feminine strengths is the only way to systematic change. This has been and should continue to be the mission of Westover." If humane qualities are ever elevated to equality with others in our society, perhaps there will no longer be a need for female communities. "But, frankly, that is going to be an incredibly long, hard struggle," she admits. "And my only fear is that if we lose girls' schools too soon, there isn't going to be a voice for those kinds of issues in the culture." And even if that day of equality comes, the experience of living in a kind of Herland for a few years deepens a young girl's understanding of her gender, of herself, and of her potential. It will be a time for all this before she returns, empowered, to the larger world.

The façade of Westover School at night. SVEN MARTSON.

NOTES

All material cited is in the archive of Westover School, unless otherwise noted. *The Lantern, The Wick,* and *The Coagess* are school publications. The diary of Theodate Pope Riddle and many other documents about her are in the archives of the Hill-Stead Museum in Farmington, Connecticut. Letters from Mary R. Hillard to August F. Jaccaci are in the collection of the August F. Jaccaci Papers 1899–1938, Archives of American Art/Smithsonian Institution (microfilm reels D118-D-126). The diary of Ginevra King and her letters to F. Scott Fitzgerald may be found in the Ginevra King Collection, relating to F. Scott Fitzgerald (C0950), Manuscripts Division, Department of Rare Books and Special Collections, Princeton University Library.

In the endnotes, a year after a name indicates an alumna's class at Westover. In the index, the letter "n" indicates that a reference is in an endnote. The following people, who are mentioned often in the notes, are identified by initials (and are not indexed after first citations):

AQE   Adele Q. Ervin '42

ASP   Ann S. Pollina

EMN   Elizabeth M. Newton

HDL   Helen D. LaMonte

JLM   Joseph L. Molder

LBD   Louise B. Dillingham

LL   Laurie Lisle '61

MRA   Maria R. Allen '42

MRH   Mary R. Hillard

1. Miss Hillard and Her Era (pages 1–20)

1. "be delighted": Pratt, diary, in "Visit with Miss Pratt Yields Pearls from the Past," by Adele Q. Ervin [AQE], *Wick*, Apr. 1950.

2. "'Taint . . . lonesome": Pratt, letter to Louise B. Dillingham [LBD], May 18, 1949.

2. "Workmen . . . activity": LaMonte [HDL], letter to AQE (early 1950s).

2. seventy or so: The number of pupils was reported as seventy in Westover's first catalog (published around 1908), as eighty by a Waterbury newspaper at the time, and as forty in a letter later written by HDL.

2. "We have been . . . beauty": Pratt, letter to Pope, Apr. 30, 1909, Hill-Stead.

2. "We are in . . . good": Mary R. Hillard [MRH], letter to August F. Jaccaci, May 24, 1909.

2–3. "It is . . . spiritual": MRH, letter to Jaccaci, July 13, 1909.

4. "vividness and aliveness": Archibald MacLeish, foreword, *Martha Hillard MacLeish*, by Martha H. MacLeish (Geneva, N.Y.: privately printed, 1949), xxxii.

4. "sweet . . . grace": Ibid., xxxi–xxxii.

4. "I can see . . . coat-tails": John T. Dallas, *Mary Robbins Hillard* (Concord, N.H.: The Rumford Press, 1944), 13.

4. "insanity . . . will": Martha H. MacLeish, *Martha Hillard MacLeish*, 14–15.

5. Hillard siblings: Emily would marry Jerry Lincoln Fenn, a Hartford lawyer, and Fanny would marry Theodore H. Morris, a Philadelphia Quaker.

5. "one hardly . . . background, too": Dallas, *Mary Robbins Hillard*, 10.

5. "simple . . . beautiful": Ibid., 14.

5–7. "very tall . . . temples": Martha Coffin, "A School Girl," manuscript (no date).

8. "a clear . . . heart" and "wealth . . . worth": Louise L. Stevenson, "Sarah Porter Educates Useful Ladies, 1847–1900," *Winterthur Portfolio* (1983).

9. "to decide . . . duty": Dallas, *Mary Robbins Hillard*, 92.

9. "some queer . . . find out": Failing, diary, Apr. 3, 1888, Hill-Stead.

9. "like a breeze . . . vitality": Ibid., Nov. 8, 1887.

10. "There was . . . restraint": Dallas, *Mary Robbins Hillard*, 61.

10–11. "There were . . . her": Ibid., 82–83.

12. "Miss Hillard . . . sin": Pope, diary, Nov. 9, 1886, Hill-Stead.

12. "Miss Hillard . . . her": Ibid., May 21, 1887.

13. "knows . . . today" Ibid., Nov. 11, 1887.

14. often with relatives and friends, including: They included Helen LaMonte, Lucy Pratt, and Mary's youngest brother, John Hillard. Around this time Theo became godmother to Mary's niece, Phyllis Fenn.

14.   Soon after her arrival . . . proposal: MRH, statement to Newton Barney and John Holcombe, July 15, 1903, Hill-Stead. Mrs. Dow was named sole principal of Miss Porter's School.

14–15. "I know . . . school": Ibid., 2, 5.

15.   "a little too exciting": Dallas, *Mary Robbins Hillard*, 83.

15–16. Years later . . . exist: Nora Borden Weare '27, letter to Westover Alumnae Office, Fall 1974.

17.   "an extremely good investment": MRH, Barney and Holcombe statement.

17.   "a true . . . influence:" MRH, letter to Whittemore, July 18, 1908, Hill-Stead.

17.   "a labor of love": Whittemore, letter to MRH, Sept. 7, 1907, Hill-Stead.

17.   "Are the girls happy": *Lantern*, June 1910.

17.   "Yellow Peril": In 1911 Henry James called the car a "fairy-godmother's gold-colored chariot," according to *Dearest of Geniuses: A Life of Theodate Pope Riddle* by Sandra L. Katz (Windsor, CT: Tide-Mar, 2003), 89.

19.   "naturally" to "to me": MRH, "Miss Hillard Makes a Formal Statement," *Waterbury American*, Nov. 20, 1907. She said she had spent $32,316.30 during her years at St. Margaret's for repairs and maintenance.

19.   "where . . . progress": *Waterbury Republican*, "Girls' Boarding School at Middlebury" (1908).

19.   quarter of a million dollars: The construction cost $509,359.48. Among the expenses were $23,000 for land, $36,956 for furniture and furnishings, $4,119 for kitchen appliances and utensils, $1,645 for china, glass, and table silver, $3,214 for laundry machinery, and $517 for reference books.

19.   "spirit": Dallas, *Mary Robbins Hillard*, prologue.

19–20. "very well . . . soda fountains": MRH, letter to Whittemore, Feb.13, 1908, Hill-Stead.

20.   Many times . . . people: MRH, letter to E. Robert Stevenson, Apr. 16, 1927.

2. Creating a School (pages 21–40)

22.   "strained nervous look": Charlotte Perkins Gilman, *Herland and Other Selected Stories by Charlotte Perkins Gilman* (New York: Signet Classic, 1992), 24.

22.   "prepossessing": David F. Ransom, "Nomination of Westover School to the National Register of Historic Places," Connecticut Historic Commission, Oct. 21, 1984.

23.   "From today . . . life": MRH, graduation remarks (no date).

24.   "a plain country school": *Sunday (Waterbury) Republican*, "Connecticut Private Schools Second to None," Sept. 27, 1931.

24.   "living . . . create": Pratt, letter to Theodate Pope (Riddle), Feb. 15, 1937, Hill-Stead.

25.   water: Nearby land with a lake, Lake Elise, was bought in the summer of 1909.

25.   In gratitude, the [Talbott] family gave the school: Louise Mead Walker Resor '34, interview by Laurie Lisle (LL), Feb. 27, 2000. Eliza Talbott Thayer '20 designed the fireplace; she was a sculptor

and received the Westover Award in 1965. Other sisters were Daisy (St. Margaret's), Lily '09, Elsie '13, Marianna '16, Katherine '22, and Margaret '24. Elsie was married in the chapel, and her daughter (Louise '34) was christened there; she received the Westover Award in 1969. At first the Lantern ceremony was always held at the school farm, but once the Seven Sisters fireplace had been built, it was held there.

25. "the right kind of girls": MRH, letter to Jaccaci, Jan. 7, 1909.

26. Agnes Irwin: Jessica Baylis '12, letter to her parents (1911–12).

26. "poorly educated . . . to us": MRH, letter to "Mr. Carry" (no date), Hill-Stead.

26. "Westover . . . back": *Fortune Magazine*, "Westover—Which Is Miss Hillard," August 1931.

26. Edith Cummings: Cummings '17 was from Lake Forest, Illinois. Called the "Fairway Flapper," she won the U.S. Women's Amateur golf title in 1923 and was the first woman to be on the cover of *Time* magazine, on Aug. 25, 1924.

26–27. "Well . . . demon:" Ginevra King '17, letter to F. Scott Fitzgerald, May 22, 1916, Princeton. See *The Perfect Hour: The Romance of F. Scott Fitzgerald and Ginevra King, His First Love*, by James L. W. West III (New York: Random House, 2005). Also, *Gatsby's Girl* by Caroline Preston, a novel based on the romance (New York: Houghton Mifflin, 2006).

27. "Unexpectedly . . . over": F. Scott Fitzgerald, "A Woman With a Past," *The Stories of F. Scott Fitzgerald*, introduction by Malcolm Cowley (New York: Macmillan, 1987), 376.

27. "an elaborate . . . home": MRH, letter to Pope (later Riddle), Mar. 4, 1911, Hill-Stead.

27. long hair: Betty Hillis Rasmussen '38, letter to LL, Mar. 17, 2000.

27–28. tuition: Transferring pupils from St. Margaret's paid its $800 tuition. Westover tuition would rise to $1,200 by 1911 and $2,000 by 1931.

28. "It is . . . *fortified*": MRH, remarks on Visitors' Day, 1923.

28–29. "I think . . . life": (Ethel) Polly Thayer Starr '22, fortieth reunion notes, 1962.

29. "creates . . . life": MRH, "The Spirit of the School and Religion," *The Education of the Modern Girl* (New York: Houghton Mifflin, 1929), 60.

29. "a code . . . [it]": Jean Defrees Kellogg '35, letter to Maria Randall Allen (MRA), Oct. 6, 1974.

29–30. "Creation . . . happiness": MRH, "The Spirit of the School and Religion," 51.

30. "Instead . . . effort": Dallas, *Mary Robbins Hillard*, 61–62.

30. "Merry . . . Christmas": Brenda Hedstrom Williams '21, letter to Westover Alumnae Office, 1974.

30. "in a wonderful way": Baylis, diary, Nov. 1909.

30. "the handle . . . morning": MRH, letter to Pope (later Riddle), Mar. 4, 1911.

30. "loveliness . . . steadiness": MRH, letter to W. S. Hillard, 1926.

30. "the solemnity . . . motherliness": Dallas, *Mary Robbins Hillard*, 61–62.

30. "she . . . experience": Eliza Talbott Thayer, letter to Westover Alumnae Office, 1974.

31. "bits . . . about": Elizabeth Clark Taft '15, letter to Westover Alumnae Office, 1974.

31. "long days of good books and invented games and sleepy, long, long thoughts": Elizabeth Choate '14, "Pilgrimage," *Atlantic Monthly*, Mar. 1922. Elizabeth "Betty" Choate Spykman took many trips with her former teacher.

31. "In the classroom, Miss LaMonte's method was one of 'enticement' . . . corridor": Elizabeth Choate Spykman, "H. D.," *Alumnae Wick,* June 10, 1958.

31. "What . . . humiliation": Kellogg letter.

32. "We . . . worthwhile": Marjorie Chase Feeter '09, letter to Westover Alumnae Office, 1974.

32. "And . . . rapture": Spykman, "H. D."

32. "An Italian . . . companions": MRH, letter to Emily H. Fenn, Aug. 31, 1907.

32. "New York . . . it": MRH, letter to Jaccaci, July 13, 1909.

32. "Our beloved . . . write": Pratt, letter to Pope (later Riddle), 1909, Hill-Stead.

32–33. "Dear Jac . . . night": MRH, letter to Jaccaci, 1910.

33. "big 'job' . . . companionship": MRH, letter to Jaccaci, Aug. 24, 1910.

33. "you read . . . manhood": MRH, letter to Jaccaci, Sept. 12, 1910.

33–34. "What . . . rather not": MRH, letter to Jaccaci, Jan. 14, 1911.

34. "the whole of Westover": Jaccaci, letter to MRH, Feb. 14, 1915. Although he was a naturalized American citizen, he spent his remaining years in his native France, where he died in the summer of 1930 at the age of seventy-four. His will revealed that he had an estranged wife, Mabel T. Jaccaci, living in Florence, Italy.

34. "troubled . . . Westover": MRH, letter to Jaccaci, 1910.

34. "Genius . . . fiercely)": MRH, letter to Jaccaci, June 24, 1910.

34. "beautifully" designed: Architect Philip Johnson (whose sister, Jeannette, was a member of Westover's class of 1918 for a year) and other architects later affirmed his praise.

35. "dissolve . . . me": MRH, letter to Jaccaci, Sept. 20, 1910.

35. "I think . . . theirs": MRH, letter to Jaccaci, Jan. 14, 1911.

35. "Theo . . . her": MRH, letter to Harris Whittemore, Nov. 11, 1913, Hill-Stead.

35. *Lusitania*: Her maid and Edwin Friend, the former secretary of the American Psychical Research Society, who were traveling with her, were both lost at sea.

36. "She . . . else": Helen Church Minton '19, interview by LL, Feb. 3, 2001.

36. a secret society: Bidda Blakeley '27, interview by Susan Willcox Mackay '64, Oct. 23, 1992.

36. "I can . . . atmosphere": Starr reunion notes.

36. "much deeper . . . spiritual": MRH, letter to Jaccaci, Sept. 4, 1910.

36–37. "exaggerated friendship": Baylis, diary, Apr. 1910.

37. "I can . . . hug": Ibid., Nov. 1909.

37–40. "an enormous . . . house" and following quotations: Vladimir Zenzinoff, "Impressions of America," *Lanterns,* May 1927 and Feb. 1932.

3. The Art of Living (pages 41–60)

41. "simple . . . natural": *Westover: Miss Hillard's School for Girls*, 1908.

41. "an education . . . Connecticut": Dallas, *Mary Robbins Hillard*, 101.

42. "A person . . . imagination": MRH, remarks on Visitors' Day, 1922.

42. "The studies . . . character": MRH, letter to "Mrs. Latta," Jan. 11, 1911.

42. "gave me . . . school": Marianna Talbott '16, diary, Nov. 1912.

43. "She . . . teacher": Katharine Van Ingen Humphrey '18, letter to Westover Alumnae Office, 1974.

43. "'this . . . was": Pauline Savage Furness '21, letter to Westover Alumnae Office, 1974.

43. "it . . . literature": Adele Chisholm Eells '16, letter to Westover Alumnae Office, 1974.

43. "to share . . . school:" MRH, Barney and Holcombe statement.

44. Helen Andrews: Born in Farmington, Connecticut, in 1872, she taught drawing and painting at Westover until her retirement in 1940.

44. "the Wise Woman": Pratt, letter to Pope (later Riddle), Mar. 8, 1909, Hill-Stead.

44. a rumor: Barbara Simonds Gwynne '32, letter to Louise McKelvy Walker '32 (no date).

45. "very affable": Helen Church Minton, interview by Mary Lois Minton '42 (no date).

46. "contact dancing": MRH, letter to W. S. Hillard, 1926.

47. "exiled from heaven" and following quotations: Mary "Polly" Willcox Wiley '18, interview by LL, Nov. 10, 1999.

48. "Victorian . . . sick": Jeannette Johnson Dempsey '18, letter, July 14, 1969.

48. "to be . . . free": MRH, remarks on Visitors' Day, 1923.

49. "bubbling . . . comfort": MRH, letter to Emily Fenn, July 29, 1920.

49. "Aunt Mary . . . anyway": Phyllis Fenn '24, letter to Mrs. J. L. Fenn, Dec. 15, 1921.

49. Betty Choate: MRH, letter to Charles F. Choate, Apr. 1, 1914.

50. "How . . . ambitions": MRH, remarks on Visitors' Day, 1923.

50–51. "with trouble . . . effort": Baylis, letter to her parents, 1911–12.

51. "I am . . . school": MRH, letter to "Mrs. Latta," Mar. 6, 1911.

51. Rachel Latta: Latta, diary, 1911–12.

51. the favor: Mary Borden McManus '27, letter to Westover Alumnae Office, 1974.

51. "Margaret . . . you": Margaret Bush Clement '18, interview by Mary Bush Clement Estabrook '48, Feb. 1993.

51. "Not . . . favorites: Dorothy Soule Milner '34, interview by LL, Jan. 8, 2000.

51. "for a girl . . . it": MRH, letter to Fenn, July 29, 1920.

52. "to exercise fortitude": Jeannette Rich Kirkham '21, letter to Westover Alumnae Office, 1974.

52. "stared . . . you'": Martha Dye Stott Diener '31, letter to Westover Alumnae Office, 1974.

52. "I have . . . funny": MRH, letter to Jaccaci, Sept. 20, 1910.

52–53. "chapel . . . throat": MRH, letter to Jaccaci, Oct. 16, 1910.

53. "I . . . letters": MacLeish, letter to Martha H. MacLeish, Aug. 4, 1924, *The Letters of Archibald MacLeish, 1907–1982*, edited by R. H. Winnick (Boston and New York: Houghton Mifflin, 1983), 145.

54. "There was . . . broken": Dallas, *Mary Robbins Hillard*, 92.

54. "It was . . . hurts": Ibid., 108.

54. "I too . . . anything": MRH, letter to Whittemore, Nov. 11, 1913.

54. "I have . . . Aunt Mary": MacLeish, letter to Martha H. MacLeish, July 19, 1925, *The Letters of Archibald MacLeish, 1907–1982*, 168.

55. "so many . . . distinction": MRH, letter to Fenn, Jan. 14, 1912.

55. "My mind . . . difficult": HDL, letter to Spykman, in *Westover*, by Elizabeth Choate Spykman (Middlebury, Conn.: Westover School, 1959), 43.

55–56. "You are . . . know it": Clark, letter to Bidda Blakeley, Sept. 15, 1927.

56. "There has been . . . effect": Dallas, *Mary Robbins Hillard*, 94.

56–57. "no certainty . . . the night": Masefield, letter to MRH, Apr. 28, 1917, as quoted in "My Aunt and Godmother Miss Mary Robbins Hillard," by Phyllis Fenn Cunningham '24, (1983), 29–30.

57. world peace: In the early 1920s, MRH rallied Connecticut high school students and later college students to the cause; at the end of the decade she organized a model League of Nations meeting at Westover. In 1928, at a lecture at Oxford University about the League of Nations, she stood up and gave an impromptu speech on the subject.

58. "dear children . . . slavedom": Henriette Coffin, "Some Memories of Mme. Breshkovsky's Visit to Westover" (no date).

58–59. "her name . . . system": Zenzinoff, "Impressions of America," 8.

59. "She would . . . topic": John Ferguson, interview by LL, Nov. 14, 1999.

59–60. "A withered . . . neglected": Dallas, *Mary Robbins Hillard*, 86.

60. trip to Europe: Ursula Ferguson's letters to her husband are dated July 2–31, 1928.

60. "your diplomas . . . souls of men": MRH, remarks at graduation, 1927.

60. "about beauty . . . went there": Blakeley interview.

4. The Spirit of the School (pages 61–78)

61. "It has been . . . matters": MRH, letter to Harris Whittemore, Nov. 11, 1913.

61. "she had . . . decisions": Dallas, *Mary Robbins Hillard*, 82.

61. "winged . . . charioteer": MRH, remarks on Visitors' Day, 1930.

62. "terror . . . hunger": Wiley interview.

63. "diaphanous . . . without": MRH, letter to Jaccaci, 1910.

64.   "the most fascinating . . . soul'": MRH, "The Spirit of the School and Religion," 47.

64.   "an exciting event . . . saying": Helen Ferguson '35, "Mary Robbins Hillard," manuscript, Dec. 9, 1935.

65.   "This vote . . . grievances": MRH, letter to Emily H. Fenn, May 8, 1912.

67.   "That settled . . . man": Williams letter.

68.   list: Her notes show that more than seventy percent were wives by the time women won the vote, and, at the last graduation she presided over in 1932, an even a larger percentage were married.

68.   "we can . . . body": MRH, remarks at graduation, 1913.

68.   "genius": HDL, letter to AQE, Feb. 18, 1964.

69.   "We are . . . presently": MRH, letter to Philip B. Simonds, Oct. 30, 1929.

69.   "awakening . . . effort": MRH, letter to Philip B. Simonds, May 10, 1930.

69.   "They . . . studies": Adeline Cole Simonds Congdon '33, letter to Philip B. Simonds (1931–32).

69.   "I've been . . . distress": Congdon, letter to Mr. and Mrs. Philip Simonds (1931–32).

69.   "we . . . people": Congdon, letter to Mr. and Mrs. Philip B. Simonds (1931–32).

70.   "the usual . . . types": Resor interview.

70.   "Her white hair . . . architecture": Rebecca Love Drew '34, "The Cherishing of Eccentrics," *Westover Alumnae Magazine*, Summer 1971.

70.   "whenever . . . them": Helen Ferguson, "Mary Robbins Hillard."

70.   "quite deaf . . . Aderlin": Congdon, letter to Mr. and Mrs. Philip B. Simonds, Sept. 18, 1929.

70.   "the most difficult . . . world": MRH, Barney and Holcombe statement.

71.   "A perfectly delightful . . . adequately": MRH, letter to Lucy Pratt and HDL, Feb. 28, 1931.

73.   "She had . . . time": John Ferguson interview.

73.   "a list . . . years": Dallas, *Mary Robbins Hillard*, 79.

73.   "No one . . . within": Ibid., 66.

74.   mastectomy: Margaret Driggs Vaughn '36, interview by LL, May 28, 2000.

74.   "married to his profession": Susan DiSesa Sheeline '75, interview by LL, June 18, 2001.

74.   "Every day . . . Aunt Mary": Helen Ferguson, "Mary Robbins Hillard."

74.   "Ask . . . way": Spykman, "H. D."

74.   "talked . . . morning": Helen Ferguson, "Mary Robbins Hillard."

75.   "Dear Mother . . . morning": Congdon, letter to Mr. and Mrs. Philip B. Simonds, Oct. 10, 1932.

76.   "absolutely . . . it": John Ferguson interview.

76.   "bereavement . . . command": Dallas, *Mary Robbins Hillard*, 89.

76.   "How . . . marvel": Ibid., 78.

76.   Helen Church Minton interview by Nevins.

77.   "There is . . . fear": Dallas, *Mary Robbins Hillard*, 91, 92.

77.   1910 letter: MRH, letter to Jaccaci, Aug. 24, 1910.

77.   "I have learned . . . nourished": MRH, letter to J. L. Fenn, Oct. 24, 1914.

77.   "nobly . . . patiently": MRH, letter to Emily H. Fenn, Sept. 9, 1932.

77–78. "I can see . . . life": Helen Ferguson, "Mary Robbins Hillard."

5. Louise Bulkley Dillingham (pages 79–98)

79.   "observing . . . traditions": LBD, "Final Report of the Head Mistress to the Trustees," May 1964.

79.   "kept . . . pleasant": Jane Cook Johnson '33, letter to MRA, Mar. 28, 1997.

79–80. "In no time . . . follow": HDL, "Ah, Did You Once See Shelley Plain?" *Westover Alumnae Magazine*, Summer 1964.

80.   "I always . . . loved": HDL, letter to the alumnae, Feb. 1933.

80.   "none . . . pleased": Jane Cook Johnson letter.

80.   "It was . . . much": Resor interview.

80.   "Now students . . . Dilly:" Adeline Cole Simonds Congdon, interview by LL, July 20, 1998.

80.   "Miss Dillingham . . . academic": Margaret Driggs Vaughan, interview by LL, May 20, 2000.

80.   "She was . . . fat": Nancy May Rennell Field '35, interview by LL, Nov. 23, 1999.

80–81. "the Truth . . . evil": LBD, "The Educational Faith That I Hold," Academic Standards Committee, Headmistresses Assn. of the East, 1934.

81.   events: Historian Arnold Toynbee and writer Thornton Wilder would also speak, as well as Archibald MacLeish, when his daughter and MRH's great-niece, Mary Hillard MacLeish '42, was unhappily enrolled.

81–82. "intellectual . . . method": LBD, "The Educational Faith That I Hold."

82.   "I knew . . . disbelief": Drew, "The Cherishing of Eccentrics."

83.   "Westover . . . alma mater": (Nancy Hale), "Ten Fashionable Boarding Schools for Girls," *Fortune Magazine*, Apr. 1936, 106.

85.   "I think . . . didn't get": Dorothy Goodwin '49, interview by LL, Apr. 10, 2000.

86.   "our failures only marry": Lillian Faderman, *To Believe in Women* (New York: Houghton Mifflin, 1999), 213.

86.   "the woman's . . . view": Helen Horowitz, *The Power and Passion of M. Carey Thomas* (New York: Alfred A. Knopf, 1994), 406.

87.   France: LBD was elected a Chevalier de Legion d'Honneur and an Officier de l'Instruction Publique in 1934.

87.   "Why . . . persuasion": HDL, *Westover Alumnae Magazine*, Summer 1964.

88.   "My own . . . location": MRH, letter to Harris Whittemore, Jan. 25, 1927, Hill-Stead.

89–90. "reminded . . . experience": Paul M. Boynton, "Report on the Evaluation of Westover School Jan.

10th and 11th, 1956," Bureau of Elementary and Secondary Education, Connecticut Department of Education.

90. "quiet liberation . . . place:" Spykman, "H. D."

90. "never said . . . she": Alison Peake Henning '36, "Memories of Helen Dean LaMonte." HDL's older, quieter sister Susan, a Barnard College graduate who had studied at the Sorbonne, had taught advanced literature and the History of Architecture and Sculpture at Westover.

91. "diminutive . . . chapel": AQE, "Adele's Remarks," *Westover Alumnae Magazine*, Fall 1976.

91. "who . . . lived": MRA, interview by LL, Jan. 26, 2004.

91. "a red-headed aesthete": Drew, "The Cherishing of Eccentrics."

92. "She was . . . effete": Drew, letter to AQE, May 16, 1971.

92. "splendid . . . interest": AQE, speech, Westover School, May 1976.

92. "remarkable . . . Dillingham": Elizabeth Fry, "Louise B. Dillingham," manuscript (no date).

93. "her crisp . . . charge": Anne Heyniger Willard '40, letter to MRA, 1997.

93. "very . . . speaking": Eunice Strong Groark '56, interview by LL, Jan. 25, 2000.

93. "When . . . shyness": Nan Morse Lyell '37, letter to MRA, 1997.

93. "She was . . . charges:" Katharine Clarkson McDonald '39, letter to MRA, 1997.

94. "My abiding . . . ways": Mary Maier Walker '54, letter to MRA, 1997.

94. "Here at Westover . . . undertaken": LBD, handwritten statement (no date).

94. "you are here . . . women": Elizabeth M. Newton [EMN], speech, Westover School, May 1985.

94. "understanding . . . troubled": Polly Hopkins Biddle '38, letter to MRA, Mar. 12, 1997.

94–95. "She may . . . side": Helen Wick Sloan '39, letter to MRA, 1997.

95. "I wouldn't . . . education": Betty Blair Mauk '37, letter to MRA, Apr. 8, 1977.

95. "Miss Pratt . . . letter": Mary Hilliard Jackson '36, letter to MRA, 1997.

95. "had high standards . . . best": Sloan letter.

95. "certainly not": Gina Miller Bissell '39, letter to MRA, 1997.

95. "the only . . . disposition": Gillet Thomas Page '52, letter to MRA, 1997.

96. "brilliant . . . school": Reinette Plimpton Phillips '35, letter to MRA, May 10, 1997.

96. "perceptive . . . qualified": Drew, "The Cherishing of Eccentrics."

96. "a woman . . . strong": Drew letter to AQE.

96. "Never again . . . her": Mavis Moore Leyrer '38, letter to MRA, Mar. 25, 1997.

96. "She was . . . woman": Audrey Oakley Johnson '38, letter to MRA, 1997.

96. "throwing . . . laughter": Ann Huidekoper Brown '41, letter to MRA, 1997.

96. "I could talk . . . privately)": Willard letter.

96. "During . . . emergency": Fry, "Louise B. Dillingham."

97. "She really . . . dissipated": Patricia Castles Acheson '42, letter to MRA, 1997.

97. "I think . . . pastimes": LBD, letter to unnamed alumna, 1937.

97. "It allowed you . . . people": Vaughan interview.

98. "to put . . . answer": *Westover Magazine*, "Helping Students Behind the Scenes," Spring 2004.

6. Encouraging Independence (pages 99–114)

100. "To the wise . . . sufficient": Virginia Anthony Soule '45, letter to MRA, 1997.

100. "provided . . . heart": Isabel Lincoln Elmer '45, letter to MRA, Mar. 21, 1997.

100. "She held . . . indeed": Eyre Heyniger Davisson '45, letter to MRA, Mar. 28, 1997.

100. "a warm and convivial hostess": Fry, "Louise B. Dillingham."

101. going to college: During much of her time at Westover, LBD was on the Academic Standards Committee of the National Association of Heads of Girls' Schools, which helped members meet college admission requirements.

101. "She simply . . . gone": Acheson, letter to MRA.

101. promising young girl: Justine Harwood Laquer '45, letter to MRA, Mar. 4, 1997.

101. "She was . . . guidance": Patricia Richardson Jamison '48, letter to MRA, Apr. 1997.

101. "if I . . . go to it": Groark interview.

102. "another student": Anita Packard Montgomery '47, interview by LL, Mar. 6, 2000.

102. "Then I think . . . course": Abigail Mason Browne '61, letter to MRA, 1997. She later got a B.S. from Sweet Briar College and a M.A. from Boston University. Her mother was Fanny Homans Mason '29.

102. "the ability . . . learning": Boynton, "The Evaluation of Westover School."

103. Eunice Strong Groark: She was Connecticut Lieutenant Governor with Gov. Lowell Wiecker on the Independent Party ticket from 1991 to 1995.

103. "she was . . . teaching": Norman, letter to MRA.

103. "her shyness . . . surrounded us": Gloria Prudden Lange '47, letter to MRA, 1997.

103. "interesting . . . subjects": Margaret Day Jones '59, letter to MRA, Mar. 20, 1997.

103. "Gertrude Stein . . . Buddha": Patricia Pollock Antich '48, letter to MRA, 1997.

103. "clear . . . eyes": Fanny Curtis Luke '41, letter to MRA, 1997.

103. "Any one . . . course:" Constance Payson Pike '43, letter to MRA, 1997.

103. "She was . . . one": Joan Pirie Leclerc '49, letter to MRA, June 22, 1997.

103. "add . . . education": Boynton, "The Evaluation of Westover School."

104. Schumacher children: Their son, Mark, was born in 1939; their daughter Noelle, born in 1946, did not attend Westover.

104–105. "stood astounded . . . face": Schumacher, "Meditation on Red Hall," speech and manuscript (no date).

106. "could laugh . . . mistake": Norman, letter to MRA, March 30, 1997.

106. "Because . . . word": Schumacher, "On Saying Farewell to Westover," manuscript (probably 1977).

106. "ignorant . . . them": Alison W. Birch, "Dr. Joachim Schumacher: Westover School's 'All 'Round Great Guy,'" *Sunday Republican Magazine*, July 28, 1974.

106. "liked . . . taught": Sylvia Schumacher, interview by Trudy Martin, Dec. 1, 1999. After a divorce in 1983, Trudy Martin dropped the name Barnes.

106. One time . . . boys: LL diary, Feb. 13 and 22, 1961.

107. "it was not easy . . . student": Schumacher, "On Being Retired—Unretiringly," *Westover Alumnae Magazine*, Spring 1978.

107. "complete freedom . . . Christian-pagan": Schumacher, "On Saying Farewell to Westover."

107. "It was balm . . . art history": Schumacher, "On Being Retired—Unretiringly."

107. "he taught us . . . it": Betsy Shirley Michel '59, speech, Westover School, May 15, 1999.

107. "Today we sing . . . joy:" Mary Germain Kenefick Graves '45, letter to MRA, 1997.

107. "self-knowledge . . . taken": Boynton, "The Evaluation of Westover School."

108. Faculty–Student Council: It consisted of the officers of the senior class, the Athletic Association, the Wests and Overs, and the Glee Club; it was also made up of two members-at-large from each class, four teachers, and four administrators, including LBD.

108. "The honor code . . . nice way": MRA interview.

109. "It is not easy . . . virtue": AQE, letter to Faculty–Student Council, 1956.

110. "When in doubt . . . thing": Anne Rindlaub Dow '56, letter to MRA, Mar. 16, 1997.

110. "I . . . grew up": Virginia Stanton Duncan '42, interview by LL, Feb. 29, 2000.

110. "I think . . . can": Davisson letter.

110. "Whatever . . . observation": Brown letter.

110. "wise . . . adolescents": Anne Clark Newbold '46, letter to MRA, Apr. 18, 1997.

110. "while . . . role": Jamison letter.

110. "The areas . . . values:" LBD, "Healthy Mental Climates," *Alumnae Wick*, April 1952.

111. "what she can do . . . about": LBD, "Forty-Third Year Opens With New Girls of Unprecedented Numbers," *Wick*, May 10, 1952.

111. "My heart . . . student": Elmer letter.

111. "She was unflinching . . . penalty": Davisson letter.

111. "She loved . . . pleasures": Goodwin interview.

112. "Never . . . spirit": Sarita Van Vleck '51, letter to MRA, Apr. 20, 1997.

112. group of seniors: Priscilla Cunningham '54, letter to MRA, Mar. 7, 2001.

113. "Miss D's eyes . . . giggle": Jerone Godfrey Paul '47, letter to MRA, Mar. 6, 1997.

113. "vindictive . . . action": Alice Bell Reid '53, letter to MRA, Mar. 10, 1997.

113–14. "dazzling display . . . moment": Van Vleck letter.

114. "greeted . . . sky": Ellen Lishman Robertson '58, letter to MRA, April 1997.

7. *The Desire for Justice (pages 115–32)*

115.   domesticity: Freudians like psychoanalyst Helene Deutsch, in her influential *The Psychology of Women,* criticized women with intellectual interests who wanted to do professional work.

115.   "It took . . . education": Barbara Miller Solomon, *In the Company of Educated Women,* 193.

115.   "Westover . . . life": (LBD), "Westover School: Statement of Objectives," manuscript, 1954.

116.   "She could tell . . . be": Lee Lort Garrison, interview by LL, June 26, 2000.

116.   "she was . . . married": EMN, interview by LL, Jan. 11, 1997.

116.   scholarship program: From 1932 to 1950, about twenty-five students a year shared around $35,000 in scholarship funds.

117.   "has reduced . . . values": LBD and Edwin C. Northrop, letter to alumnae, parents, and friends of Westover, May 1, 1950. Northrop was an insurance executive and the husband and father of alumnae.

117.   tuition: In the late forties the endowment was around $100,000. Tuition was $2,250 in 1950, and it gradually rose throughout the decade.

117.   Westover Alumnae Association: In 1950 LBD asked to be replaced by an alumna, and in 1951 Marion Savage Heyniger '14 became president. It is also known as the Westover Board of Governors.

117.   "to spark . . . someone": Drew letter to AQE.

117–18.   "While I felt . . . considered": Don Ross, "Westover School Ready to Take a Small Group of Negro Girls," *New York Herald Tribune,* May 25, 1949.

118.   "equality . . . democracy": LBD, letter to parents, June 1, 1949.

118.   "a matter of principle . . . publicity": Ibid.

118.   "It's as simple . . . things": Ross, *New York Herald Tribune.*

118–19.   "In a small community . . . problems": AQE, letter to alumnae, May 25, 1949.

119.   "I have always felt . . . same": Spykman, *Westover,* 122.

119.   "still the same place . . . bird": HDL, letter to unidentified alumna, May 29, 1949.

119–20.   "so that I could mix . . . need": Roberta West Waddell '52, letter to Tamora Groves Noyes, May 26, 1949.

120.   "this important . . . took": Waddell, letter to Richard Beebe, Feb. 23, 2000.

120.   "taught us . . . world": Marion Macmillan '50, letter to MRA, May 29, 1997.

120.   "her intense energy . . . life": Mary Maier Walker letter.

120.   "she was a powerful . . . all": Dow letter.

120–21.   "I have known . . . easy": LBD, letter to Emma Morel '48, June 24, 1949.

121.   "snowball . . . thinkers": George P. Bissell Jr., letter to LBD, July 7, 1949.

121.   "unfortunate" . . . living": LBD and Northrop letter.

122.   "a more realistic . . . past": Ibid.

122.   "perilously . . . under": AQE, interview by LL, Oct. 15, 1998.

122–23. "Grandchildren . . . rewarding": HDL, letter to AQE, Apr. 22, 1951.

123.   "The way men . . . guess": HDL, letter to AQE Aug.14, 1961.

123.   "a very good student": LBD, "Negro Students at Westover," Aug. 1961.

123.   Warings: See *A Passion for Justice: J. Waties Waring and Civil Rights* by Tinsley E. Yarbrough
         (New York: Oxford University Press, 1987), and *The Atlantic Sound* by Caryl Phillips (New York:
         Vintage, 2001). After Judge Waring's retirement in 1952, the couple moved to New York City,
         when Mrs. Waring asked Westover's alumnae office to strike her from its records to help her
         avoid hate mail and telephone calls.

124.   "unpleasant . . . *against*": Miriam DeCosta-Willis '52, interview by LL, Feb. 9, 2000. She went on to
         graduate Phi Beta Kappa from Wellesley College, earn a Ph.D. in Comparative Literature from
         Johns Hopkins University, and become a college professor, an author, and the mother of four
         children.

125.   students: Intelligence, personality, and achievement tests were given to incoming students. Intel-
         ligence tests at the time showed an I.Q. range from 124 to 94, with many more at the higher than
         the lower end of the scale.

125.   "jubilant headline": Audlyn Higgins Williams '56, interview by LL, Feb. 27, 2000.

125.   "very successful": LBD, "Negro Students at Westover."

125.   "immensely frustrated": AQE, interview by LL, Dec. 14, 2003.

125.   "awe . . . intelligence": Roger Lort, interview by LL, May 4, 2000.

125–26. "good hard . . . judgments": *Waterbury American*, "Tribute Paid to Ex-Head at Westover," Jan. 18,
         1965.

126.   "She had no . . . fools": AQE, interview, Oct. 15, 1998.

126.   "She wasn't . . . people": Henry, interview by LL, August 16, 1999.

126.   Barbara Cushing: It's uncertain whether she raised more money than usual. In 1951–52, $112,999
         was raised, but in 1952–53 gifts fell to $44,309.

126.   Elizabeth Newton: Born in Chicago in 1919, she went to Girls Latin School and, after college,
         taught at Miss Porter's and Dana Hall prior to Westover.

127.   "the controlling abstraction": EMN, interview, Jan. 11, 1997.

127.   "the place . . . beautiful:" EMN, interview by LL, Feb. 23, 2000.

127.   "One occasionally . . . forceful": EMN, letter to MRA, Mar. 21, 1997.

128.   "it was a remarkable performance every year": Lois Cameron, interview by LL, Mar. 5, 2000; also,
         Garrison interview.

128.   "a living . . . that": Wallace "Polly" Bartlett, manuscript (no date). She was a former WAAC who
         had arrived in 1950 to teach music, current events, and other subjects.

128.   "everybody's grandmother": EMN, interview, Feb. 23, 2000.

128–29.   "dirty . . . Dillingham": Sherrill Williams Mills '59, letter to MRA, Apr. 2, 1997.

129.   "a quiet . . . encouragement": Constance Seely-Brown McClellan '56, letter to MRA, 1997.

129.   "Your light . . . it": Berrell "Babs" Mallery '60, "'Your Light is Burning Brightly,'" *Hillard Herald*, Summer 2005.

129.   "Do any of you . . . women": Groark, letter to MRA, March 8, 1997.

130.   Terry Hallaran: Hallaran, letter to LL, Mar. 3, 2002.

130.   "Of course": EMN, "Westover Award . . . Elizabeth Newton," *Westover Alumnae Magazine*, Winter 1986.

130.   "in small things . . . large": LBD, "Final Report of the Head Mistress to the Trustees."

130.   "Academically . . . place": Groark interview.

131.   "high caliber": Boynton, "The Evaluation of Westover School."

131.   "rigorously . . . brilliant": EMN and others, "Westover School Academics 1951–1985," 1987 or 1988. In the late 1950s, AP French and AP calculus were added to the curriculum.

131.   newspaper reporter: *Milwaukee Sentinel*, "School Leader in City to Check On Graduates," Jan. 15, 1953.

131.   "a friendly household with high ideals": (LBD), "Westover School: Statement of Objectives."

131.   "not so much . . . culture": EMN, interview, Feb. 23, 2000.

132.   "we were told . . . men:" Michel speech.

8. A Great Lady (pages 133–50)

133.   portrait: It was painted by artist Sally Moffat to help pay the tuition of a granddaughter, Frances Welch '56, the daughter of Marion Moffat Welch '33.

133.   Westover Award: The first recipient in 1954 was Virgilia Peterson Paulding '21, author, literary critic, and host of a television program, "The Author Meets the Critics."

133.   LBD Chair: The first grant would go to history teacher Marjorie Pratt (niece of Lucy Pratt), who planned to retire the following spring. Subsequent winners were: Evelyn Merrimon, 1958; Elizabeth Cushman, 1959; Elizabeth Kellogg, 1960; Gladys Haring, 1961; Julie McLintock, 1962; Adela Prentiss, 1963; Emma Hibshman, 1964; Patience Norman, 1965; and Elizabeth Newton, 1966.

134.   "She didn't . . . drinker": Goodwin interview.

134.   "to dispel . . . rejuvenating": LBD, "Head Mistress Sends Message to Alumnae," *Alumnae Wick*, Dec. 1958.

135.   "I'm sure . . . with": Garrison interview.

135.   "child-like . . . transparent": Jones letter.

135–36.   "keen . . . headmistress": Elizabeth G. Baldwin and Rita Faust, "25 Years a Leader of Young Women," *[Hartford] Courant Magazine*, Dec. 14, 1958.

136.   "masterful": Patience Norman, letter to MRA, Mar 6, 1997.

136.   "Miss Hillard . . . secure": Spykman, *Westover*, 97.

136.   Bishop Gray: He was the husband of Virginia Hutchinson Gray '25, who was president of the alumnae association.

137.   "Miss Helen . . . about": Spykman, "H. D."

137.   "What a birthday . . . afraid": HDL, letter to AQE, Marion Griswold '23, Shirley Foote '38, and others, Sept. 25, 1962.

137.   "Here I am . . . race": HDL, letter to Joseph L. Molder [JLM], 1973.

138.   "You . . . Lulu": Goodwin interview.

138.   "valued . . . Court": HDL, letter to Louise McKelvy Walker '32, Jan. 28, 1974.

138.   "as she got older . . . that": AQE, interview by LL, May 18, 2002.

138.   "with total glee . . . deed": Antich letter.

139.   "She was . . . models": Jamison letter.

139.   "It was always . . . feminine": Deborah Morgan Luquer '58, letter to MRA, 1997.

139–40.   "There was a sense . . . kind": Jones letter.

140.   "highest . . . imagination": LBD, "The Educational Faith That I Hold."

140.   "The most exciting . . . age": Garrison interview.

140.   "Pleides . . . liveliness": Meredith Medina Murray '61, "Letters to My Cousin Ann," June 1994, 27–28.

140.   "in my own . . . world": Katrina Rauch Wagner '61, interview by LL, Feb. 9, 2001.

140.   "to fight . . . way": Wagner, "Chapel Talk," May 2006.

140–41.   "'nailing . . . place to be": Carole Hayes Williams '62, letter to MRA, 1997.

141.   "she had me pegged": Drayton Grant '66, letter to MRA, May 9, 1997.

141.   "I have always . . . missed": Browne letter.

142.   "the *content* . . . religions": LBD, letter to unidentified alumna, 1937.

142.   fundraising: Annual fundraising had fallen in 1957–58 to $133,176, and stayed at that level through 1960–61. The capital campaign for the LBD building raised $573,445 in 1961–62 and $409,651 in 1962–63.

143.   "lewd": Pamela Ray Vaughan '64, interview by LL, Jan. 15, 2004.

144.   "phenomenal . . . word": Lort interview.

144.   "a professional estrangement . . . areas": AQE, letter to HDL, June 21, 1963.

144.   "over time . . . renewed": AQE, letter to LL, Apr. 28, 2000.

145.   "more for Westover . . . person": HDL, letter to AQE, Apr. 21, 1964.

145.   being pushed out": EMN, interview, Feb. 23, 2000.

145.   "The most casual . . . see": Elizabeth Choate Spykman, letter to AQE, Nov. 15, 1963.

146.   "no woman . . . Head": HDL, letter to AQE, Feb. 18, 1964.

146. "younger, fresher outlook": LBD, "Final Report of the Head Mistress to the Trustees."

146. "hypnapogogic . . . say": LBD, "Thank you, Thank you," *Westover Alumnae Magazine*, Summer 1964.

147. "mental awareness . . . abilities:" Elizabeth H. Kellogg, "Process of Growth—New Girl to Alumna: Some Observations of a Teacher," *Westover Alumnae Magazine*, Summer 1964.

147. "What was sound . . . added": HDL, "Ah, Did You Once See Shelley Plain?"

148. "strong lines . . . stern:" Grant letter.

148. "a completely different . . . younger:" Pamela Whittemore Bell '64, letter to MRA, Mar. 11, 1997. Her grandfather, Harris Whittemore, had followed his father as president of the board of trustees from 1914 until his death in 1928. Several of her relatives also attended Westover, including Helen Whittemore Adams '17 and Gertrude Whittemore Upson '22.

148. "I remember . . . irresistible": Virginia Lionberger '66, letter to MRA, Mar. 6, 1997.

148. "a beloved great woman": Elizabeth Harnischfeger Ogden '39, letter to MRA, 1997.

148. "and then . . . laugh": Montgomery interview.

149. "as energetic . . . look": Cunningham, letter to Julie Kirlin (no date).

149. "a great shock to me": HDL letter to Elsie Bristol, Feb. 2, 1965. Elsie (Mrs. Ralph) Bristol had graduated from St. Margaret's School in 1901.

149. "It was a beautiful service": Cunningham, letter to unidentified classmates, Feb. 28, 1965.

150. "a great lady": *Waterbury American*, "Tribute Paid to Ex-Head at Westover," Jan. 18, 1965.

150. her relatives: They included: Dorothy's children, Dorothy Goodwin '49, Frank Smedley, and Nancy Smedley Arney; Tom's daughter, Florence Dillingham Howe '52; Helena's daughter, Barbara Flanagan; Hope's children, Louise Garfield Muranko '46, Edward Garfield, and Dorothy Garfield Stivers; and Sherburne's children, Melita Dillingham Brownell '55 and Peter Dillingham.

9. Days of Desperation (pages 151–72)

152. "I felt . . . be": HDL, letter to Elsie Bristol, Sept. 10, 1964.

152. "Westover . . . hostess": HDL, letter to Elsie Bristol, Feb. 2, 1965.

152. "However . . . alterations": *Wick*, "New Headmaster—Mr. Iglehart," Dec. 1963.

152–53. "strange figure . . . manner": Jennifer Martin '66, interview by LL, Feb. 13, 2005.

153. "to look . . . leer": Abigail Congdon '68, letter to LL, Nov. 16, 1999.

153. "was supposed . . . corridors": EMN, interview, Feb. 23, 2000.

153. "ghastly temper": Elysabeth Barbour Higgins '40, letter to AQE, Jan. 7, 1965.

153. "irreparably . . . Iglehart": AQE, letter to Louise McKelvy Walker '32, Aug. 2, 1973.

153. "They were . . . school": EMN, interview, Feb. 23, 2000. The next year Miss Kellogg became head of the English department at a preparatory school in Texas, headed by the husband of

Anita Packard Montgomery '47. The teacher returned to Westover to teach nineteenth-century literature for another year or so before retiring.

153.   "I felt . . . changes": EMN letter.

154.   "an all-time low": Schumacher, letter to Lee, Mar. 23, 1966.

154.   "ways . . . disagree": Schumacher, "On Saying Farewell to Westover."

154.   "Several reunioners . . . standards": HDL, letter to Elsie Bristol, June 3, 1965.

154.   "taken . . . system": Pamela Whittemore Bell, interview by LL, Jan. 31, 2004.

154–55.   "It has been harder . . . exist for": Norman, letter to Lee, Mar. 24, 1966.

155.   "Genuine morality . . . wrong": Schumacher, letter to Lee, Mar. 23, 1966.

155.   "bedroom trustees": Jane Iglehart, interview by LL, Nov. 1, 1999. Alumnae on the board included Gertrude Whittemore Upson '22, Nancy May Rennell Field '35, and Virginia Hutchinson Gray, '35. Alumnae wives included the former Frances Jackson '13, wife of Elliott H. Lee; Margaret Elizabeth Kennedy '31, wife of G. Keith Funston, the former president of Trinity College and now president of the New York Stock Exchange; the former Jean Van Sinderen '39, wife of Donald W. Henry; and the former Marjorie McComb, '29, wife of Dorrance Sexton.

155.   "maybe . . . missed": Norman, letter to Lee, Mar. 24, 1966.

155.   "His unctuous . . . defects": AQE, letter to Elysabeth Barbour Higgins '40, Jan. 12, 1966.

155.   "Make no mistake . . . love": AQE, letter to Virginia Hutchinson Gray '35, Mar. 23, 1966.

156.   "a delicate pass . . . time": Iglehart, editorial, *Westover Alumnae Magazine*, Dec. 1964.

156.   "a curator . . . headmaster": Jane Iglehart interview.

156.   "As you . . . year": HDL, letter to Elsie Bristol, Apr. 25, 1966, with a copy of the prayer, "Desiderata."

156.   father of three daughters: At the time his daughters were fifteen, nineteen, and twenty-one; the youngest was at the all-girl Hewlett School.

157.   "We were . . . ahead": John W. Alexander, "For All of Us It is a Matter of Being Faithful": *Westover Alumnae Magazine*, Summer 1967.

157.   "heroic": Frances Welch '56, interview by LL, Mar. 19, 2000.

157.   "has done . . . out of it": Alexander, "For All of Us . . ."

158.   "It is not . . . *eyes*": *Westover Alumnae Magazine*, "Commencement Address, June 8, 1967," Summer 1967.

158.   retirements: Adela Prentiss had retired in 1964 after thirty years, the same year as Miss Dillingham. Emma Hibshman lived for the next two decades in her home in Woodbury, Rose Dyson returned to her hometown of Winsted, Connecticut, and Marion Griswold joined her aunt, Helen LaMonte, in the family home in Owego, New York.

158.   "shocked": Diana Strawbridge Crompton '57, letter to JWA, June 13, 1967.

158.   "slovenliness": Alexander letter to Crompton, June 28, 1967.

158.   "a very sensitive . . . to be": Alexander, interview by LL, July 16, 2000.

158.   "She has . . . about": Alexander, "Message from Headmaster to Alumnae Magazine for Fall, 1967."

158.   "I don't have . . . may be": Alexander, "For All of Us . . ."

159.   "at rest . . . once more": HDL, letter to Elsie Bristol, Feb. 11, 1968.

159.   "We sensed . . . brave": Abigail Congdon, interview by LL, Nov. 15, 1999.

159.   "subversives . . . to do it'": Karin Lawrence Cord '68, interview by LL, Jan. 16, 2005.

159.   civil rights: In the 1960s he was a trustee of Spelman College in Atlanta and worked desegregat-
       ing schools with the American Friends Service Committee.

160.   "really . . . see": Elizabeth Stern '69, interview by LL, Jan. 4, 2007.

161.   "what may . . . history" and other comments by evaluators: "Chief Strengths and Weaknesses of
       Westover School Evaluation Report," 1968.

161.   "it doesn't . . . strengthen it": Alexander, "Chapel Remarks Feb. 12, 1969," *Wick*, Mar. 1969.

161.   "sad . . . self-indulgence": (unnamed author), "Random Thoughts," late 1960s.

161.   "more appropriate . . . behind": Alexander, "From the Headmaster . . . ," *Westover Alumnae
       Magazine*, Spring 1969.

161.   Victoria DiSesa: DiSesa '70, interview by LL, Jan. 16, 2005. She and three sisters went to Westover.
       Her mother, Rose Pelliccia '35, was the niece of Mary Hillard's close friend and physician, Dr.
       William F. Verdi. Her father, New Haven lawyer Joseph DiSesa, was president of the Westover
       Fathers Association and then a trustee.

161–63. "often emphasized . . . teaching": EMN and others, "Westover School Academics 1951–1985."

162.   Rewis and Clark: Rewis soon left Westover, divorced, and married a member of the class of 1970.
       Clark, who was married with a young son and daughter, also left Westover, divorced, and married
       a student in the class of 1971. Neither marriage lasted.

163.   "pied-pipers": Trudy Martin, interview by LL, May 26, 2000.

163.   "such restrictive . . . full": Alexander, letter to the chairman of the Commission on Independent
       Secondary Schools, Oct. 15, 1970.

163.   "male domination": Alexander, "Headmaster's Report to the Trustees," May 4, 1970.

164.   "Taft wanted . . . join Taft": Duncan interview.

164.   "gained tremendously . . . in vain": B. M. Belcher, "Memorandum on the Future of Westover
       School," Dec. 1, 1969.

164.   "to educating . . . way": Alexander, "From the Headmaster . . . ," *Westover Alumnae Magazine*,
       Winter 1970.

165.   "constructive freedom . . . school": Alexander, "From the Headmaster . . . ," Spring 1969.

165.   "an attempt . . . possibilities": EMN and others, "Westover School Academics 1951–1985."

165.   "a catalyst . . . this": Alexander interview.

166.   "unraveled . . . pieces": EMN, interview, Feb. 23, 2000.

166.   "The chapel . . . the line": Alexander, "Headmaster's Report to the Trustees," May 4, 1970.

167.   "her emotional . . . energy": Martin interview.

167.   "revolt of our offspring": Belcher, "Memorandum on the Future of Westover School."

167.   "an utterly alien . . . quadrangle": Nancy May Rennell Field, memorandum to unnamed trustee, 1971–72.

167.   "worldly . . . sharp": AQE, letter to Elysabeth Barbour Higgins '40, Jan. 12, 1966.

168.   "a tragedy . . . destroyed": Alexander, "Statement to Westover Students by the Headmaster," Sept. 27, 1970.

169.   "horrified . . . wrong": Betsy Shirley Michel, interview by LL, Mar. 2, 2000.

169.   "in essence, died": AQE, letter to Louise McKelvy Walker, Feb. 17, 1971.

169.   "There was very little . . . happened": Duncan interview.

169.   "ricocheting . . . heritage": Nancy May Rennell Field memorandum.

169.   "the old world . . . sex:" Alexander interview.

169–70. "I think . . . Dictator": HDL, letter to Alexander, Mar. 31, 1970.

170.   "Becky Love . . . musician." Drew, letters to AQE, May 16 and 24, 1971.

170–71. "As a young . . . her future": Drew, "The Cherishing of Eccentrics," May 1971.

171.   "discipline . . . tradition": "Random Thoughts."

171.   "It wasn't only the chapel . . . guidelines": Nancy May Rennell Field; memorandum.

171.   "When I reached the end . . . day": JLM, "Memorial Service for Helen LaMonte," Westover School, May 8, 1982.

172.   "It was . . . mission": Alexander interview. After he left Middlebury, he took administrative positions at the University of Maryland and at SUNY-Albany. After retiring in Chapel Hill, North Carolina, he died at the age of eighty-eight in 2006.

10. *Regaining Balance (pages 173–95)*

173.   "torn . . . women's lib": Nancy May Rennell Field, memorandum, 1971–72.

173.   "Westover . . . now": Drew, letter to Dorrance Sexton, July 20, 1971.

173.   "For some . . . desired": AQE, letter to Sexton, Aug. 1971.

173.   "Women's Lib overtones": Higgins, letter to AQE, Aug. 15, 1971.

173–74. "leave me . . . them": Sexton, letter to AQE, Aug. 27, 1971.

174.   "in the velvet glove . . . Westover": AQE, letter to Sexton, Sept. 18, 1971.

174.   "an excellent . . . Have-Faith": MRA, letter to AQE, July 25, 1971.

174.   "next to no experience . . . answers": Higgins, letter to AQE, Aug. 15, 1971.

174.   "was like a shining . . . faculty": Edith Noble Bacon '72, letter to LL, Apr. 1, 2005.

174.   "What was impressive . . . carefully": Michel interview.

175. "Is everybody happy . . . happy": Sally Kreger '72, "Mr. Molder is Permanent Headmaster," *Wick*, March 1972.

175. "a wonderful . . . endurance": JLM, "Headmaster's Remarks," *Westover Alumnae Magazine* (date unknown).

175. Equal Rights Amendment: First drafted in 1923, it was finally passed by Congress in 1972, but it did not become law because it was not ratified by enough states.

176. "he became sad . . . against:" Susan Ray Busby '72, interview by LL, Jan. 24, 2006.

176. "calmness . . . affection": Gerster letter to LL, Apr. 1, 2005.

176. "He took over . . . way": EMN, interview, Jan. 11, 1997.

176. "My attitude . . . different": JLM, interview by LL, June 22, 2005.

177. "very helpful": JLM, interview by LL, Jan. 27, 1997.

177. "individuality . . . essential": JLM, "Remarks Made to Westover Alumnae," Oct. 7, 1971.

177. "They were a giggly . . . skill": JLM, "At Westover the Headmaster Coaches . . . ," *Westover Alumnae Magazine*, Fall 1976.

177. "a kind . . . us": Claudia Rawal Morris '78, letter to LL, Mar. 28, 2005.

177. "an amazingly talented . . . reminders": Margaret Thayer '81, letter to LL, Apr. 8, 2005.

177. "about adroitness . . . result": EMN speech.

178. "quick wit . . . voice": Cynthia Travis Metzger '74, letter to LL, Mar. 28, 2005.

178. "It's good . . . see": Devin Brown, "Three Who Teach at Westover," *Westover Alumnae Magazine*, Spring 1985.

178. "From then on . . . problem": Rothman, interview by LL, Sept. 27, 2005.

178. "informal dress . . . extreme": JLM, "Remarks Made to Westover Alumnae," Oct. 7, 1971.

178. "And I would . . . go up": Rothman interview.

178. "Discipline . . . school life": *Hillard Herald*, "Thirty Years of Mrs. Rothman's 'Special Way,'" Summer 2002.

179. "At lunch . . . home": Bruce and Maria Coffin, interview by LL, Sept. 19, 2005.

180. "in his heart of hearts": JLM, interview by LL, Jan. 27, 1997.

180. "someone . . . illegal": Groark interview.

180. "another way . . . shock": Richard Uhl, interview by LL, May 7, 2000. He was married to the former Emily Detwiler '41; their three daughters would go to Westover.

180. "I shall never forget . . . waters'": Walker, speech, Hartford, Connecticut, Nov. 1978.

180. "a tremendously good . . . away": AQE, interview by LL, Apr. 25, 2005.

181. "The rug . . . filthy": Jeannette Brown, interview by LL, Feb. 14, 2006.

181. "She could turn . . . eyes": Groark interview.

181. "It was . . . needed": Barbara Loveridge, interview by LL, Feb. 8, 2006.

181. "a wonderful . . . everybody": JLM, interview, June 22, 2005.

182.   "were not recognizing . . . program": JLM, interview, Jan. 27, 1997.

182.   "its very . . . teachers": Paul O. West, "Students, Graduates, Parents, Community," New England Association of Schools and Colleges, Spring 1978.

182.   "It is here . . . experience": Ann S. Pollina [ASP], "Mathematics: Do We Know What We Are Talking About? Is What We Say True?" *Westover Alumnae Bulletin,* Fall 1976.

183.   "I was dying to teach . . . teacher": ASP, interview by LL, Aug. 2, 2005.

183.   "She was very sweet . . . teacher": Wadsworth '73, letter to LL, May 1, 2006.

183.   "Math . . . things": Debra Gartzman Gottlieb '77, letter to LL May 4, 2006.

183.   "sweet young teacher . . . compassion": Ivette Caldera Esserman '78, letter to LL, Apr. 29, 2006.

183.   "Ann was like . . . way": Margaret Perrow '80, letter to LL, June 11, 2006.

183–84.   "We came with . . . difference": ASP, interview, Aug. 2, 2005.

185.   "He was tough . . . English": Holly Kennedy Passantino '74, "Westover Honors Faculty & Staff . . . Bruce Coffin," *Westover Magazine,* Fall 1992.

185.   "run . . . East": Terry and Alice Hallaran, interview by LL, July 6, 2005. LBD's youngest sister, Hope, married Theodore Garfield of Cleveland, whose sister is Terry's mother.

185.   "Well, chief . . . go": JLM, interview, June 22, 2005.

185.   "Well . . . that": Hallaran interview.

185–86.   "a pretty . . . feelings": Metzger letter.

186.   "quiet, dignified manner": Susan Schorr '74, letter to LL, Mar. 10, 2005.

186.   "Sometimes . . . bond": Margaret Thayer letter.

186.   "universal human liberation": Schumacher, "Ad Libbing On the Lib Movement," *Wick,* Dec. 1970. He retired to his home in Woodbury in 1977; he died in 1984.

187.   "And it's not . . . you were": Rothman interview.

187.   "We were very creative . . . now": Mary Jane Mitchell Hemmings '77, letter to LL, Mar. 28, 2005.

187.   "both a loving . . . headmaster": Margaret Perrow '80, letter to LL, Mar. 24, 2005.

188.   "It was as if . . . family:" Elizabeth Darlington '73, letter to LL, Apr. 10, 2005.

188.   "We were entrusted . . . trust": Gerster letter.

188.   "Of course . . . now": Hemmings letter.

188.   "drama and craziness . . . soul": Margaret Thayer letter.

188.   Beth Molder: Her father and mother met in New York City when he attended Union Theological Seminary and she, from a Mennonite family in Illinois, attended Columbia Teachers College. Mrs. Molder also restarted Career Day, organized Founders' Day, and worked with parents of day students.

188.   "She was extremely nice to everybody": Jean Van Sinderen Henry '39, interview by LL, Aug. 16, 1999.

189.   "The sudden shift . . . bridge it": JLM, interview, Jan. 27, 1997.

189.   "exceptionally active . . . atmosphere": JLM, "Report to the Board of Trustees," Sept. 1978.

189.   "You could correct . . . way": JLM, interview by LL, Mar. 11, 2000.

189.   "persuasion . . . coercion": JLM, "Thoughts Concerning the Future Direction of Westover" (no date).

189.   "we work . . . shaped by]": JLM, "What is Headmastering all About?" *Westover Alumnae Magazine*, Fall 1979.

190.   "that sudden awareness . . . judgment": Walker, Hartford speech.

190.   "as if . . . place": Holly Kennedy Passantino '74, interview by LL, Feb. 12, 2006.

190.   "I feel . . . outrageously": JLM, "Memorial service for Helen LaMonte."

190.   "You will give . . . growth": HDL letter.

191.   "close . . . gracefully": Sexton, letter to Walker, Oct. 31–Nov. 1, 1974.

191.   "I knew . . . stubborn": Walker, speech, Westover School, June 1973.

191.   "Joe . . . articulated": AQE, interview by LL, Apr. 25, 2005.

191.   "angled . . . problem": Jerry Van Voorhis, interview by LL, Apr. 27, 2005.

191.   "He was silent . . . deep": Groark interview.

191–92. "if you have . . . anything": JLM, interview, Mar. 11, 2000.

192.   "Rightly . . . aid": JLM, letter to LL, May 9, 2006.

192.   "We used . . . students": Groark interview.

192.   "saved me . . . could be:" Hemmings, interview by LL, Feb. 2, 2006.

192.   "Mr. Chips . . . headmaster": Uhl interview.

193.   "to build . . . person": JLM, interview, Mar. 11, 2000.

193.   "a bit of a pied-piper . . . pride": Jonathan O'Brien, letter to Walker, Feb. 27, 1974.

193.   "No one . . . good": HDL, letter to Walker, Jan. 28, 1974.

193.   "like it or not . . . itself": (no author), "Some Thoughts on Conversations With Weedie and Admissions and Development and Trustees" (no date).

193.   "a kind of Mr. Outside": Michel interview.

193.   "'bare its soul' . . . public": (Van Voorhis), "Westover: Ripe for the Risk, Ready for CBS," *Westover Alumnae Magazine*, Spring 1977.

193–94. "I felt . . . sense": Walker, letter to AQE, Jan. 18, 1977.

194.   "it got the school . . . game": Van Voorhis interview. He would resign in the spring of 1981 to become headmaster of Chatham Hall School in Virginia.

194.   "is a good place . . . telling": JLM, "The Headmaster's Alumnae Day Address," *Westover Alumnae Magazine*, Fall 1977. HDL died in 1981 at the age of 109.

194.   fund drive: Walker gave as much as a quarter of a million dollars. Mandeville also gave money for scholarships for the daughters of teachers and for a playing field in honor of his daughter.

194.   "held her feet . . . cheerleader": Michel, letter to Charlotte Beyer Fiveson '65, Feb. 6, 1999.

195.   "I have been bold . . . sight": Walker, letter to Acheson, Jan. 20, 1978.

195.   "As it turned out . . . depth": Michel letter.

195.   "a time of disaster . . . today": West, "Students, Graduates, Parents, Community."

11. Classroom Innovations (pages 196–214)

197.   "a mind . . . trap": Acheson, letter to AQE '42, Jan. 31, 1980.

197.   "a unique mission": Jerry Van Voorhis, letter to PCA, Apr. 25, 1981.

198.   "a pretty gutsy . . . afford to": Michel letter.

198.   "perhaps . . . school": JLM, memorandum, Feb. 28, 1980.

198.   "If we make our goal . . . building": Acheson, letter to Walker, Sept. 14, 1981.

198.   "Nothing . . . partnership": JLM, interview, Mar. 11, 2000.

198.   "I knew I was going . . . school": Eleanor Dean Acheson '65, "This Astonishingly Beautiful, Immensely Enduring Place," speech at Westover School, May 20, 2000. In 1993 President Bill Clinton's Attorney General, Janet Reno, appointed her an assistant attorney general at the Department of Justice, where she headed the Office of Policy Development.

199.   "After . . . place": Acheson, letter to AQE, Oct. 11, 1980.

199.   "the perfect plan": Acheson, letter to AQE, Feb. 14, 1981.

199.   Adams Library/Whittaker Science building: The Reed/Whittaker family donated about a half million dollars. Hugh Adams, whose mother, Mary Trumbull Adams, was a friend of Mary Hillard's, gave about the same amount. Over the years, he was a generous donor to Westover, giving funds for a carillon, a memorial garden in honor of his mother, a twelve-acre woodland, and many other gifts. "T" Mandeville also gave a quarter of a million dollars to endow the building. The observatory is named the Acheson Tower.

199.   Archibald MacLeish: Patricia Acheson's husband, David, was the brother of her Westover roommate, Mary Acheson Bundy '42. Mary and David Acheson were children of diplomat Dean Acheson. Dean Acheson was a friend of Archibald MacLeish's, and the poet was David's godfather.

200.   "tall figure . . . this room:" MacLeish, "The Building and the Spirit," manuscript, May 19, 1979.

200.   "a sense of integrity . . . ethic of care": Gilligan, *In a Different Voice: Psychological Theory and Women's Development* (Cambridge, Mass.: Harvard University Press, 1993), 171. Gilligan was influenced by Jean Baker Miller, a Boston psychiatrist whose 1976 book *Toward a New Psychology of Women* (Boston: Beacon Press) noted the importance of relationships to females. *Women's Ways of Knowing*, by M. F. Belenky, B. M. Clinchy, N. R. Goldberger, and J. M. Tarule, first published by Basic Books in 1986, elaborated on and enlarged many of these ideas.

200–201. "Joe . . . audience": ASP, interview, Aug. 2, 2005.

201.   "brilliant": EMN and others, "Westover School Academics 1951–1985."

201.   "charmingly . . . cultivated": EMN interview, Jan. 11, 1997.

201.   "Real life . . . us": ASP, interview, Aug. 2, 2005. There would eventually be a Jane Austen Book and Movie Club at Westover.

201.   "not always . . . thing": Ibid.

201.   "Not only . . . formulas": Deidre A. Sullivan '76, "Westover Honors Faculty & Staff," *Westover Magazine*, Fall 1992.

202.   Elizabeth Newton: She died at the age of eighty-seven in 2006.

202.   old guard: Patience Norman had retired in 1980. Still very much intellectually alive, she was wistful about giving up teaching for volunteer work at the museum and library in her home town of Norwich, Connecticut. As she prepared to depart—filling trash bags with all the clippings and newspapers in her room—she expressed gratitude for Westover's high teaching standards, interesting fellow teachers, and gratifying students. She read a book a day well into retirement before her death at the age of ninety-two in 2006.

202.   "There was no doubt . . . position": Hamill, letter to Margaret Velie Kinney '54, May 18, 1985. Polly graduated magna cum laude from Radcliffe, then earned a master's degree in romance languages, then a law degree, and became a judge of the tax court of New Jersey. Tragically, she died of cancer in 1996 at the age of fifty-four. One of her classmates, Mimi Sammis Webster '59, gave in her memory a sculpture of a female figure, "Embrace of Life," which was installed near Virginia House.

202.   committee: Members were Ann Pollina, Shamus Weber, Terry Hallaran, Anneke Rothman, history teacher Jill Freeland, and art history teacher Sonja Osborn.

202.   "It was time . . . advantage": EMN and others, "Westover School Academics 1951–1985."

202.   "the competence . . . strength": New England Association of Schools and Colleges, "Report of the Visiting Committee," Apr. 10–13, 1988.

203.   "a magical . . . serenity": Laura Nash Volovski '83 interview by LL, May 31, 2005.

204.   "great freedom": West, "Students, Graduates, Parents, Community."

204.   "formal writing . . . students": Weber, interview by LL, Aug. 8, 2005.

204.   "Given his head . . . ways": EMN and others, "Westover School Academics 1951–1985."

204.   "made sense . . . intellectual ecstasy": Mary Gelezunas '84, interview by LL, Jan. 15, and letter to LL, Jan. 17, 2007.

205.   "personal support . . . times": EMN and others, "Westover School Academics 1951–1985."

205.   "When I first arrived . . . manner": Yates, manuscript, June 1983.

205.   "I . . . anything": Ann Vileisis '85, interview by LL, Sept. 14, 2006.

205.   "might be . . . spoon-feeding": EMN and others, "Westover School Academics 1951–1985."

206.   "individualist and relationalist": Valerie E. Lee, Helen M. Marks, and Tina Byrd, "Sexism in

Single-Sex and Coeducational Independent Secondary School Classrooms," *Sociology of Education*, Apr. 1994.

206.   "What . . . much": ASP, interview by LL, May 23, 1997.

206.   "We started . . . wonderful": Vileisis interview. After getting degrees in history and environmental studies from Yale, and a master's degree in history from Utah State University, she wrote *Discovering the Unknown Landscape: A History of America's Wetlands* and *Kitchen Legacy: How We Lost Knowledge of Where Food Comes From and Why We Need to Get It Back*. In 2001 she was the first recipient of Westover's Distinguished Young Alumna Award.

207.   "all came . . . family": Thomas Hungerford, interview by LL, Aug. 30, 2005.

208.   "There are all kinds . . . individuality": ASP, interview, May 23, 1997.

209.   "I appreciate . . . profaned": Higgins '40, letter to JLM, Aug. 27, 1971.

209.   "If the chapel . . . no one": Hungerford, "Chapel and Westover," manuscript (no date).

210.   "a spirit of rivalry": Ibid.

210.   "When there are problems . . . be": Hungerford interview.

211.   "the conditions . . . language": Rich, "Taking Women Students Seriously," *On Lies, Secrets, and Silence: Selected Prose 1966–1978* (New York: W. W. Norton & Co, 1979), 238.

211.   "I would suggest . . . powerlessness": Rich, "Taking Women Students Seriously," 240.

211.   "listen . . . unfeminine": Rich, "Taking Women Students Seriously," 243.

211.   "If you had said . . . furious": ASP, interview, May 23, 1997.

211.   "If I populated . . . engineers": ASP, "Single Sex Education Debate," speech, Westover School, Jan. 5, 1999.

211.   "a very masculine field . . . girls": ASP, interview, May 23, 1997.

212.   "To teach girls . . . minds": ASP, "Educating Our Daughters for the 21st Century," *Education Register*, 1998–99.

212.   "What was extraordinary . . . enjoyed it": Vileisis, letter to LL, June 2, 2006.

212–13.   "The good teacher . . . teach": ASP, "On Teaching," *Westover Magazine*, Spring 2001.

213.   "she would help . . . for that": Alexandra Conway Marks '91, letter to LL, May 10, 2006.

213.   "If I want . . . growth": ASP, interview, May 23, 1997.

213.   "altruistic . . . learners": ASP, "No Place to Hide: Women in Mathematics and Science," *Westover School Magazine and Annual Report*, Winter 1991.

213.   "to synthesize . . . intelligence": ASP, "Gender Balance: Lessons from Girls in Science and Mathematics," *Educational Leadership*, Sept. 1995.

213.   "will do . . . same way": ASP interview, May 23, 1997.

213.   "What I propose . . . radical": ASP, "Women In Math and Science . . . Where are They?" *Westover Magazine*, Spring 1990.

213–14.   "Suddenly . . . vocabulary": Christian Daviron, letter to LL, May 20, 2005.

214. "may be unique . . . schools": Westover School, "A Survey of Advanced Placement Performance of Westover Students," July 6, 1987.

214. "You do . . . different": ASP, interview, Aug. 2, 2005. For her work with girls and math, ASP received a College Board AP Recognition Award in 1991 and an award from the National Coalition of Girls' Schools in 1993.

12. Backlash (pages 215–30)

215. "polarization . . . intelligence": Rich, "Taking Women Students Seriously," 243.

215. "If there . . . They are not": Rich, "Taking Women Students Seriously," 241. In his 1990 book, *Girls and Boys in School: Together or Separate?* (New York: Teachers College Press), sociologist Cornelius Riordan called coeducation "ideologically egalitarian and effectively inegalitarian."

215–16. "Ours . . . professionals": Rachel P. Belash, "Why Girls' Schools Remain Necessary," *New York Times Magazine*, Feb. 22, 1988.

216. "women are still . . . primal level": ASP, Westover Web site (no date).

216. "We are . . . best": ASP, "No Place to Hide: Women in Mathematics and Science."

216. "I find . . . growth": Judith Jacobs, "Women's Learning Styles," *Math and Science for Girls: Convening the Experts, Reforming the Classroom, Finding the Right Equation*, National Coalition of Girls' Schools, 1992.

217. "to celebrate . . . dreams": American Association of University Women Educational Foundation, *Growing Smart: What's Working for Girls in School*, 1995.

217. "We didn't . . . there": JLM, interview, Jan. 27, 1997.

217. Arnold Cogswell: He was married to Jessie Batchelier Cogswell '45 and is the father of Jessie Cogswell Tichko '75.

218. "as a tool, not a toy": ASP, "Gender Balance: Lessons from Girls in Science and Mathematics."

218. W.I.S.E. program: In 2006 it was honored by the National Association of Independent Schools as a "leading edge program."

218. "In English classes . . . principles": New England Association of Schools & Colleges, "Report of the Visiting Committee," Apr. 5–8, 1998.

219. "Women . . . worthwhile": *Westover School Magazine*, "Judy Chicago Visits Westover," Winter 1995.

220. complaints: The New York chapters of NOW and the ACLU, along with the New York Civil Rights Coalition, complained to the civil rights division of the U.S. Department of Education that the YWLS was in violation of Title IX of the Education Amendments of 1972 and 1975, which ordered public schools to provide equal opportunities to both genders in academics and athletics. Their complaints were never acted on. In fact, more all-girl public schools would open around the country, eased by provisions in President Bush's No Child Left Behind legislation.

220. "culture shock": Izukanne Emeagwali '01, interview by LL, May 2006.

221. "The part that saddens me . . . value": ASP, Westover Web site (no date).

221. "we face . . . difference": ASP, "The Education of Girls and Women," *Westover School Magazine*, Spring 1994.

221. "Regardless . . . goal:" ASP, interview, May 23, 1997.

221. "both disheartening and understandable": ASP, Westover Web site (no date).

221. "a culture . . . strengths": ASP, interview by LL, Aug. 22, 2006.

222. "learning . . . fantastic": Hallaran interview.

222. "Once you've gotten . . . up": Lucille Rundin Evans '56, interview by LL, Feb. 2, 2007.

222. Harvard: Catherine G. Krupnick, "Women and Men in the Classroom: Inequality and Its Remedies," *On Teaching and Learning*, 1985.

222. Kate Walker: Relatives include her mother, Ann Wigglesworth Walker '64; two aunts, Dr. Pauline Sweet '57 and Sally Sweet Wylde '61; two grandmothers, Louise "Weedie" McKelvy Walker '32 and Elise Sortwell Wigglesworth '35; two great-aunts, and a number of cousins.

222. "cool" and "dragon lady": Kate Walker '00, Sarah Cugini '00, Meredith Renda '98, and Cathleen Cheung '97, interview by LL, Apr. 29, 1997.

222. "exciting and expansive": New England Association of Schools and Colleges, "Report of the Visiting Committee."

222. "a little flower . . . blossomed": Monique Corbat Brooks '66, interview by LL, May 19, 2006.

222. "You put women . . . themselves": ASP, interview, May 23, 1997.

223. "a different species": Hallaran interview.

223. "I think we are . . . teachers": Robert Havery, interview by LL, Jul. 25, 2005.

223. "Our girls . . . class" JLM, interview, Jan. 27, 1997.

223. "my friends . . . women": Stern interview.

224. "Westover . . . place": ASP, interview, Aug. 2, 2005.

224. A senior that year: This alumna wishes to remain anonymous.

224. "it was . . . imagined" and following quotations: Montgomery interview. In 1994, Myra and David Sadker's *Failing at Fairness: How America's Schools Cheat Girls* (New York: Scribner's), and Mary Pipher's *Reviving Ophelia: Saving the Selves of Adolescent Girls* (New York: Ballantine Books) were published.

226–27. "Even for a close observer . . . *there*": EMN, "Westover Salutes Joe and Beth Molder," *Westover School Alumnae Magazine*, Spring 1987.

227. "He told us . . . Mr. Molder": Victoria Campbell '94, letter to LL, Mar. 21, 2005.

228. "Now . . . great moms": JLM, "Charge to the Senior Class," June 6, 1997.

228–29. Rose Gatling Williams: Williams, interview by LL, Feb. 20, 2007. Molder asked her, a neurosurgical physician's assistant, to stay involved with the school; she joined the board of governors in 2000. Her daughter, Brittany Williams '06, is the first legacy daughter of an African-American alumna.

228.   "Apparently . . . us": Gerster letter.

228.   "single-handedly . . . marvelous man": Bacon letter.

228.   "I think . . . center": JLM and ASP, "Westover: A Conversation with Joseph Molder and Ann Pollina," Westover School, June 1996.

228.   "weathered . . . right:" ASP, interview, Aug. 2, 2005.

229.   "At first . . . them": Martin interview.

229.   "gadfly": JLM and ASP, "Westover: A Conversation . . ." After ASP became head of school, she continued to be a consultant, speaker, and writer about girls in math, science, and technology. Over the years, she has held leadership positions at the Connecticut Girls & Technology Network, the Connecticut Association of Independent Schools, the AAUW Educational Foundation, the Connecticut Academy for Education in Mathematics, Science & Technology, and the National Coalition of Girls' Schools. In 2000, she received two awards from the AAUW, and in 2002 she was named "Woman of the Year" by the Connecticut AAUW.

229.   "with great joy . . . community": Montgomery, letter to alumnae and friends of Westover, May 1996.

229.   "the reception . . . break": Montgomery, letter to Priscilla Cunningham, May 12, 1996. The next board president was Charlotte Beyer Fiveson '65, a financial consultant, who had chaired the search committee.

230.   "which in some ways . . . worlds": ASP, interview, May 23, 1997.

230.   "you are here . . . school": ASP, "Installation as Head of School," Oct. 16, 1997.

230.   "depth and richness:" ASP, "From the Head of School: A Look back at her First Year," *Hillard Herald*, Summer 1998. It was decided that the mission of the school was "to provide an environment that inspires the intellectual, artist, athlete and philosopher in each student. Westover challenges young women to think independently, to embrace diversity, and to grow intellectually and spiritually. Westover encourages in each student integrity, responsibility and commitment to community."

230.   "Westover . . . birthday": ASP, letter to friends of Westover, Sept. 10, 1997.

13. The Ethics of Care (pages 231–46)

231.   "a case history . . . country": "Review & Outlook: Schools for Girls," *Wall Street Journal*, Mar. 13, 1998.

231–32.   "Since their inception . . . professions": Kaminer, "The Trouble with Single-Sex Schools," *Atlantic Monthly*, Apr. 1998. She also challenged the way an earlier AAUW report measured girls' self-esteem, suggesting that when girls say they are less satisfied with themselves than do boys, it may mean they are more self-effacing or have higher aspirations.

232. "What Kaminer sees . . . androgyny": ASP, letter to the editor, *Atlantic Monthly*, July 1998.

232. "in my heart . . . girls": ASP, interview, May 23, 1997.

232. "We get further . . . questions": ASP, "Single Sex Education Debate."

232. "This is a *very* . . . across": ASP, interview, May 23, 1997.

233. males: It's said that learning styles range along a continuum and about twenty percent of each gender learns like the majority of the other.

233. since the schools educate relatively few pupils: In 2007 there were 46,636 pupils in the 114 member schools of The National Coalition of Girls Schools. The U.S. Department of Education says that in 2003–04 there were 64,367 pupils in 136 private elementary and secondary girls' schools throughout the country.

233. "Why is not . . . education": ASP, Westover Web site (no date).

233. "almost sexist": ASP, interview, Aug. 25, 1999.

233. "gynergy": Carey Goldberg, "Facing Forced Retirement, Iconoclastic Professor Keeps on Fighting," *New York Times*, Aug. 15, 1999.

233–34. "a traditional philosophy . . . Harkness table": ASP, "Single Sex Education Debate." Afterward, ASP was invited to be on the board of the AAUW's Education Foundation, where she served four years. As the methodologies at Westover and other girls' schools spread to classrooms throughout the country during the next decades, she continued to feel frustrated that the female institutions did not get credit for creating them.

234. "*all* my children . . . dream": ASP, "An Exciting Time for Westover," speech, May 19, 2006.

234. "a part of my soul . . . classroom": ASP, interview, Aug. 22, 2006.

234–35. "a long, hard conversation . . . Mom": ASP, interview, Aug. 2, 2005.

235. "No matter . . . Westover": Alyssa Siefert '05, letter to LL, May 5, 2006.

236. "Architecturally . . . cliquish": ASP, interview, May 23, 1997. Day students have been assimilated by assigning lounges on corridors and residents (or dorm parents) to them, and by encouraging them to stay for meals, study hall, and overnight.

236. "not an option": ASP, letter to Vincent W. Durnan, New England Association of Schools and Colleges, May 28, 1998.

236. "one of the finest . . . country": "The Strengths and Weaknesses of Westover School."

237. "True education . . . structure": ASP, interview, May 23, 1997.

238. "It was a wake-up call . . . complacency": ASP, interview, Aug. 22, 2006.

238. "scary" . . . like that": Chromik, Siefert, and Zheng, WTNH radio, "Harvard President's Speech Still Draws Controversy," Feb. 28, 2005.

239. "Every gain . . . hook": Pollitt, "Summers of Our Discontent," *Nation*, Feb. 21, 2005.

239. "richer, broader, better": ASP, "The Culture that Surrounds our Mathematics and Science is the Real Problem," *Waterbury Republican-American*, Mar. 1, 2005.

239. "joyless": ASP, interview, Aug. 22, 2006.

239. "emotional intelligence . . . feeling brain": Gilligan, "'Mommy, I Know You,'" *Newsweek*, Jan. 30, 2006.

240. "abilities . . . intelligence": ASP, "Gender Balance . . ."

240. "The work . . . along": ASP, interview, Aug. 22, 2006.

240. "The real culprit . . . culture": ASP, interview, Aug. 2, 2005.

240. top scores: Forty-two percent of the class of 2006 did so well on Advanced Placement tests that they were named AP Scholars.

240. "We've lost . . . way": Weber interview.

240. "too driven . . . BE": Alice Hallaran, New England Association of Schools and Colleges, "Report of the Visiting Committee." The committee noted that it found no more pressure at Westover than at other schools or, for that matter, in their own lives: "Achieving an appropriate balance of thinking, doing, and being is a challenge to each of us."

241. "part . . . Westover": ASP, minutes of board of trustees meeting, Jan. 1996.

241. "If I have . . . work": ASP, "Westover Graduation Address," June 2, 1995.

241. "It may be . . . can": ASP, speech on alumnae weekend, May 19, 2001.

241. "You don't have to marry . . . woman": ASP, interview, Aug. 22, 2006.

241. college: College competition is tougher for girls today because more girls than boys are graduating from high school and applying to colleges.

241. "Who cares . . . take'": ASP, interview, Aug. 22, 2006.

241. "Like play . . . thing": Hungerford, "Chapel and Westover."

242. "wasn't the time . . . happier": Vileisis interview.

242. "slightly . . . something": Zwack, as quoted in Hungerford.

242. "never learned . . . education": Stern interview.

242. "deeply good kids:" ASP, letter to Westover parents, Oct. 8, 2002.

242. "serenity . . . her": Christian Daviron letter.

243. "When I think . . . evil'": Hilary Bibb Porado '80, letter to LL, Mar. 11, 2005.

243. "you will be asked . . . goodness": ASP, letter to Westover students and parents, May 6, 2005.

243. "mean girls . . . competitiveness": ASP, interview, May 23, 1997.

243. "absolutely . . . women": ASP, interview, Aug. 2, 2005.

243. "The school . . . spirit:" Hallaran interview.

244. "quirky": Weber interview.

244. "There's a way . . . place": Rachel Bashevkin, interview by LL, Oct. 23, 2006.

244. "the dumbing down": Stern interview.

244. "a different kind . . . experiment": Jeannette Q. Byers '69, speech, Westover School, May 1999.

245. testimony: Whitney Ransome and Meg Milne Moulton, "Why Girls' Schools," *Fordham Urban Law Journal*, Dec. 2001. Over the years, the National Coalition of Girls' Schools has commissioned polls of thousands of alumnae who graduated from 1955 to the present. Response rates have been thirty to forty percent.

245. "exhilarating . . . capability": Vileisis interview.

245. "Westover let me . . . help you" and following quotations from the poll: Westover School, "2004–2005 Alumnae Survey," 2006. It had a fifty percent response rate.

246. "Unlike the eye . . . interaction": Belenky, Clinchy, Goldberger, and Tarule, "Introduction: To the Other Side of Silence," *Women's Ways of Knowing* (New York: Basic Books, 1997).

246. "We need to send . . . girls": ASP, interview, May 23, 1997.

246. "Infusing . . . Westover": ASP, letter to friends of Westover, Sept. 10, 1997.

246. "But, frankly . . . culture": ASP, interview, May 23, 1997.

INDEX

Italicized page numbers indicate illustrations. The letter "n" following a page number indicates a note.

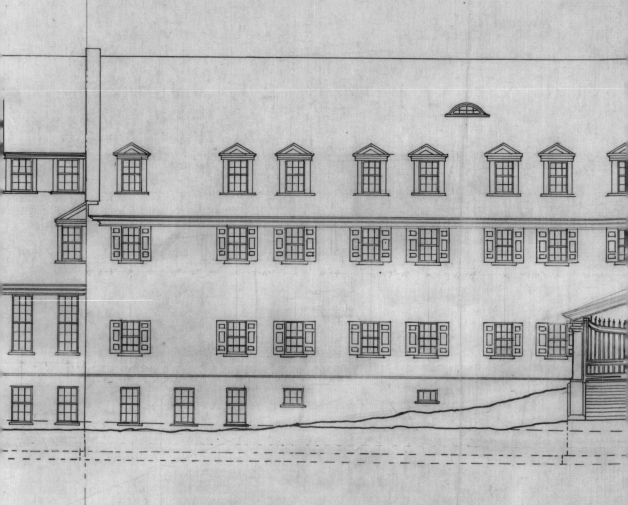

SHEET N.º 7.
SCALE: ONE INCH = 8 FEET.

SOU
WESTOVER, MIS
MIDDL